The Art of Surrender

The Art
of Surrender

DECOMPOSING SOVEREIGNTY
AT CONFLICT'S END

Robin Wagner-Pacifici

The University of Chicago Press · *Chicago and London*

Robin Wagner-Pacifici is professor of sociology at Swarthmore College. She is the author of *The Moro Morality Play: Terrorism as Social Drama; Discourse and Destruction: The City of Philadelphia versus MOVE;* and *Theorizing the Standoff: Contingency in Action.*

The University of Chicago Press, Chicago 60637
The University of Chicago Press, Ltd., London
© 2005 by The University of Chicago
All rights reserved. Published 2005
Printed in the United States of America

14 13 12 11 10 09 08 07 06 05   1 2 3 4 5

ISBN: 0-226-86978-4 (cloth)
ISBN: 0-226-86979-2 (paper)

Library of Congress Cataloging-in-Publication Data

Wagner-Pacifici, Robin Erica.
    The art of surrender : decomposing sovereignty at conflict's end / Robin Wagner-Pacifici
        p.   cm.
    Includes bibliographical references and index.
    ISBN 0-226-86978-4 (cloth : alk. paper) — ISBN 0-226-86979-2 (pbk. : alk. paper)
    1. Sovereignty. 2. Capitulations, Military. 3. World War, 1939–1945—United States. 4. United States—History—Civil War, 1861–1865. 5. Thirty Years' War, 1618-1648. I. Title.
    JC327.W25   2005
    355.02'8—dc22

                                                            2005008023

This book is printed on acid-free paper.

*To my dear sister Alicia and to my enduring
friends from childhood, Natalie and Lauren*

Contents

Preface ix
Acknowledgments xi

1   THE PROBLEM OF SURRENDER   1

The End 2 / *Archetypes in Action: A Word on Method* 3 / *Cases of Surrender* 8 / *The Archaism of Surrender* 11 / *The Conditions of Surrender: Toward a Political Semiotic* 13 / *Converging to Convert* 15 / *The Etymology of Surrender* 17 / *Etymological Coda* 22 / *Surrenders as Actions in the Interstices* 23 / *The Copies of Surrender* 25

2   WITNESS TO SURRENDER   29

Bearing Witness at Breda 29 / *What Is a Witness?* 36 / *The Visual Order of the Witness* 41 / *Where Is the Witness?* 44 / *What Does the Witness Do?* 47 / *Signatories to the Scene* 48 / *Witness to a Disappearance* 50 / *Looking at the Vanishing Point* 52 / *Paper and Responsibility* 56

3   THE EXCHANGES OF SURRENDER   59

The Dangers of Surrender 61 / *The Case of the Unconditional Surrender* 64 / *The Nature of the Surrendering Exchange* 69 / *The Objects of Exchange* 74 / *Originary and Secondary Objects of Contention* 74 / *A Note on the Work of Maps* 76 / *Civil War Territory* 77 / *The Fates of Warriors and Civilians* 78 / *Transactional Objects of the Process of Surrender* 82 / *Pledges, Oaths, Promises, and Pardons* 86 / *Instruments and Weapons of War* 88 / *Symbolic Objects of Authority and Solidarity* 90 / *Tributes, Demonstrations, and Gestures* 91 / *Sites of Exchange* 94 / *Convergence and Divergence* 96

4   SOVEREIGNTY AND ITS AFTERLIFE   98

What Is Sovereignty? 100 / *Types of Sovereignty* 101 / *Erotic Exchange and Vicarious Surrender* 105 / *Actions of the Sovereign* 107 / *Assumption and Divestment of Responsibility* 109 / *The Itinerant Sovereign* 111 / *How to Recognize the Sovereign* 114 / *Mapping Sovereign Relations* 118 / *Agency without Sovereignty* 119 / *How to Represent the Sovereign* 120 / *The Multiplicity of Singularity* 122 / *Sovereignty at the Scene?* 126 / *The Uncopied* 128

5   THE DEEP STRUCTURE OF SURRENDER   133

Borderline Scrutinies 135 / *Uneasy Appearances* 137 / *The Political Semiotic at Conflict's End* 138 / *Demonstration and Deictics* 139 / *Deictic Deferrals* 142 / *Performatives and Transformations* 144 / *Representations* 145 / *Copies and Their Inversions* 147 / *Underrepresentation and the Civil War* 149 / *On the Threshold of Assumptions and Divestments* 149

Notes 153
Bibliography 189
Index 199

Color plates follow page 148.

Preface

FORGET the utopian notion that a brave new world without power politics will follow the unconditional surrender of wicked nations.

—Hans Morgenthau, *In Defense of the National Interest*

VIOLENT CONFLICTS, be they "wars of position" or "wars of maneuver," ultimately come to an end. Even the wildest violence finds limits in time, space, and target. Conflicts may end with clear winners and losers, or they may conclude with more equivocal forms of social relationships forged through treaties, peace accords, or withdrawals. One mode of ending wars and other violent encounters is surrender, the apparent submission of one party to another. This book focuses on just that kind of ending.

Perhaps it is ironic to write about surrender from deep within the heart of a regnant political superpower. The United States of America solicits surrenders from others—it does not traffic in them itself. But today's transfers of power after violent conflicts are often confounding, and just when a conflict seems to have come to a conclusion, new forms of resistance and contestation emerge. More than ever, perhaps, we need to review how violent conflicts have been concluded in the past. Surrenders seem to have promised distinct and definitive conclusions. But irony, double vision, and reversion turn out to be the very argot of this study of surrender's forms and meanings. *The Art of Surrender* plants its analytic "white flag" in a number of superposed interstices: between victory and defeat, between war and peace, and between violence and law. It asks the question, What actually occurs there in the space and time of transition? How do the parties to a war or violent conflict navigate these transformations?

This book develops what I term a "political semiotic" analysis of this key social action and archetypal social form—military surrender. An act of power transfer that appears to entail unmitigated abjection for the vanquished and glory for the victor, surrender actually comprises a complex configuration of social and cultural forms. Surrenders are moments of victory, but they are marked by the pathos of loss. They appear to stanch violence and force, but perhaps they simply displace them. While our contemporary era seems more attuned to expedition in concluding conflict than to ritual, it is nevertheless important to pay attention to the older models of endings. These models highlight the way force and power seek rearticulation and reinforcement after the shooting stops. Ultimately, surrender highlights defeat as much as it does victory. To thus regard winning through the lens of defeat is the goal of *The Art of Surrender*.

Acknowledgments

I WOULD LIKE to thank the following people for giving assistance, advice, or disciplinary expertise as I was writing this book. Several of these scholars are experts in the specialized fields I draw on (art history, classics, French, Spanish, and English literature, political science), and I am particularly grateful for their consultations, translations, and references (of course, all errors are my own): Nathalie Anderson, Jean-Vincent Blanchard, Joy Charlton, Randy Collins, Michael Cothren, Míguel Diaz-Barriga, Aya Ezawa and Kennosuke Ezawa, Marion Fourcade Gourinchas, Roger Friedland, Edward Fuller, David Gibson, Jeffrey Goldfarb, Bruce Grant, Pam Harris, Constance Hungerford, Tessa Izenour, Suzanne Jablonski, T. Kaori Kitao, Jonathan LeBreton, James Maraniss, Ann Mische, Barbara Mujica, Charles Muntz, Jeffrey K. Olick, Patricia Reilly, Marc Howard Ross, Magali Sarfatti Larson, Barry Schwartz, Susan Schifrin, William Turpin, Phil Weinstein, and Sarah Willie.

I also thank the organizers (Eviatar Zerubavel and John Gillis) and members of the "Beginnings and Endings" seminar group at the Center for the Critical Analysis of Contemporary Culture at Rutgers University, where I was a fellow during the 1999–2000 academic year, for their extremely perceptive and useful comments at the inception of this study of military surrender. This book benefited as well from opportunities to present material at colloquia at New School University, the University of North Carolina–Chapel Hill, Princeton University, the University of Pennsylvania, Northwestern University, Amherst College, Yale University, University of California–Davis, and Columbia University. Many thanks to those scholars who offered me such rich arenas in which to engage the ideas of this book: Austin Sarat, Jeffrey Goldfarb, Vera Zolberg, Jeffrey Alexander, John Hall, Gary Alan Fine, Jeffrey Olick, Andrew Perrin, and Michèle Lamont.

Parts of the book were published elsewhere. Part of chapter 2 appeared as "Dilemmas of Witness" in *The Blackwell Companion to the Sociology of Culture,* edited by Mark D. Jacobs and Nancy Weiss Hanrahan (Malden, MA: Blackwell, 2005). Another part of chapter 2 will appear as "Witness to Surrender" in *Visual Worlds,* edited by John Hall, Lisa Tamaris Becker, and Blake Stimson (New York: Routledge, forthcoming).

Special thanks and appreciation go to Rose Maio, administrative coordinator of the Sociology and Anthropology Department at Swarthmore College, for her efficient and generous assistance in all phases of this book's preparation.

Once again, I thank Douglas Mitchell, editor extraordinaire, for his enthusiasm, his intelligence, and his humanity. Doug has brought his erudition and intellectual engagement to this project from its early stages of conception through to completion. He has at times definitely rerouted my thinking, and I hope this book reflects his wisdom.

The Pacificis have done more than provide succor and love and humor. Maurizio is, as always, my truest friend and love. He is generous with his brain, heart, and brawn, and I love him for it. I thank Adriano, Laura, and Stefano for their respective gifts and for just being our wonderful children.

CHAPTER I

The Problem of Surrender

Therefore no no, for I resign to thee.
Now, mark me how I will undo myself.
I give this heavy weight from off my head,
And this unwieldy sceptre from my hand,
The pride of kingly sway from out my heart;
With mine own tears I wash away my balm,
With mine own hands I give away my crown,
With mine own tongue deny my sacred state,
With mine own breath release all duteous oaths . . .
Long may'st thou live in Richard's seat to sit,
And soon lie Richard in an earthy pit! . . .
What more remains?

—William Shakespeare, *Richard II,* 4.1.202–22[1]

Perhaps there exists, in this painting by Velázquez [*Las Meninas*], the representation as it were of Classical representation, and the definition of the space it opens up to us. And, indeed, representation undertakes to represent itself here in all its elements, with its images, the eyes to which it is offered, the faces it makes visible, the gestures that call it into being. But there, in the midst of this dispersion which it is simultaneously grouping together and spreading out before us, indicated compellingly from every side, is an essential void: the necessary disappearance of that which is its foundation—of the person it resembles and the person in whose eyes it is only a resemblance. This very subject—which is the same— has been elided. And representation, freed finally from the relation that was impeding it, can offer itself as representation in its pure form.

—Michel Foucault, *The Order of Things*

In viewing the shot, the reader had to look over the shoulders of the German civilians in order to see the bodies, creating a layering between the shot's foreground (where the Germans were standing) and the background (where the victims and liberators stood). The effect was magnified by the middle of the shot, where a seemingly impassable white space kept the groups at a distance from each other.

—"German civilians view corpses at Buchenwald, April 16, 1945,"
in Barbie Zelizer, *Remembering to Forget: Holocaust Memory through the Camera's Eye*

THE END

We begin with a consideration of ending. All endings are difficult, whether endings of wars or meetings or relationships. Endings are actions that terminate actions; thus they do double duty as markers and unmakers. The philosopher J. L. Austin briefly considered the verbal formulas that end actions or events and noted their slide from markers to "performatives." "There is a transition," he wrote, "from the word END at the end of a novel to the expression 'message ends' at the end of a signal message, to the expression 'with that I conclude my case' as said by Counsel in a law court. These, we may say, are cases of marking the action by the word, where eventually the use of the word comes to be the action of 'ending' (*a difficult act to perform, being the cessation of acting,* or to make explicit in other ways, of course)."[2]

Endings are difficult practically and conceptually. And surrenders are quite particular and paradoxical forms of ending. They depend on a resistant cooperation and mutuality. They draw on an authority in the very process of undoing that authority. They raise a series of questions. For example, what does it mean to be a subject who says "I surrender," or to be a recipient of the statement "I surrender," or to be a witness to an interchange of surrender? What happens to the subjecthood of the surrendering self, the surrendering army, the surrendering sovereign, and the surrendering state as they surrender their selves to others? And what, analytically, does it take to grasp these social entities performing and interacting in such a moment of extremis?

Surrenders are never quite what they seem. They may be part relinquishment of power and identity, part exchange (handing over), part termination of conflict or resistance, part degradation ceremony, or part salvage operation. For all the variations on modalities of surrender (more or less emphatic asymmetry between the victor and the vanquished, more or less severe consequences incumbent on the act), surrenders entail performances of the self in a moment of existential extremis. Hinge mechanisms of the flows of power, they illuminate the adjudication of victory and defeat in social life.

Shame and social death, with their corrosive powers, hover at the edges of all surrenders, where the self must be simultaneously present and self-absenting/abnegating. The vanquished are, after all, giving up and giving over. In *Remnants of Auschwitz,* Italian philosopher Giorgio Agamben writes that in shame "it is as if our consciousness collapsed and, seeking to flee in all directions, were simultaneously summoned by an irrefutable order to be present at is own defacement, at the expropriation of what is most its own . . . It is nothing less than the fundamental sentiment of being a subject, in the two apparently opposed senses of this phrase: to be subjected and to be sovereign. Shame is what is produced in the absolute concomitance of subjectification and desubjectification, self-loss and self-possession, servitude and sovereignty."[3]

Surrenders are thoroughly paradoxical affairs in just the way that Agamben means: the vanquished self must "present his credentials" in order to divest himself of his credentials. His *sovereign* self exposes and delivers up his *subjected* self in his own undoing. Thus, on the verge of losing his kingship and kingdom, Shakespeare's Richard II begins his surrendering soliloquy with a series of statements in the first person singular: "*I* resign to thee"; "*I* will undo myself"; "*I* give away my crown." He ends the speech in a hortatory and prophetic mood, signaling his undone status as he switches to the third person: "Long may'st thou live in Richard's seat to sit, / And soon lie Richard in an earthy pit!" The "I" gives way to "Richard," a king who already begins to seem a figure from the past, subject now to other rulers.[4]

With all its paradoxes and existential extremities (another key paradox: one is both *forced* to surrender and *allowed* to surrender),[5] the complex negotiations of surrenders reveal identities in moments of transition. Such negotiations also point to the fault lines of resignation and forced consent that underscore the realm of the "normal" to which all parties return at conflict's end. This book highlights the way such fault lines are vividly and richly illustrated in these fleeting moments of unguarded power. This is true both for individuals and for collectivities (and often simultaneously relevant at both levels, since I will show that the surrender of collectivities must be transacted through the medium of the surrender of the individual representative or proxy). The complex relational dynamics of selves surrendering to other selves must therefore be charted across an array of affectual, even sentimental, couplings. This is so even when the focus, as here, is on surrender of the military type. The flows of power, the meetings and exchanges, and the consequent merging of formerly autonomous entities in surrenders anticipate an analytical role both for force and for the erotic. In early modern nation building, for example, the exchange of women in royal marriage agreements frequently combined the sexual with political forms of surrender.

Archetypes in Action: A Word on Method

This book's goal is to illuminate a complex, evolving archetype. It is an archetype of political probity, but one that inevitably operates asymptotically to its apparent goals of permanent conflict resolution. While archetypes refer generally to origins and templates, in practice they, like genres, develop through their situational manifestations.[6] Thus the archetypal illumination of surrender must view surrender as an evolving phenomenon. Shifts occur at the level of practices, technologies, discourses, and genres of representation with each new enactment of a surrender.

Beyond the apparently paradoxical attention to archetypal evolution, there are several obvious intellectual challenges associated with the analysis of an archetype. Perhaps the biggest challenge is generalizing across disparate historical periods, cultures, languages, and practices. How do we even know that we are talking about the "same thing" when we categorize actions from different settings under the same conceptual rubric? Can we assume certain invariants across all human societies—beyond reproduction? Although it may be safe to proceed inductively and follow the tracks of such phenomena as "conflict" across historically and culturally diverse societies, how justified are we in naming diversely configured endings of conflict "surrender" just because they resemble each other in certain aspects?

I am not the first to grapple with these conundrums of comparative analysis. Discernment of similarities and differences has posed epistemological problems for social scientists since the inceptions of the various disciplines. The hermeneutic tacking back and forth between general definitions and specific cases does a lot of the work of making the case for reasonable comparisons. But variations in language, practices, and symbolic forms make this work complicated and, inevitably, somewhat speculative. It may be that, as we shall see, it is often the clashing of two diverse definitions of the situation that makes for the most interesting cases—one party to the end of a conflict thinks he is getting a new political partner, the other thinks he is getting a loyal vassal. At another, nominal level, both parties may understand that they are participating in a "surrender." But such agreement only begins the process of meaning making.

It may seem self-evident that surrenders work only when both the victor and the vanquished participate in the same military, legal, and cultural paradigm. From the conventions of leave-taking (weapons in certain positions, exiting a besieged town in a certain manner), to the forms of interaction and exchange, to the transfers of sovereignty, successful transactions of surrender seem to rely on mutual comprehension and interpretation. Nevertheless, this mutuality is qualified by several factors: (1) Even parties operating with the same paradigm can dissimulate and fail to live up to agreements. Sometimes this may involve the signatories of the agreements themselves, and sometimes it may involve the subordinates who must carry out the orders of their signing superiors.[7] (2) The encounter of different paradigms can promote hybridization rather than unintelligibility, eventually leading to new paradigms.[8] (3) The bias of historical archives means that most of the material that survives a surrender reflects the victor's point of view, regardless of the paradigmatic coordination between victor and vanquished.

Given all these qualifications, the question remains: How do we recognize an action as a surrender and not as something else? Regardless of the competing paradigms "on the ground" of history, the comparative analyst must appeal to some overarching (however emergent) paradigm whereby similar actions can be recognized as such despite their different appearances. One exemplary study is that of historian Patricia Seed. In *Ceremonies of Possession in Europe's Conquest of the New World, 1492–1640,* Seed compares the bases of claims and the mechanisms by which claims were pursued by the English, Dutch, French, Portuguese, and Spanish forces involved in overseas conquests. There were significant differences across this group of separate, often competing, powers. The English built fences and thus "improved" the land for habitation; the French performed both religious and political-military ceremonies in which they planted crosses and carried royal standards; the Spaniards read the "Requirement" and ordered native peoples to submit to Catholicism; the Dutch "discovered" lands and claimed them through trade and mapmaking; the Portuguese engaged in trade and commerce. In each case, these practices and discourses had a bifurcated audience—native peoples who were acquiescing to or resisting (in ways both overt and covert) the acts of possession, and other European powers who were sometimes competing for the same territory. Recognition was thus complex and multivocal. This is a meticulous historical study, but on two points it is more suggestive than definitive. First, the relation between ceremonies of possession and violent encounters is not developed. Second, and most relevant here, the very question of an emergent international discourse of conquest and possession is only implicitly introduced through discussions of recognition.

My own study of surrender aims to foreground the mechanisms of recognition and its contestation, since forms of surrender do different work in different contexts. I will keep the epistemological question active as cases are examined. The theoretical apparatus is one that provides a precise framework for analyzing such adjudication.

A couple of examples may indicate the high stakes of interpretation. Participants to a siege and analysts alike might view the collective suicide of a besieged group as a form of surrender to an enemy that the group knows it cannot defeat (though the defenders deny the enemy the "gift" of themselves as subjects or slaves). Some might view this action as a form of resistance or martyrdom rather than a form of surrender. Some might contest the very terms "suicide" and "surrender."[9] Yael Zerubavel has traced these historically contingent recognitions and misrecognitions in the case of Masada, where in 70–73 CE a group of Jews holding out against the conquering Romans on a high plateau overlooking the Dead Sea and Judea killed each other rather than face slavery, torture, or death at the hands of the Romans.[10] Zerubavel tracks the coming and going of paradigms of explanation and justification as the actions of the Jews are lauded or critiqued.

A more contemporary example comes from the standoff in Texas in the early 1990s between the forces of the Federal Bureau of Investigation and the Bureau of Alcohol, Tobacco, and Firearms and the Branch Davidians. At points this standoff appeared to be moving in the direction of a surrender of the religious group, but that movement was propulsive, intermittent, and difficult for the FBI negotiators to recognize as a surrender. The FBI maintained a literalist, quantifiable idea of surrender, as evinced in this poststandoff interview with two agents:

> Jeff Jamar: We worked out a surrender plan in minute detail . . . See you want a plan, you want a surrender plan because you put that in their heads.
> Byron Sage: If they can visualize—and you actually use those words— "Can you picture this? Can you—can you visualize—okay, you're going to come out the front door. You're going to turn left."[11]

Meanwhile, operating within another interpretive frame, religious scholars claimed that David Koresh, the leader of the Branch Davidians, had a very different sense of surrender, one mediated and made possible through biblical hermeneutics: "What the authorities never perceived was that Koresh's preaching was precisely such to him, the only matter of substance and means through which to work out a 'surrender.'"[12] Both sides were theoretically searching for a gestural and discursive language through which to effect and communicate a surrender. Translation problems of an epistemological sort prevented mutual recognition—with all the tragic consequences of misrecognition.

These two examples do not just demonstrate the interpretive difficulties associated with different epistemological and ideological paradigms; they also reveal the high stakes for recognition in situations of conflict and violence. Analysts enter the historical stream at a particular bend of the river. The necessarily retrospective gaze of the analyst can seek out evidence of prior changes in typification, and it must do so on several levels simultaneously.

At one level, conventions of behavior and social organization develop and change over time. At another level changes in genres and media of representation also occur, but often in ways that are contingently coordinated with changes in the former. In studying surrender, changes in military conventions and technologies—the way wars are actually fought—may be correlated with changes in the ways wars are depicted. Peter Burke notes one such coordinated development that followed on the early seventeenth-century invention of the military drill in Europe: "Battles were becoming less like an agglomeration of single combats and more like collective actions in which groups of soldiers marched, charged or fired as one man. The new pictorial trend, in step with military developments, was to show a scene which could be read like a diagram—and was indeed influenced by the diagrams printed in books on the art of war."[13]

In this way the developments in the field were mirrored and reinforced by the developments in their representations as diagrams and maps came to have new prominence. Along similar lines, Chandra Mukerji argues for the seamless way French territorial ambitions incorporated both the military and the "domestic" landscape. Louis XIV's interest in the gardens of Versailles was neither frivolous nor merely ceremonial "but rather [involved] engaging in a search for territorial control that was continuous in his projects (and passion) for building and war . . . Allées and bosquets often had double rows of trees along their boundaries, reproducing the style of planting used on the barricades of French fortified towns. These long lines of trees constituted a kind of symbolic standing army, guarding garden features, just as trees along barricades stood sentry, guarding and standing in for French soldiers, along the walls of Vauban's fortresses."[14]

When the landscape itself demonstrates and represents military power and ways of making war, when diagrammatic or cartographic renderings of battle become predominant, when particular literary genres tend to identify with either the besieger or the besieged town in battle, the analyst is advised to develop an apparatus of analysis that is capable of "reading" these various levels of change.[15]

Reading individual surrenders through their media of presentation and representation involves several types of discrimination and contextualization. The extant aesthetic and rhetorical conventions and technologies determine the range of generic options at particular historical moments. We need an analytic language that can identify the choices made and the consequences of these choices at the level of meaning. A first pass through this issue simply demarcates the different genres and their languages; for example, the generic conventions of history paintings are different from those of maps. Additionally, we must identify trajectories of generic development, since new genres emerge when ideologies and technologies of representation change. Finally, it is the combination of modes of presentation and representation (combinations that can co-occur and those that are sequenced over time) that gives a sedimented meaning to specific events. Thus ceremonies of surrender that engage and generate gestures, conventionalized oaths, paintings, plays, maps, and journals find their meaning in just these various modalities of presentation and representation. It is thus incumbent on an analyst to explicate these modalities in any given case, to be clear about what they can and cannot conjure, and to articulate the way they both track and constitute power.

If the implicit claim here seems to be that events cannot be distinguished from their representations, it is a claim that needs qualification. By centering a study on a transhistorical concept of surrender, I am indeed asserting a certain degree of freedom for such events. Surrenders retain something of their archetypal essence regardless of the particular genres in which they are transacted. Looked at from the other end of the telescope—the point of view of forms of representation—they too have a relative autonomy. Changes at one level do not completely determine changes at another. Social and cultural forms may perdure in the face of what appears to be their practical obsolescence. Tracing the transition from chivalry to courtesy, Jorge Arditi notes, "For example, in terms of their usefulness for combat, the transformations in warfare would indeed render the chivalrous practices developed in the princely courts obsolete—although their continuation indicates that their significance lay elsewhere; in their embodiment of a collective self. More importantly, the actual blending of chivalry and courtesy transforms the technologies of the body in whose operations the military element takes shape."[16]

Acknowledging the challenges of historical and cross-cultural comparison, I thus nevertheless aim to differentiate surrender from other modalities of ending conflict, including extermination and large-scale retreat. To a large extent, following Paul Kecskemeti's distinctions, surrender in this reading requires that the enemy is not destroyed altogether: "Annihilation does not mean the physical extermination of the enemy, but merely neutralization of his combat strength. In surrender agreements, immunity of life is expressly guaranteed to members of the surrendering force."[17] This baseline understanding of surrender as some kind of privilege in defeat provisionally leaves open a precise definition.

Cases of Surrender

As a modality for ending conflicts in the West, codified military surrenders took their most elaborate ceremonial form in the early modern period—a period, according to such scholars as Norbert Elias and Jorge Arditi, of evolving ceremonies and conventions that civilized and domesticated power and violence generally.[18]

The moments of surrender are indeed moments of statecraft. This book approaches those moments of history as they were rendered by participants, witnesses, and correspondents of a wide variety of types. In developing this analysis I will refer to many actual surrenders, but three are highlighted. These selected surrenders have left significant trails of documents, maps, paintings, plays, lithographs, photographs, and films for us to track, and they offer several variations on themes that prove important: witnessing, rendering, exchange, humiliation, magnanimity, recognition, translation, resolution, and sovereignty. The cases are the surrender of the Dutch to the Spanish at Breda in 1625; the surrender of Lee's Army of Northern Virginia to Grant's Union army at Appomattox in 1865; and the surrender of the Japanese to the Allied forces on the USS *Missouri* in Tokyo Bay in 1945.

Breda

The siege and surrender of Breda, a city now in Belgium, was one of the most emblematic, if not the most strategically significant, of the many sieges of the Thirty Years' War between Spain and the Dutch Republic (1618–48). The famous Spanish general Ambrogio Spinola mounted a siege of the city and successfully overcame Dutch resistance and (re)conquered the town for the Habsburg King Philip IV. This siege involved innovations of both a technical and a political nature. The Spaniards built intricately engineered siege-works (even attempting to turn the course of a river), and they implemented an explicitly liberal and magnanimous surrender agreement. When the Dutch finally gave up after some nine months of encirclement, the town maintained economic autonomy, and the Protestant clergy were allowed to depart unharmed.

Sieges generate highly codified forms of surrender, even with the variations of mentality and terms in each case. Thus it is useful to draw preliminary attention to some essential aspects of siege warfare in order to begin to connect the types of battle with the types of surrender. Siege warfare grew in frequency in the medieval to early modern period in Europe. It was also during this period that the codified customs and laws of war rapidly evolved. A siege necessarily pits an immobile place (a town, a garrison, a castle) and its inhabitants against a more mobile force seeking to assault or encircle it into submission.[19] Sieges can end with the destruction of the walls of the town or fortress, the starvation of the inhabitants as their food and water supplies are cut off, the depletion of the resources of the encircling foe, or the rescue of the besieged by an external friendly force that causes the besiegers to retreat. If those inside the town do surrender (for whatever reason) to those outside, the demarcations of inside and outside are most explicitly marked. These surrenders after a siege are thus among the most highly diagrammatic. They also bring clear territorial rewards and were recognized to do so historically: "Until the French Revolution, which changed the character of war, the number of sieges exceeded the number of battles, as the possession of a hostile fortress was of greater positive value than the results of the average field victory; and the fortress served as a counter of exchange at the peace."[20] The dynamics of siege warfare and surrender will be explored in the following chapters.

Appomattox

Nearly two and a half centuries after the surrender of Breda, General Robert E. Lee surrendered his Army of Northern Virginia to Lieutenant General Ulysses S. Grant at Appomattox Courthouse in Virginia to begin the end of the American Civil War. On April 9, 1865, after four years of pitched battle in fields and cities in the North and the South, it was finally the unequivocal loss of two besieged Southern stronghold cities, Petersburg and Richmond, that convinced Lee he should surrender. Nevertheless, this conflict also presented both guerrilla warfare and a scorched-earth policy.[21] The surrender of Lee to Grant was highly ceremonial and, thanks largely to President Lincoln's and Grant's explicit desire to heal the rift between the North and South, highly magnanimous in its terms (e.g., Confederate officers and enlisted men alike were allowed to keep their sidearms and their horses in order to return home and take up civilian life, and Lee himself was not arrested for treason). There was, as we shall see, no official pictorial rendering of the scene of surrender and no photographs (in a much-photographed war). There were many unofficial, unsanctioned imagined and imaginary renderings in many media. These variable renderings and their meanings will be explored.

Tokyo Bay

Finally, the most recent highlighted historical case of surrender, and one noted as the last clear and unmitigated surrender in modern warfare, was that of Japan at the end of World War II. On September 2, 1945, a formal Instrument of Surrender was signed by government ministers and military officers of Japan and signed and accepted by General Douglas MacArthur and other officers of the Allied forces on the deck of the USS *Missouri,* anchored in Tokyo Bay. This surrender followed that of Nazi Germany by three months and also followed, by less than a month, the dropping of atomic bombs on Hiroshima and Nagasaki. While demanding unconditional surrender, as had been required of Germany, the surrender agreement nevertheless provided for the continued sovereignty of the Japanese emperor (a sovereignty dependent on Allied supervision, however). The signing of the surrender was highly ceremonial and was filmed and photographed by a corps of journalistic photographers.

Photojournalists played a major role in officially witnessing the battles, surrenders, and liberations during World War II. Barbie Zelizer brilliantly analyzes the role of reporters and photographers in bearing witness to the opening of the concentration camps. She notes that "photos are important tools for constructing moral consensus, particularly about events newly named or classified for public discourse."[22] Given this high-profile role of photographers in documenting the course and meaning of the war, it is not surprising that special arrangements were made to allow sixty-eight photographers from approximately a dozen countries (including, significantly, Japan) to be positioned on board the USS *Missouri* to photograph and film the surrender.[23]

All these surrenders generated rich archives, including paintings, plays, maps, photographs, and memoirs. I weave an analysis of the multimedia dossiers of these three historically marked surrenders through this exploration of the larger meaning of surrender.

The Archaism of Surrender

In spite of transformations in the technologies and modalities of war, from besieged battlements with *trace italienne* to atomic bombs dropped on entire cities, a certain archaism seems to attach itself to surrenders, even those occurring in the modern era. Surrenders still evoke images of white flags, swords, signings, and kneeling figures rather than helicopters and insurgents. Even legal officials attached to United States Army troops in Kuwait (at the aptly named "Camp Virginia") on the brink of the 2003 war against Iraq specifically referenced Lee's surrender to Grant at Appomattox in explaining the anticipatory "articles of capitulation" being drawn up for surrendering Iraqi troops.[24] The task of the analyst of surrender is to trace the origins of these apparently archaic evocations and to detail the mechanisms generating them. Then we might understand the afterimage of this surrender apparatus and track its appearance in contemporary social, political, and military realities.

And indeed, the afterimage of this ceremonialized form of surrender is still with us in both military and political spheres of action. In mid–December 2000, as Vice President Albert Gore finally acknowledged defeat in the United States presidential election after the Supreme Court definitively stopped the recount of votes in Florida, one question remained: Would he use the word "concession" in his concession speech, or would he simply say that he would now withdraw? In other words, would he sign bona fide "articles of capitulation"? After the heated, vexed, and highly partisan vote-counting debacle of November and December, the media commentators made much of the necessity for Gore to concede explicitly, lest the legitimacy of the Bush presidency be forever in doubt and Bush's power be viewed as unfairly won, illegal, and provisional. In the terms of this book, the question was whether, in the speech's narrative of the conflict and the contest, Gore would actually *surrender*. And indeed, even as he stated his disagreement with the Supreme Court decision, he did surrender with the following words: "I accept the finality of this outcome, which will be ratified next Monday in the Electoral College. And tonight, for the sake of our unity as a people and the strength of our democracy, I offer my concession."[25] Victor and vanquished were declared as the grudging gift of Gore's surrender marked the conclusive end of the contest.

The uncertainty and anxiety about Gore's lexical choices, about the nature of his speech act, concretely raise the issue of the contemporary relevance of surrender. In spite of the felt need for Gore to concede, the live possibility that he might merely withdraw resonates with the claim of many contemporary conflict negotiators that surrender *is* actually an archaic concept, no longer appropriate to the ways we now end conflicts—conflicts that do not, and should not, necessarily have decisive winners and losers. These conflicts end with "peace accords," or they may merely peter out. Reflecting on this situation, one military historian was led to write that "since World War II, hostilities have terminated less conclusively than in the past. Armistices, cease-fire lines, suppression of insurrection, acquiescence in de facto territorial changes, or a contested status quo have been provisional and hostilities have often been renewed."[26]

Such an analysis recalls the muddled end of the Vietnam War or of the first Gulf War that left Saddam Hussein in power despite his military defeat; of the second Gulf War, in which there was no obvious authoritative political or military body in Iraq to surrender to the coalition forces; of wars between Israel and its Arab neighbors in which victory either is not declared or is declared by all; and of the Dayton Peace Accords that were meant to end the conflicts in the former Yugoslavia without simultaneously announcing victory or defeat for the various antagonists. We may think of all the recent wars (declared and undeclared) that have ended—but not really. Indeed, as the very nature of the wars changes, it becomes almost impossible to imagine surrender. For example, in a general war on "terror," who surrenders?

In matters of social and military conflict, then, we may ask when and how surrenders are deemed desirable and relevant, and when they are not. What kinds of conflicts militate against identifying the victors and the vanquished? When do the pragmatic impulses associated with a pluralistic world or relativized notions of right and wrong, aggressor and innocent override the desire for clear and asymmetrical endings? When does it seem politically and philosophically more sophisticated to see the exaggerated clarity and political asymmetry of surrender as archaic, unproductive, and unnecessary? (Those in the field of dispute resolution avoid the term altogether.) And when, as in the case of the 2003 Gulf War, does surrender reappear as a desideratum of the conqueror?

I would argue that surrenders—their signings and exchanges, their ceremonies, and their symbolic representations—are acts that mark and redraw the conceptual edges of social and political time, space, and identity. They emerge out of the disordered spatiality and temporality of the battlegrounds and besieged cities of violent conflict and assert a reordering. In this edge-work, they are akin to other transactional encounters that demand a convergence and a divergence at a designated boundary. These include foundings, resignations, secessions, inaugurations, and marriages. All of these are events that reconfigure the world as they enact a transformation. They constitute both ends and beginnings and map the material landscapes of political, territorial jurisdiction and the symbolic landscapes of solidarity and power. The assumed clarity of the structural intervention of a surrender seems intuitively to contrast with the ambiguous leveling of such things as "peace accords." Yet surrenders are themselves complicated ways of ending conflicts, with many contingent variations on their enactments and with their own ambivalence and ambiguity.

The Conditions of Surrender: Toward a Political Semiotic

This book follows what I identify as the semiotic phases of surrender in order to grasp surrender's deepest meanings and mechanisms. Such an approach to the conditions of surrender is not materially incompatible with a more straightforward chronological charting of the sequence of actions that constitute a military surrender. And indeed, I address these more conventional conditions in tandem with its main analytic foci. A strict chronological or causal approach would track and account for the decision to surrender on the part of the vanquished (or the offer of surrender terms on the part of the victor, or both); the communication of these decisions, offers, and acceptances; the meetings to negotiate terms; the ceremonies of signing and exchange; the resulting actions of punishment or imprisonment, or of freeing and exoneration; and finally, the commemorative representation of the surrender in various aesthetic media.

These are strategically critical decision points in the trajectory toward war's termination. And they may heighten the already considerable stock of tension that has built up and surged forward ("forward panics," in Randall Collins's terminology) over the course of the war's proximal armed encounters. As Collins writes, "Confrontational tension builds up as persons in conflict come close to each other, and not merely because that is the point at which one might be hurt; it is at the point that one has to face the other person down, to put him or her under one's violent control against their resistance."[27] According to Collins, there is a marked tendency for victorious troops to kill their opponents just as these opponents are attempting to surrender.

As a consequence of such perils, the dangerous decision to surrender by fighting units involves a series of calculations about risk and benefits. Historian Niall Ferguson outlines the issues:

a) likelihood of one's being killed if one continues fighting
b) likelihood of one's being killed by one's own side if one attempts to surrender
c) likelihood of one's being killed by the enemy if one attempts to surrender
d) differential between the recent quality of life as a fighting soldier as compared with the anticipated quality of life as a prisoner, including the possibility that one might sooner or later be killed.[28]

As significant as such issues are, my alternative analytical framing of these same events will highlight the semiotic and pragmatic conditions of surrender rather than the exclusively strategic conditions. Thus surrender will here be considered according to its semiotic conditions: the *performative* conditions, the *demonstrative* conditions, and the *representational* conditions. These conditions highlight the dynamism of surrenders understood as indeterminate archetypes, and they are all necessary elements of transactional encounters playing off each other in the field they establish.[29] In fact, an important theoretical advance deriving from this approach to surrender is to highlight the ways performative actions existentially depend on preexisting, legitimating constative (or, in the language I am employing, demonstrated) entities, themselves relying on predetermining performative actions, and so on and so forth.[30] Social and political interaction derives its propulsive force from this dialectic.[31]

The fundamental issues of these alternative "conditions" of surrender encompass sovereign selfhood, identity loss and reformulation, and reorientation. These reorientations are of both a temporal and a spatial nature. Surrenders interrupt and reroute specific historical timelines and alter identities and fealties as much as they cartographically reroute territorial entities.

The perspective afforded by the political semiotic highlights such edgework as that of surrenders. And these are exactly the kinds of interactions that risk being overlooked in analyses preoccupied by searches for causes. While not divesting itself of all questions of causality and consequentiality, the political semiotic highlights the mechanisms through which social meanings are forged.

Converging to Convert

The participants in a surrender must converge on a point of exchange in order to successfully convert conflict into peace. The nature of the exchanges effected at and by a surrender will be analyzed at length in chapter 3. In this chapter the focus is on the necessity for convergence and conversion. One highly conventionalized social setting in which conflict undergoes a conversion is the juridical field. As Pierre Bourdieu writes, "The juridical field is a social space organized around the conversion of direct conflict between directly concerned parties into juridically regulated debate between professionals acting by proxy."[32] Other social settings do similar work in alternative idioms. The social space of the surrender is unique in its mixture of conventionalized and contingent mechanisms of converting conflict into peace. To get a handle on this emergent and ephemeral structure, we ought to begin from the ground up—on the one hand appealing to a basic semiosis of figures in space, and on the other appealing to the social-psychological experiences of actual conflict.

Thinking in the most axiomatic terms about subject orientations in space, semioticians like A. J. Greimas have developed a strict, bare-bones conceptual schema for describing the figure in its spatial context.[33] These axiomatic descriptions are extremely useful in thinking about the semiotic conditions of the fundamentally disorienting and reorienting act of surrender. Greimas proposes three axiomatic concepts: displacement, orientation, and support. Figures displace other figures (since no two figures can occupy the same space); they are oriented in either an inward or an outward direction vis-à-vis the parameters of that space (as well as being oriented either toward or away from other figures in that space); and they are supported by that space and the other figures in it as they stand, sit, kneel, lie down, and so forth. How can these concepts be deployed in an analysis of the military, political, and social frames of actual surrenders?

If one thinks about the spatial, temporal, and action parameters of surrenders, in ways that have already been advanced, several modes of working with the semiotic figural program present themselves.[34] To take an example, the concepts of *orientation, displacement,* and *support* offer a mechanism for analyzing the very possibility of surrender itself. A colloquial sense of surrender suggests that one surrenders only when one's back is against the wall. Thus surrender in its purest conceptual form seems to be possible only when one is in a defensive posture (literally and figuratively). This is one reason, as we shall see, that the siege warfare of early modern Europe provided the most highly elaborated formulas and forms for surrender. In contrast, when one is in an offensive stance, attacking the targeted center and seeking to displace its current occupants, the concept of surrender becomes nearly oxymoronic (suggesting that retreats and routs constitute de facto surrenders and thus are both conceptually and politically problematic, as I will show). William Ian Miller suggests just such an impossibility in his analysis of the confounding phenomenon of soldiers' experience of "weak legs," the sudden paralysis of one's legs, an inability to move, in the midst of combat: "Weak legs may be the only way of raising the white flag on offense. When I asked [the Korean war veteran] about his fears going up the hill he answered impatiently: 'What the hell was I supposed to do? Raise a white flag on an assault? . . .' Weak legs move in to fill the void raised by the comic incomprehensibility of surrendering as you go forward in an attack."[35] The "weak legs" experience identifies a semiotically untenable program of surrendering on assault. It announces the short-circuiting of action when *orientations* (inward vs. outward,[36] offense vs. defense) and aims (to literally *displace* the enemy) encounter a lack of psychophysiological support on the part of the attacking soldier, who has the political and semiotic intuition that it is impossible to surrender on assault.

Beyond this, the consideration of the temporal dimensions that orient and reorient actors in such situations both suggests the extension of the *semiotic* program to the concept of time and makes clear the necessity for adding a *pragmatic* theoretical apparatus. Thinking about the example of "weak legs" in temporal terms, we get the sense of a project in which the sequence of actions is out of phase. An assault suggests the beginning of an action, not its conclusion. Surrenders seek just such a conclusion, though they also harbor new beginnings within themselves. Thus surrenders must perform and demonstrate phase appropriateness as various competing timelines converge and resolve themselves in the transfer of power.

The issue of phase appropriateness brings us back to the analytical rubric being proposed here. A complex of mechanisms must be employed to convert a violent conflict or war into a surrender. And these must occur at the right time and the right place. This book aims to follow the semiotic conditions of surrender: the *performative* aspect (in which the act of surrender is accomplished with speech acts—"I surrender," "I promise to lay down my arms"—signatures on documents, and strategic exchanges of weapons and troops); the *referential-demonstrative* aspect (in which speeches, gestures, ceremonies, postures, positions, and so forth do the work of pointing out and recognizing the transformations that are about to be, are being, or have been performed); and the *representational* aspect (in which the accomplished surrender is "copied" and its meaning is launched toward history and posterity). All three aspects provide mechanisms for the sedimentation of the meaning of the event, although they are not all explicitly interpretive in nature. Demonstrations, for example, aim to draw attention to an arena of action or of transformation. They are indexical and directive. They are explicitly interpretive only insofar as they differentiate between the important and the unimportant, the familiar and the unfamiliar, the figure and the background.

While any event of social or political transformation can be interpreted by applying this rubric, the specificity of surrender as an event that is an undoing as much as a doing pushes this analytic scheme to its epistemological limits. The surrender, first and foremost an event at the extreme of worldmaking, becomes an ontological telling of the halting of violence and resistance, of an undoing, or of the loss of an ongoing situation.[37]

The Etymology of Surrender

The English language is full of terms of authoritative transaction that derive their authority from language itself: juris-*diction;* sub-*scribe;* re-*sign*. Sur-*render* is one of these terms, and we turn to linguistic roots to begin examining the meaning of surrender. Embedded in the etymology and use of the word "surrender" are several themes that flow through the political semiotic analysis of acts of surrender. Such themes as repetition, return, and translation are already traceable in the term itself. Further, key inscriptions condition historical acts of surrender and appear in documents of all sorts, the most central of which are the articles of capitulation. Surrenders thus work through the medium of language as much as through gesture and pictorial representations (media of importance to this analysis in their own right).

The Oxford English Dictionary, in its entry for "surrender"[38] as a noun, lists "sure render" and "surrendre" as other forms of the word. The etymological roots of surrender are given as the Anglo-French *surrender* and the Old French *surrendre*. The first meaning listed pertains to law: "The giving up of an estate to the person who has it in reversion or remainder, so as to merge it in the larger estate . . . specifically the yielding up of a tenancy in a copyhold estate to the lord of the manor for a specified purpose." Thus surrender is immediately linked to jurisdictional *space,* by way of its territorial referent, to *time* and the idea of temporary or contingent holdings, in its signifying of re-version or re-mainder, and to the accumulations of *power* ("so as to merge it in the larger estate"). The second, more general, meaning is given as "the giving up of something (or of oneself) into the possession or power of another who has or is held to have a claim to it; especially (Military, etc.) of combatants, a town, territory, etc. to an enemy or a superior. In wider sense: Giving up, resignation, abandonment."

Three things are striking about these meanings. First is the persistent suggestion of a *prior* claim in the essential meaning of surrender—there are always those who are held to have a claim to the self or thing surrendered. Superior force is never sufficient, at least by definition. Second, one is always surrendering something to someone else—whether that be the lord of the manor, the sovereign,[39] the court, another claimant, or the enemy or assailant.[40] And finally, the concept "enemy" is linked to yet also distinguished from "superior."[41] These issues demonstrate the relational nature of surrender—there is always a recipient of the surrendering act, which recipient must be recognized as some kind of sovereign authority.[42] They also suggest an ambivalence about the nature of that relationship between victor and vanquished, an ambivalence that is contingently resolved through the literal and figurative conditions of each surrender. Does an enemy transmute into a superior upon the surrender of the defeated to the victor? Or does an enemy remain an enemy in spite of the submission to the enemy's authority?

A clue to the first issue (that of the prior claim) can be found in the etymology of the root word "render" in surrender. Render is identified as a verb with the Old French root *rendre,* the popular Latin root *rendere* (an alteration of *prendere*), and the classical Latin root *reddere,* whose meaning is "to give back." In fact the very first of some seventeen meanings for "render" that are provided in the *OED* is "to repeat (something learned); to say over, recite." Repetition is, then, at the very linguistic heart of surrender. But not just rote repetition, for the second definition of "render," though noted as now somewhat rare, is "to give in return, to make return of." Here repetition is return, as one renders thanks for some prior gift. Thus notions of recompense and proportionality are brought to bear as "render" gets drawn into the modality of the gift and gift giving, a modality that will prove critical for this analysis.

Meanings 7 and 8 of "render" are actually synonymous with "surrender" itself: "to hand over, deliver, commend, or commit, to another, to concede," and "to give up, surrender, resign, relinquish." But another meaning, between "render" as return and "render" as surrender, is "to reproduce or express in another language, to translate." Translation turns out to be central for the renderings that occur in acts of surrender. The concept of translation captures the potential problems of identity transformation in exchanges mobilized by claims of return. Land, property, language, legal systems, or populations may have been altered during the lapses of a time now retrospectively recognized as alienated. As time passes between the so-called originary time of the prior possessor and the so-called fallen time of the pretender possessor, something happens to what is possessed. Thus, even with the successful assertion of the "giving back" of the rendering up of surrender, the surrender participants and structure must also engage in an act of translation as one system repossesses the object. Here social, cultural, and linguistic differences are put into high relief.

Does this complex of meanings of the word "surrender" appear in the etymology of the term in languages other than English? The *Dictionnaire de la langue française* carries forth a similar constellation of meanings for *rendre,* the French root of "render" and "surrender" (*sur rendre*), as does the *Oxford English Dictionary.* Important meanings of *rendre* are to make someone become; to give back something to the one it belongs to in the first place; to bring something, to transmit; to have respect; to represent; to witness and certify. In so many of these meanings there is the clear sense of transformation, yet of transformation connected to a return to origins. In fact it is the French reflexive verb *se rendre,* translating into the English "surrender," that most clearly suggests an implicit return of the self to its true sovereign, a surrender to the self made sovereign. Throughout, there is a sense of a recovery of an original state that either is true in its essence or is made true by the work of witnesses who certify a rightful state through the imposition of consensus.

What is clear even from these etymological excavations is the fundamental tension revealed by the oscillation between meanings that point to a transsituational legitimation of the social acts of rendering and surrendering (the mythological notion of return) and meanings that are derived from, and enacted by, consensually validated performances/performatives subscribed to by witnesses. I explore this tension as I take up the several cases of surrender under examination. As for the latter meaning, as I noted earlier, the role and presence of witnesses is critical to the legitimacy and success of surrenders. Indeed, witnesses figure prominently in the enactments and representations of these scenes, visually as well as discursively. But as the former meaning suggests, complicated understandings of temporality (surrenders that look back as well as forward) also flow into the exchanges of surrenders. These discrepant and sometimes contradictory temporal frames will also be addressed.

Jacques Derrida, in his intricate meditation on the world of the gift, works through Marcel Mauss's classic text, *The Gift,* to notice that the French word *rendre* carries within itself the idea of a temporal pause or gap as well as the idea of repetition. He quotes and comments on a passage from Mauss: "The notion of a time limit or term is thus logically implied when it is a question of paying or returning visits [*rendre des visites,* an interesting expression in the French idiom: a visit is always repaid or returned even when it is the first], contracting marriages and alliances, establishing peace, attending games."[43]

If even what appears as a discrete historical surrender is actually a restitution of a prior act of extension or alienation, there can be no real first occasions of this sort within human history. The first mover must be out of time itself. And sense must be made of the gap in coherently narrated time before the repayment is both possible and actually transacted. In other words, one needs to come to terms with the essential mythos of return in the linguistic and symbolic roots of such situations of social exchange as surrender. With all the assumed glory of the victor in a surrender, it is puzzling that the very terms of the scene themselves ("sure render," "surrender," *sur rendre*) do not allow the victor the claim of being first mover. Perhaps a clue to this lies in the obligations that accrue from receiving gifts. If the items exchanged in surrenders (swords, soldiers, populations, territory) are viewed through the model of the gift, if the vanquished makes a "gift" of this bounty in the surrender ceremonies and agreements, this may create an unwanted and unwarranted sense of the superiority of the defeated, to whom the victor now owes a debt. Maurice Godelier examines the complex of relationships established by gift giving and gift receiving: "A relationship of solidarity because the giver shares what he has, or what he is, with the receiver; and a relationship of superiority because the one who receives the gift and accepts it places himself in the debt of the one who has given it . . . and to a certain extent becoming his 'dependent' at least for as long as he has not 'given back' what he was given."[44]

Thus must surrenders be framed as returns, as regivings. In this configuring, the victor avoids becoming the unwilling dependent of the vanquished and can receive the gifts without incurring debt. Finally, this etymologically embedded notion of the cycle of return obviously suggests ideas about a nonlinear temporal order, one perhaps of eternity and the divine (to whom all objects of human exchange are ultimately referred and returned) as well as the annexing of these ideas into human projects of conquest. These projects then become retakings.[45]

Similarly, there is no last mover or final surrender—even as each new victor hopes to have put the matter to rest with each surrender received. By their very cyclical natures, surrenders cannot be definitive.[46] They must be repaid. While surrenders may, in their extremism, seem to be the very essence of conclusiveness and finality, they are revealed to harbor an idea of provisionality. Today I surrender to you—tomorrow you will surrender to me. As the wheel of military and historical fortune turns, the idea of retaking is too much at the heart of the surrender, and the vanquished must of necessity be drawn back into the cycle. This suggests that any analysis of surrender must explore the complex and deeply existential relationships between events and repetitions.[47] As a first parsing of these issues, it is useful to think of surrenders as, simultaneously, historical events (occurring within a linear and progressive notion of time and history), symbolic events (occurring within a metaphorical frame of competing sovereign authorities and hierarchical systems), and political events (occurring within the strategic frame of the victor's superiority of force rhetorically configured as the legitimacy of rightful return). Of course, by highlighting the strategic framing of return in the political aspects of surrender, this conceptualization introduces a reading in which the violence of the victor is legitimated via its displacement—that is, via its reference to the authority of origins.

Since one of the three main historical cases this analysis will develop around is the surrender in 1625 of the Dutch-held city of Breda to the Spanish Habsburgs, it is useful to take note of the Dutch terms for surrender. The Dutch words for surrender are *overgeven* and *afstaan*. *Overgeven* translates as "hand over" and *afstaan* as "cede territory, yield possession or one's place, resign an office or a right, surrender a privilege." Handing over and ceding recapitulate some of the previously examined meanings of "surrender" in English and French—that of exchange and that of giving up. The idea that one must surrender to another, hand something over to one who receives it, is as crucial to these meanings as it is to the others.

Surrender agreements are written in as many languages as there have been antagonists in conflict that have ended with some kind of acknowledgment of victory and defeat. Sometimes one language serves for both parties. Sometimes, as we will see, the surrender instrument is simultaneously written in the respective languages of the former combatants. It is not my purpose to survey the dictionary meanings of all languages; I elucidate only those relevant to the selected cases. More to the point, it is the reflexive deployment of terms toward the conclusion of conflict that is of ultimate interest. Sometimes the highlighted terms focus on the concrete acts that will be recognized as surrender, as in the term used in Allied broadcasts to Germany near the end of World War II. Aiming to persuade Germany to unconditionally surrender, the broadcasts demanded the total *Bedingungslose Waffenniederlegung* ("laying down of weapons").

Sometimes the terminological focus is on the nature of the subordination of the vanquished to the victor. Kyoko Inoue notes that there was some subtlety at work in selecting the best Japanese phrase to communicate the English requirement that "from the moment of surrender the authority of the Emperor and the Japanese Government to rule the state shall be subject to the Supreme Commander of the Allied Powers who will take such steps as he deems proper to effectuate the surrender terms." Inoue writes: "The English phrase 'shall be subject to,' which clearly implies subordination, was translated *seigen-no moto-ni okaruru-mono-to su*. This phrase, which literally means something like 'will be placed under the restraint of,' does not carry the same implication of direct subordination . . . This 'translation' thus made it possible for the military to save face, while enabling the Japanese government to accept the substance of the Allies' terms."[48]

Niall Ferguson also parses the Japanese reticence toward linguistic acknowledgments of subordination in surrender. He writes that "even at the end of the war there was extreme reluctance to make use of Surrender Passes bearing the word 'surrender' in either Japanese (*kosan, kofuku*) or English: 'I cease resistance' was the preferred euphemism."[49] According to the linguist Kennosuke Ezawa, both *kofuku* and *kosan* have the component *ko*, which indicates descent, or going down from high to low. *Kofuku,* used exclusively to describe military surrender, actually is rarely articulated, since the literal and figurative lowering it entails often led in the past to suicide or to being killed by the enemy. In post–World War II discourse about the surrender, the most common term is *shusen,* which indicates quite simply "end of war."[50]

Etymological Coda

Etymological archaeology is extremely valuable, partly for connections discovered and partly for connections that are given the lie. One might assume that the roots of "render" are somehow linked to the roots of "rend" and that both provide some of the meaning of the word "surrender." Were this commingling indeed to be linguistically "natural," it would further complicate surrender's meaning. For, as we have seen, "render" means to "give back," to restore to wholeness what was rent. And "rend" means to "tear or pull violently or by main force, to tear off or away" (*OED*). So it appears at first that there is a dynamic contradiction at the heart of the surrender. Surely it marks the site of a fissure or a tear as the vanquished loses what it previously possessed. But surrender also announces the restoration of the peace, the end of hostility, the merging again of what was torn asunder. However, "render" and "rend" actually inhabit different etymological families. They are not related, though they look alike. "Render" has its roots in the Latin *reddere,* and "rend" has its roots in the Old Frisian (Friesland, Netherlands) *renda* and the Old English *rendan.* So this assumed linguistic dynamism is actually a false linguistic consciousness, and we are left with the notion of restoration devoid of the fissure. There is *no* recognized fissure in "sure render," and therefore no first mover is allowed. Yet there is something uncanny about the accidental encounter of these terms that mirrors the uncanniness at the heart of the surrender—something that marks a breach, a loss, a rupture of a war and conflict becomes a return, a repetition, a giving back, a translation to make legible. The opposed meanings of "render" and "rend" shadow each other in ways that are nevertheless meaningful for our general understanding of surrender, and they raise important questions about the various objects that are conventionally and necessarily exchanged in surrender ceremonies—the swords, the batons, the keys to the city, the letters, and so forth. Simply, are the transfers across the antagonists' divide best understood as exchanges that mark a loss and a rift or as sutures that draw the sides together and assist in healing the rift? And how do we come to recognize these transfers and objects as one or the other?

Surrenders as Actions in the Interstices

> When the terms were completed, they were carried to a designated
> point beyond the fortress walls and were here considered. All work on
> the fortifications and trenches ceased. At this critical moment both
> sides were on alert; . . . If the garrison were not watchful, there could
> be a sudden assault from the trenches; if the guards of the trenches re-
> laxed for a moment, the garrison might sally out and spike the hostile
> cannon.[51]

Armed conflict and war are by definition dangerous states of affairs. They are
dangerous both for participants and for the inhabitants of the territories
where the conflicts occur. But within these social states, certain moments are
more dangerous than others. In the statement quoted above, historian John
Wright notes how very dangerous the moment right before a surrender can
be, that moment when the promise to surrender can be exposed as perilously
"infelicitous" (in the "speech-act" terminology of J. L. Austin). The period
during which the surrender is to occur can thus be understood as an interval
or an interregnum ("interregnum" defined both temporally and spatially in
the *Oxford English Dictionary* as "a breach of continuity; an interval, pause, vacant space"). And as such it entails the sense of *suspense* that all suspensions of
action bring. All parties are waiting to see if this transaction that promises to
end the hostilities will actually occur.

Surrenders are situated in the interstices of history and are primarily oriented to the present, to the momentous stopping of the conflict. And yet the
narratives of the past and the terms of the future must enter into this present
to give it meaning and to redirect it. They occur at the switching points of
historical chronologies. Surrender as a rendering up of meaning over time,
then? How is that defining moment to be rendered, when the present is
forged through a particular rendering of the past to declare a future, with all
of its realignments? How do we capture and navigate the pause in the action
of war or conflict, see it as a time in itself?

All codified terminations of hostilities function as pauses. Some—cease-
fires, for example—may be self-consciously temporary and brief, as hostilities are halted to retrieve the dead and the wounded from the battlefield.
Others, such as truces or armistices, may be formally construed as temporary,
as formal negotiations are entered, but may evolve into a situation of de facto
permanence when hostilities are not resumed. The parties to these pauses
may try to anticipate their duration and their stability, but their true nature
can be known only retrospectively. So these pauses are entered with the inevitable uncertainty and anxiety of all waiting to see.

The pauses of surrenders, unlike suspensions of arms or truces, appear to gather themselves or concentrate around the point of exchange at their centers. Arms must be laid down, promises to refrain from future fighting must be made and witnessed. The vanquished must accept the reality of loss (at least for the present). These actions, of both a performative and a demonstrative nature, take place *within* the pause and allow the parties to traverse it. Unlike other types of termination, surrenders as pauses seem to involve more than the usual suspense about surprise resumption of fighting, about sneak attacks and so forth. Because the nature of surrender entails the radical submission/abnegation of one self to another (the collective self and the individual self are both relevant here and often synecdochically linked), the pause of surrender brings with it the earlier noted transformation of social and political identities and existential orientations. Thus the pause of surrender constitutes a truly liminal space and time during which the new order can emerge only once the old order goes through a kind of historical vanishing point.

As one might expect, the atmosphere around such vanishing points is confused and distracted. Social agents, already exhausted by the conflict, suspect that things are about to change radically. One Confederate army soldier in the American Civil War, sent by the president of the Confederacy to deliver dispatches to General Robert E. Lee on the battlefield in the days before Lee's surrender to Union general Ulysses S. Grant in April 1865, wrote about his impressions of the Confederate troops he encountered on the road: "The roads and fields were filled with stragglers. They moved looking behind them, as if they expected to be attacked and harried by the pursuing foe. Demoralization, panic, abandonment of all hope, appeared on every hand. Wagons were rolling along without any order or system."[52]

This condition of distraction and confusion is both strategic and symbolic. I will call this suspended state of being at the border of the surrender "deictic deferral," inasmuch as social agents are at a loss to indicate place, time, and identity with certainty. Chapter 5 will take up this question of deictic deferral at length in its analysis of the deep structure of surrender.

Here, though, I remain with the concepts of interval and delay. The nature of the delay is first one of *interpretation,* since competing frames of meaning are still in play while the surrender enters history. It is also that of a possible delay of *resolution,* since infelicitous performative acts (or others' refusal of their uptake) can potentially derail the surrender and send the parties back into conflict. The delays both in interpretations of the meaning of what is happening and in the resolutions of events themselves highlight the radical contingency of surrender transactions.

All of social life is contingent: plans are made and thwarted, relationships are entered and abandoned, promises are made and broken. The social life of the interregnum of surrender is suffused with the even greater, radical contingency of the self-consciously liminal. Surrender is an event on the threshold. One area of contingency concerns the promise to surrender. Among theorists concerned with the general role of promises in the public sphere, Hannah Arendt most precisely articulated the risks associated with this performative gesture in her analysis of action. Even as they function as "isolated islands of certainty in an ocean of uncertainty," promises hold only insofar as they "arise . . . directly out of the will to live together with others in the mode of acting and speaking, and thus they are like control mechanisms built into the very faculty to start new and unending processes."[53]

So in the promise to surrender lie two risks. One risk is that the defeated group's promise to surrender and the victors' promise to accept the surrender, with all the agreed-on exchanges and terms, will not be upheld in that great ocean of social uncertainty, exacerbated by violence and war. The second risk is that the "will to live together" on which all promises are premised will founder on the uncertainties and confusions about sovereign identities in the postconflict period. Who is the "we" who will live together? Chapter 2, devoted to understanding the significance of the witnesses to surrender, will analytically approach the tenuous stability of the "isolated islands of certainty" that promises to surrender can constitute. Accordingly, such speech acts as "I promise" will be highlighted, together with that of the more ontologically problematic "I surrender."

Yet another area of the contingency of surrender concerns the instability of all transfers involving force. While surrenders aim to suspend violence, they also operate with the presumption of greater (withheld) force on the part of the victors, who disengage their instruments of force in accepting the surrender. What happens to this force that is held in suspended animation for the duration of the surrender? Is it merely withheld, or is it transmuted into something else (perhaps law or humanitarianism) as the performative and demonstrative exchanges of the encounters do their work?[54] Here we need to think deeply about the concept of symbolic violence, described by Bourdieu as "that form of domination which, transcending the opposition usually drawn between sense relations and power relations, communication and domination, is only exerted through the communication in which it is disguised."[55] Chapter 3 will develop an analysis of the exchanges of surrender as a specific type of communication, one that specifically deflects and sublimates the violence being withheld.

The Copies of Surrender

The afterimage—the presence of sensation in the absence of a stimulus—and its subsequent modulations posed a theoretical and empirical demonstration of autonomous vision, of an optical experience that was produced by and within the subject. Second, and equally important, is the introduction of temporality as an inescapable component of observation.[56]

As participants and witnesses make their way through the ordeal of surrender, performing and demonstrating (showing forth) the transformations in identity, fealty, hierarchy, and power, they both follow and forge a trail of texts and pictures.[57] Official documents are written, signed, and witnessed. Maps are recovered and redrawn. Correspondents draw, paint, photograph, or film (depending on the available technology of reproduction) the encounters and exchanges. The actions of surrender claim singular existence and general meaning only as they come to life within typifying genres. Further, a well-tuned analytic framework must be cautious not to approach these diverse media in a reductionist manner. As Roger Chartier writes, "Recognizing that past realities are for the most part accessible only through texts intended to organize them, describe them, prescribe or proscribe them does not in itself oblige us to postulate that the lettered, logocentric, hermeneutic logic governing the production of the discourses is identical to the practical logic regulating behaviors, or the 'iconic' logic governing works of art."[58] The diverse idioms and codes of these media are simultaneously political, diplomatic, and aesthetic. The inevitable semiotic gap between performance and interpretation is intensified by the self-consciousness of the suspense of surrender.[59] Thus do the performative, the demonstrative, and the representational phases of surrender constantly draw from and feed back into each other as assurances of success and successful rendering are sought.

Of course, mixed in with the suspense and the danger and the shame, there is also the pleasure of surrender—the pleasure of the victor who accepts the submission of the enemy. This pleasure, intimately connected to the flows of power and desire in the exchanges, must be transcribed and translated into objects of contemplation. Otherwise the victorious sovereign has no evidence of their having happened in any particular way at all. The objects then form a dossier, copies in the strongest sense of the term (the word "copy" appearing in medieval Latin in such phrases as "dare vel habere copiam legendi" and meaning having the *power* of reading and the *power* of transcription). This is exactly where the role of the witness figures so prominently—indicating and recording in a variety of ways and media that the surrender occurred at a specific time and place, in a specific manner, and with a specific outcome. As I noted above, chapter 2 moves the witness from the periphery to the center of attention.

A preliminary question may be posed here: Who or what is the ideal witness, the ideal copying spectator? Theories of language, and their extrapolation onto other symbolic media of representation, may hold the key. Following Émile Benveniste's linguistic model of distinguishing modes of discourse from modes of enunciation, art historian Louis Marin seeks to apply this model to an analysis of pictorial material, specifically the history painting (of which paintings of military surrenders figure as one iteration). Marin quotes Benveniste on the presumed objectivity of the mode of enunciation in which "nobody is speaking. Events seem to narrate themselves from the horizon of the past."[60] What does it mean to say that events narrate themselves? Does it assume no particular point of view on the event itself? Does it, alternatively, presume a unique, ideal point of view that provides a unique truth (say that of the victor at the moment of the submission of the vanquished)? Or does it, impossibly, aspire to an ideal, aperspectival spectator, one not encumbered by a particular point of view but merely occupying a place in a balanced system of places?[61]

Ultimately, the high stakes for power and identity in acts of surrender, and in the copies they spawn, must invoke a theory of sovereignty itself. Of course, the sovereign is both the ideal (though often absent) actor and the ideal (though often unlocatable) spectator. Chapter 4 will explore the afterlife of the sovereign, that unique, nonsubject subject who coincides with the Nobody of the objective reality that narrates itself. This sovereign divests himself of a point of view precisely in his investment in power—a worthy paradox taken up by such theorists as Ernst Kantorowicz and Giorgio Agamben, and one I will address at length in chapter 4.

Returning to the reading of surrender as a temporal interval, the representative phase of surrender has the problem of copying that interval and its transformative exchanges as a moment in time rendered in space. Theorists of vision and visuality, like Jonathan Crary, Wendy Steiner, Louis Marin, Michel Foucault, and Svetlana Alpers,[62] have taken on this issue of the inter-translatability of the temporal and the spatial in pictorial renderings. In his examination of the modern mechanisms of visual representation such as the camera obscura, Crary notes that "movement and time could be seen and experienced, but never represented."[63] And yet the essence of surrender is its signaling of definitive historical change and requires the authoritative seeing of movement in time. Capturing this seeing is a fully paradoxical affair, whose paradoxes are only suggested in this chapter and will be examined throughout the book. Copies must capture the unique event of this specific surrender and also must be recognized as participating in a wider genre of such renderings. Copies must thus be both time bound (political and historical) and timeless (symbolizing the claim of the rightness of the surrender—a return, as we shall see—that must aspire to eternal fixity).[64] These epistemological challenges often translate into media and genre challenges. Writing about the genre of history paintings, Louis Marin notes that they must "express diachrony, temporal relationships yet can do so only through the network of a whole that generates its parts logically or achronically by its own signifying economy that represents only the logical relationships of elements subordinated to a center."[65]

Even as they are all replete with representational constraints, each codification of the surrender is also a copy. And each copy (maps, signed documents, paintings, and so forth)[66] is a kind of royal pretender, combining and confusing its pragmatic, demonstrative, and representative functions as the meaning of the surrender is historically sedimented. Following Marin's understanding of "representational systems as apparatuses of power," it is critical that representation be linked to issues of recognition and misrecognition, familiarization and defamiliarization.

Ultimately, surrenders have unstable representability: they are by nature suffused with deictic deferral and transformations and thus short-circuit any codified formulas for portraying such adverbs as here and there and then and now (already naturally difficult to translate from language to pictorial idioms). The unstable representability of surrender also derives from what might be called the shame factor—the urge to look away from shameful encounters. Submission of one human to another involves a certain quotient of shame, and witnesses (even those of the victorious sort) must overcome diffidence in order to copy the event.

The power of the copy to effect a reality more powerful than the original (already, in its use of ceremonial templates and conventional performatives, not entirely an original itself) is largely attested to in the realization that the reality of historical surrenders can be approached only through their copies. As their meanings sediment or alter over time, a sense of constant deferral or delay is inevitable. The gap or interval of surrender seems to yawn wider. Such deferrals and their associated recognitions and misrecognitions connect most widely to the difficulty of studying the state and statecraft in any of their manifestations.

My analytic strategy follows the semiotic phases of surrender through their performances, their demonstrations, and their representations. The deictic deferrals of surrender create a kind of visual unconscious (foreshadows and afterimages) around the action. This visual unconscious, resonating as it does with a political unconscious of the state, calls forth a heightened examination of the visual representations of surrender. But not only surrender—my ultimate aim is to draw affinal scenes of encounter and transformation into its analytic orbit. A first attempt at this will be developed in chapter 5. These scenes include inaugurations, coronations, annunciations, marriages, resignations, and foundings. All these scenes both entail and suppress a sense of an interregnum—a break in the narrative flow of history. And they all struggle to be competent in navigating and successfully signifying this middle ground where an end meets a beginning, where one world meets another.[67]

CHAPTER 2

Witness to Surrender

Bolingbroke: Are you contented to resign the crown?
King: —I, no; no, I; I for I must nothing be.
Therefore no no, for I resign to thee.
Now, *mark* me how I will undo myself.

—William Shakespeare, *Richard II,* 4.1.202–3 (italics mine)

OUGHT WE NOT to begin with the main protagonists of surrender, the victorious leader and the undone, vanquished foe? Clearly the transfers of power and sovereignty flow through them and their actions. Those whose task it is to bear witness to these actions are situated in the margins, literally and figuratively. Witnesses are held to observe the actions of other, more central actors who are the protagonists of social and historical progress and transformation. The archetypal witness, the Greek chorus of the ancient tragedies, recounts and extols—or more often laments—the fates of those more exposed individuals who dare to throw themselves directly into the pitch of the universe.

But where would history be without witnesses? These figures do not simply watch. They ratify and notarize. They escort the principals to sites of exchange and transition. They comment on the events, evoking and interpreting them for those not present. They sanction deals and documents and signatures, and they so very importantly *co*sign or *counter*sign.[1] Thus we must also read history through the eyes of those who bear witness to it.

Bearing Witness at Breda

In the sixteenth century, the Spanish Crown came to possess all of the Burgundian Netherlands (the Netherlands and Belgium) through a series of dynastic alliances. Late in the century, Holland and the northern provinces fought for independence from Spain and successfully formed the Dutch Republic. Spain, a Catholic power impelled by religious as well as dynastic imperatives, intermittently persisted in trying to recapture this Protestant territory through the first half of the seventeenth century. These attempts at independence and retaking respectively constituted one arena of the Thirty Years' War (1618–48) in Europe.

After a twelve years' truce broke in 1621, the war in the Netherlands resumed, and in 1622 the Spanish general Ambrogio Spinola captured the town of Julich. But then the war got bogged down "in the waterlogged fields of Flanders outside the walls of cities impregnable to assault."[2] In 1623, despite what seemed to be optimistic circumstances for a renewed Spanish land initiative, Spinola made no move. Bitterly criticized for this by the Consejo de Estado in Madrid, in February 1624 Spinola gave orders for a renewed assault on such towns as Groningen, Cleves, and Gennep. Finally, in August 1624 Spinola encircled Breda, on the border of the southern, securely Spanish Netherlands. Breda, strategically important for its location on the main route to Utrecht and Antwerp, was a heavily fortified town, and a long and militarily complex siege began.

As I noted in chapter 1, this siege was a spectacle of military engineering and strategizing. Historians Jonathan Brown and J. H. Elliott write, "Distinguished visitors came from all over Europe to watch the progress of the operations, which were conducted with great skill and technical ingenuity by both Spaniards and Dutch. Trenches were dug, complicated engineering schemes undertaken, and both sides attempted to turn the rivers to their own account . . . The results of these various dyking and damming operations can be clearly seen in a later painting of the siege by Peter Snayers and less clearly in Velázquez's picture [plate 1], although the famous Black Dike across the artificially flooded Vucht polder is easily visible in the line across the waters above the head of Justin's horse."[3]

Although Spain lagged behind the Protestant states and France in absorbing the military innovations of the drill (introduced in 1619 by Maurice of Nassau in his military training academy), it did not lag behind in the other technological innovations of warfare—the use of guns and the development of siege warfare that "depended on the engineering of military victories through the construction and destruction of battlement systems, not individual heroics and equestrian skills."[4] In spite of the massive construction and reconfiguration of water and land, this siege involved minimal fighting. Jonathan Israel writes, "Breda was simply an exercise in starving the defenders out . . . There was scarcely any fighting, little bombardment, and few casualties."[5]

Of all the diverse modes of conducting wars, the siege is perhaps the most conducive to surrender as a method of resolution. As I noted in chapter 1, the emergent territorial consolidations of early modern Europe made sieges the most logical form of warfare. Fortresses and walled cities mapped the landscape into clearly demarcated proprietary zones. The walls, doors, and spaces of the besieged town or fortress established a visible zone of inside and outside and made legible the lived phenomenology of such concepts as friend and enemy, attacker and defender. The revived interest in ancient Roman military strategies of digging ditches and erecting ramparts led to series of concentric perimeters that recapitulated the zoning of the inside and the outside of the siege: "By systematically digging ditches and erecting ramparts to defend its outer perimeter, a besieging army could protect itself against a relieving expedition while continuing to press the siege."[6] Mapping, calculating, and reconfiguring spatial relations become more important in the conduct of warfare.

In the late spring of 1625 General Spinola, victorious, but exhausted and with depleted forces of his own, negotiated with Justin of Nassau, the Dutch general who led the defense of Breda, to effect a surrender of the town to the Spanish forces. The terms of the surrender were generous: Justin was allowed to leave the city with his officers and survivors of the garrison; according to Gerrat Barry's English translation of the account, they left the city "after the accustomed manner of war with their colors displayed, the drums beating, after the accustomed sound."[7] No Spanish soldier was allowed to shout invectives or make remarks as the Dutch passed by, and a personal escort was appointed to accompany Justin's party. In addition, the town of Breda was allowed to retain a significant amount of economic autonomy. Historical opinion is mixed on the practical impact of Spinola's victory at Breda. Certainly the campaign was a massively expensive undertaking, stretching the resources of the Spanish Crown. Spinola's own troops suffered from food shortages. Nevertheless, it was an unmitigated symbolic triumph—for Spinola, for Isabella, the regent of the Spanish Netherlands, and thus, indirectly, for Philip IV.

Ambrogio Spinola is generally viewed as the proximate architect of the chivalric display of magnanimity toward Justin and the Dutch (having been deputized by Philip IV and his chief minister, the ambitious Count Olivares). This was in accord with seventeenth-century Spanish ideals regarding the treatment of the vanquished enemy and was to be broadly compensatory for the very unchivalric legacy of the previous century (known as the *legenda nera*), in which the Spanish troops had treated their vanquished enemies with cruelty. In his contemporary book *Politica militar*, Francisco Manuel de Melo, a proponent of the magnanimous victor, wrote, "For there is no doubt that such men would feel more deeply their decline in fortune as the result of receiving insufficient esteem, than they feel the loss of their possessions. Therefore it is just that the man who has been instrumental in depriving them of the latter should preserve them in the former . . . And also because in this way the glory of the victory is increased."[8]

Thus the terms of the surrender treaty at Breda were magnanimous, with the economy of the city basically left in the hands of its inhabitants and with only minimal pressure to abandon their Protestant faith.[9] Nevertheless, it is important to keep in mind that by the time Diego Velázquez came to paint his painting some ten years later (*The Surrender of Breda,* 1634–35), the town was on the verge of being retaken by the Dutch, and Spinola's prestige and power had dissolved.[10]

That many distinguished, even noble, visitors came from afar to witness the siege has already been noted. But it is important to examine the recordings of several of these witnesses to this siege and surrender to get at something crucial about the settling in of the reality of transformative moments in history more generally. Witnessing, as we shall see, takes many forms and makes an action reverberate in many media. Beyond the actual witnesses to the signing of the surrender treaty and the ceremony of surrender, other witnesses extended its reality through time and across space. The Jesuit priest Hermannus Hugo, Spinola's personal chaplain, wrote a detailed eyewitness journal of the siege and surrender called *Obsidio Bredana*. Its title page was designed by the artist Peter Paul Rubens and consisted of an allegorical scene of Breda as a maiden being strangled into submission by Famine. It also contained etchings of maps and diagrams of the siege works and battlements by the brothers Theodore and Cornelis Galle. The mapmaker Jacques Callot drew information from the *Obsidio Bredana* to create his well-known *Map of the Siege of Breda*. Another primary source was the anonymous *Carta tercera que vino a un cavallero* (published in Valladolid, 1625); its consideration raises the issue of the credibility and functionality of *anonymous* witnesses.

Further, three years after Justin's surrender to Spinola, in 1628, the renowned playwright Pedro Calderón de la Barca wrote a play titled *El sitio de Breda*. In his play, Calderón has Justin of Nassau offer the keys to the city to Spinola (something only the *Carta tercera* mentions and that may not have occurred).[11] Spinola responds by saying, "Justino, I receive them, and I know how valiant you are and that the valour of the conquered makes famous the conqueror."[12] Finally, six years later, Diego Velázquez, court painter for Philip IV, was commissioned to paint *The Surrender of Breda* for the Hall of Realms in the Palace of the Buen Retiro in Madrid. It was to be one of twelve paintings of victories won during the reign of Philip IV, hung together to symbolically reconstitute the Spanish Habsburg empire. Velázquez's painting thus comes at the end of a line of renderings of the Breda surrender scene.

One can follow the trail of official and unofficial witnesses to this scene of surrender as it proceeds through a variety of textual and pictorial genres—journals, maps, plays, paintings. Each successive iteration hands off its own version of the history of the event witnessed and gets drawn up into the larger sedimented history that aims to transcend its particulars. But each iteration in this relay also has its own generic conventions that constrain the kinds of actions and intentions it is capable of expressing. Sometimes we find an artist who is able to successfully absorb the expressive conventions of other genres in creating a transcendent combinatory work. For example, in *El sitio de Breda* Calderón implicitly references Callot's map and the kind of intimate knowledge that maps can bring. In discussing a long speech in act 2, during which Spinola identifies various landmarks in Breda for the visiting Prince of Poland, Renaissance scholar Shirley Whitaker notes an interesting aspect of the forms of speech Calderón uses: "As Spinola explains, the siege enclosed an area thirty miles in circumference; hence the natural assumption is that he and the prince would have been standing fairly close together looking off into the distance. If this is the case, it is puzzling—indeed incomprehensible—that Spinola should employ *aqui* and forms of *este* throughout the speech . . . The only explanation consonant with the use of equivalents of 'here,' 'this,' and 'these' is that Spinola was indicating positions on a plan [or map] of the city and its environs beside which he and the prince were standing."[13] Supplementing this notion, one can hear the familiarity associated with a place that is referred to with the closer forms "here" and "this." These speakers seem to know this place, a place they have mapped, and their knowledge buttresses claims of ownership. Calderón's imagining of such speech in the play performs this claim through a merging of the demonstrative and the performative in these deictical choices.

Here it is useful to think about the place of maps in the seventeenth century, particularly in northern Europe. Art historian Svetlana Alpers makes the case for a historically unique coinciding of mapping and picturing in seventeenth-century Dutch art. This period saw the production of maps for use as wall hangings—part decoration, part geographical pedagogy, part inscription of the world on the domestic interior surface of the walls. I would argue that these maps operated much like the history paintings of victory and surrender that lined the walls of such buildings as the Sienese Palazzo Pubblico, the Sala Grande in the Medici Hall of State of the Palazzo Vecchio in Florence, and the Hall of Realms in the Palace of the Buen Retiro in Madrid.

Nevertheless, a map on a wall creates a different vision than does a history painting. As Alpers writes, "Such mapped images have a potential flexibility in assembling different kinds of information about or knowledge of the world which are not offered by the Albertian picture."[14] Expanding on the role of maps, art historians Gridley McKim-Smith and Marcia Welles note that "from the frequent display of mapped imagery in Spain in the 16th and 17th centuries, one concludes that a map had a special valence, a truth value to the 17th century onlooker that resembled the documentary value of a photograph to the modern viewer."[15] This idea of documentary value suggests that maps did more than help people find their way in space—they also assisted in finding one's way in history: here is where the battle took place; this was the landscape; here the walls of the town, and so forth. Detail becomes politically significant, and an emphasis on detail links directly to ideologies of discovery and ownership. Historian Patricia Seed notes, "While in other 16th century European languages . . . to discover meant simply to view from afar, in Dutch discovery implied far greater meticulousness."[16] While the Dutch took to the cartographic vision of reality most enthusiastically, they also were the largest producers of maps for other European powers of the time, including the Spanish.[17]

It is important to note, however, that the specific kind of mental compassing involved in cartography suggests that Dutch maps and their makers (along with their eventual viewers) constituted particular kinds of witnesses, invested in what Alpers calls "the art of describing." When it came to understanding themselves and their relation to their territorial possessions, the map provided an instrument for trade and commercial relations rather than a monarchical imprimatur. Writing about the importance of the municipal charter for the Dutch state, Seed notes that "other Europeans usually accepted a king's rights to create a political authority on his own initiative, of his 'own motion, certain science and special grace or authority,' a custom rejected in 16th century Dutch political practice."[18] In like manner, writing about the cartographic tradition of rendering, Martin Jay notes that while it rejects "the privileged, constitutive role of the monocular subject, it emphasizes instead the prior existence of a world of objects depicted on the flat canvas, a world indifferent to the beholder's position in front of it."[19]

Another way to view maps may be as a kind of halfway house between actual text documents like articles of surrender and ethnographic reports of battles and such pictorial representations as paintings. Seventeenth-century maps contained words, legends, symbols, and images, all deployed together. Scholars have identified allusions to Callot's map in *The Surrender of Breda* in Velázquez's inclusion of topographical details as well as a tiny second image of Spinola in the background, still engaged in the siege battle[20] (plate 2). In addition, we see the Dutch defenders exiting through the breach in the wall, giving cartographic evidence that the commander did not surrender prematurely (for which there were severe penalties).[21] Velázquez thus takes the very northern style of painting—attuned to maps and landscapes—and builds his *Surrender of Breda* as if the scene of the surrender with its main protagonists were actually standing in front of a map of the siege that had been hung up on a wall. In doing so he is able to reference both Callot's map and Calderón's play.[22] The foreground is temporally situated in the present, the mapped and landscaped background in the past. Perhaps one thing revealed by this hybrid aesthetic is that in spite of stylistic, religious, and political differences, the worldviews of the victorious Spaniards and the defeated Dutch were not necessarily incompatible and, at least for this one unique historical moment, could be reconciled in a work of transcendent political and aesthetic daring.

Why daring? The two central figures in the painting, the generals Ambrogio Spinola and Justin of Nassau, convey, respectively, magnanimity and gratitude. Yet being grateful to one's victorious enemy clearly is at best an ambivalent attitude. There is a keen sense of dignified humiliation[23] here that gives the scene its particular poignancy. Scholars have interpreted the gestures of Spinola and Justin as indicating that as Justin goes to kneel before Spinola, Spinola puts his arm on Justin's shoulder to prevent him from doing so. Hierarchy, as expressed through mutual bodily alignment, is muted (though not altogether erased) as the vanquished is saved the humiliation of kneeling before the victor. In this forestalling, the exchange of keys to the city is *also* deferred, and thus the frame of magnanimity inserts itself into the conventional, if humiliating, operation of the act of surrender. It literally interrupts the surrender, interposing a new normative framework of conventions as the gestures seek to carry out the action. It is important to note the relation between the aesthetic aspect and the normative aspect that is developed in this painting. Velázquez's portrayal (witnessing) of the surrender at Breda is unusual in placing the victor and the vanquished on the same plane. Typically, paintings of surrender visually exaggerated the asymmetry between former foes: "The ceremony of surrender could take many forms. But in art it was almost always represented as a pageant of triumph and humiliation, in which the victor was shown as standing or seated on a throne or horseback and accepting tribute from the kneeling and submissive general."[24] Indeed, General Spinola himself had been portrayed in this more conventional way in a painting of the surrender of Julich by Jusepe Leonardo (plate 3). Several reasons might account for Velázquez's unconventional representation, including the explicit turn away from the *legenda nera* and, more proximally in 1635, the emphasis on Spinola's humanity.

But in this chapter focused on the witnesses to surrender, it is to the groups of soldiers and nobles flanking the two principals that we must turn. At this moment of surrender, these figures are the most obvious and proximal witnesses to the act.

Groups of men stand on each side of the painting, flanking and buttressing the two generals. On the right stand the victorious Spaniards, nobles in the foreground, looking back and out from their congested ensemble—soldiers massed in the middle ground with their mass of lances straight up all across, exemplifying the strength, resolve, and solidarity of the Spanish troops. On the left, the Dutch have their pikes and halberds tilted, staggered, and akimbo, reflecting the disorganization and disorientation of the defeated. Even with all these lances and pikes clearly evident in the foreground and the middle ground of the painting, we do not see this scene as one dominated by the weaponry and artifacts of war, especially of siege warfare. In fact, only two muskets are visible—one held by a Dutch soldier looking out at us on the far left of the painting and one held by a Spanish soldier behind Spinola. What is interesting is that both muskets are held in the same manner, over the shoulder and pointing away from the center where the former enemies are involved in the acts of surrender and exchange. Conventions of war carefully calibrated the ways the defeated could carry weapons out of a siege, with the "at carry" position (sabers and muskets resting on the shoulder pointing up-ward) as the most honorable. In this case the symmetry and lack of aggres-sion of the position of the muskets held by both the Dutch and the Spanish soldiers reiterate the mutual recognition of the ceremony, the magnanimity of the terms, and that of Spinola himself.

The soldiers are there to bear witness to the rendering up of surrender, to the transmission of the key to the city from Justin's hand to Spinola's. Here is a case in which former protagonists of the conflict must transmute into witnesses in order for the act of surrender to succeed. What is involved in such role switching, and what are the singular burdens on witnesses to sur-render? To answer these questions, we must first examine what it means to be a witness.

What Is a Witness?

All witnessing involves a combination of performative, demonstrative, and representational acts. Through such actions as the signing of official docu-ments, witnesses coauthor events; through their demonstrative gestures and attentions, they locate the focal points of action and direct others toward them; through their recountings in various media, they represent what has happened, rendering it historically legible. In sum, by taking up a point of view, witnesses make the world intelligible.

Playing this crucial hinge role in moments of social and political transfor-mation, witnesses are both necessary and an encumbrance. The central ac-tors in an ongoing event must count on the witnesses to see what they are supposed to see, to record the event in a particular way, to sign their true names in the appropriate way on the right document. The quasi autonomy of the witness is both required and a source of anxiety. What will the witness record? Will the witness attend to the scene, or will he or she turn away? How will the witness recount and represent the act after its occurrence? In this re-gard, artists like Velázquez and writers like Hermannus Hugo and Calderón de la Barca are particular kinds of witnesses. Their paintings, plays, poems, and journals are essentially the signatures by which they subscribe to (under-write) the scene.

The word "witness" has several etymological roots and historical mean-ings. Giorgio Agamben notes that "the Greek word for witness is *martis, mar-*

tyr (derived from the verb meaning 'to remember'). The first Church Fathers coined the term *martirium* from *martis* to indicate the death of persecuted Christians, who thus bore witness to their faith."[25] There is a paradox to this root meaning of "witness." The act of witnessing faith, borne by martyrs in their very martyrdom, must rely on second-order witnesses to record and remember it. This paradox draws out something key to this book, namely what it means to bear witness to a scene of surrender. Wherever selves are undergoing processes that can be understood as undoings or abnegations, the task of the witness becomes doubly complicated. In such events as martyrdoms, resignations, or surrenders, it is not unreasonable to claim that witnesses are asked to bear witness to a disappearance—even, at times, to their *own* undoing.

In his reflections, Agamben goes on to note that "in Latin there are two words for 'witness.' The first word, *testis,* from which our word 'testimony' derives, etymologically signifies the person who, in a trial or lawsuit between two rival parties, is in the position of the third party (*terstis*). The second word, *superstes,* designates a person who has lived through something, who has experienced an event from beginning to end and can therefore bear witness to it."[26] First let us consider witnesses as third parties.

Third parties are crucial to the structure and progress of disputes. They stand outside the intense standoff of the charge and countercharge that pits the main protagonists against each other. This "outside" is both temporal and spatial. Third parties can be figures linked to the past in their representation and embodiment of tradition and institutionalized authority. They can open an escape hatch to the future by subscribing to a way out of the conflict. Or, given their structural position, they can simply operate in the present as spectators with an autonomous vantage point. Credible testimony comes from third parties, or witnesses in this sense. And the variable dynamics and forms of testimony reflect the different demands placed on witnesses—moral, political, and legal.[27] The report of the witness needs to be accurate to some standard (epistemological or political) of reality. And the witness must take responsibility for ratifying that this event happened in this way rather than in some other. Of course, the third-party witness often finds a kind of situational zone of discretion—discretion in two senses of the word. There may be discretion in the face of action that undoes identity or is shameful. Can and does the discreet witness look away from a scene of degradation, humiliation, or dispossession? Further, to what extent does the witness have the discretion to testify, to sign, to subscribe or to withhold from doing so?

Since vantage points turn out to be key for credibility and intelligibility of witness reports, it is important to *locate* third parties spatially and temporally. Are they close enough to see or hear the exchanges and transactions at the center? Are they oriented correctly to the action? How do we latter-day witnesses account for their presence? After all, it seems the essence of the witness to be an acknowledged presence at the scene (even, and especially, when the scene's very boundaries are fluid).

Situational boundaries are not simply spatial, however. There are temporal boundaries as well that determine the relevance of incumbents' roles. The role of the witness can be temporary—witnesses are created or called forth in situations when principal actors and actions claim both attention and center stage. Historically, however, social-organizational developments turned the contingent role of witnessing a specific act into a professional identity. Hillel Schwartz writes that during the epoch of the Roman Empire, a gradual transformation occurred that turned copyists and public scribes into notaries and administrators and then, by the fourth century, into senators: "But the shorthand route to power was so clear that the title of notary would mark rather a political than tachygraphic skill. Petronius Maximus, Emperor in 455 had started off as a notary."[28] Schwartz notes that this trajectory for notaries continued into the medieval culture, as they became "the chief repositories of legal precedent."[29]

Thus there is a continuum of involvement and agency of third parties to conflicts. Donald Black has developed a typology of third parties that "classifies third parties along two dimensions: the nature of their intervention (whether partisan or not) and the degree of their intervention. It identifies a total of twelve roles, including five support roles (informer, advisor, advocate, ally, and surrogate) and five settlement roles (friendly peacemaker, mediator, arbitrator, judge, and repressive peacemaker)."[30] But even lacking the more formal and authoritative statuses, onlooking third parties can have their presence felt in several ways. One potentially significant way for this presence to be felt, particularly in the context of conflict, is for central actors to anxiously anticipate the transmutation of witnesses into central actors like themselves. Here the role contingency of witnesses in a moment of danger is vital. For example, political scientist H. E. Goemans analyzes the presence of third parties in ongoing two-party wars: "The presence of a potential intervener allows winners to credibly commit to limit their war aims if both winners and losers know that any further demands would invite balancing behavior by a third party. The anticipation or actuality of third-party intervention in war provides the first mechanism that makes a self-enforcing agreement to end war possible."[31] In gauging the impact of witnessing, including witnessing that might develop into active participation, it is thus essential to specify, spatially, temporally, and semiotically, the meaning of such presence and attention.

Taking up the second Latinate meaning of "witness," that of *superstes,* it is clear that this meaning emphasizes less the *position* and more the *experience* of the witness. The witness in this sense is one who has lived through an event and can bear witness to its having occurred. Thus the witness is a survivor, one who bears the event within himself or herself. These witnesses combine experience with meaning, survival with judgment.

Several dilemmas are associated with this meaning of witness. What, for example, happens when not one of those who see and experience the event survives to record and remember it? In *Remnants of Auschwitz,* Agamben addresses just this problem when he considers the Shoah: "The Shoah is an event without witnesses in the double sense that it is impossible to bear witness from the inside—since no one can bear witness from the inside of death, and there is no voice for the disappearance of voice—and from the outside— since the 'outsider' is by definition excluded from the event."[32] Here is the deeply political and moral problem of the absence of testimony when presence is necessary.

Another problematic feature of this understanding of witness is that of individuals recognized as inhabiting mutually exclusive roles. What happens, for example, when those who were, or who might have been, protagonists are called on to bear witness to that event? They had the experience under one optic and are called on to give it meaning under another. The Fifth Amendment to the Constitution of the United States weighs in on this question when it takes up the problem of self-incrimination, stating that "no person . . . shall be compelled in any criminal case to be a witness against himself." In the case of the role of the public in the political sphere, historical transformations wrought by social or political change might suppress the agentic role in a moment of general amnesty or reconciliation. We are all, or almost all, witnesses *now.*

In his analysis of the 1996 series of newspaper articles that reproduced the "Report of the Commission on Truth and Reconciliation in South Africa," Philippe-Joseph Salazar raises a question about the identity of the reading public. Can these newspaper readers simultaneously be the *subjects* of the narrative of the Report and be *witnesses* subscribing to it? He writes, "The series of articles cogently argue for an argumentative fiction . . . by which readers have already removed themselves from the past and moved beyond the Truth and Reconciliation Commission. In sum, the new citizens are no longer subjects of the TRC's narratives."[33]

Political dilemmas of this type recapitulate the sociolinguistic parsing of authorship of speech acts. Erving Goffman's famous concept of "footing" tracks the varieties on a theme of identity—when a speaker is alternatively understood to be the author (or not) of the words that are spoken, the animator (or not) of the utterance, and the principal (or not) who adheres to the sentiment of the utterance.[34] These gaps, or degrees of freedom, that are opened up by the role, position, and actions of the witness raise a crucial question. Can witnesses ever be thoroughly implicated in the events they are called on to bear witness to? Or are they always positioned slightly to the side, thereby necessarily afforded a degree of freedom we might call the zone of autonomy?

In her detailed analysis of the emerging conventions of visual documentation on the liberation of the Nazi concentration camps at the end of World War II in Europe, Barbie Zelizer draws attention to the self-reflective role of images of witnessing. These witnesses included American journalists, American military officers, German camp officials, and German civilians. They were called on to witness the atrocities in and of the camps. For the journalists in particular, the linguistic choices they made in narrating their stories highlighted their witnessing role. Zelizer pays close attention to their grammatical and lexical choices, and of one wire service reporter's use of pronouns she writes, "His shift to first person enhanced the narrative's credibility by muting his professional role as neutral observer, signified in third person, and acknowledging instead his role as witness."[35]

Published photographs of all the various witnesses established different visual angles for individual constituencies. For example, concentration camp survivors were photographed frontally, staring directly at the camera, while German perpetrators were photographed in side views. Zelizer writes: "Perpetrators were generally shown at odd angles to the camera, which showed large uniform bodies—angry stares, colorless prison garb . . . German civilians were also frequently depicted witnesses, and they too were photographed in various encounters with the atrocities, reburying the bodies of Nazi victims, looking at the cremation ovens, or 'being forced to gaze' at stacks of corpses."[36] In these photographs, framed, as Zelizer describes, in formal, conventionalized tableaus, the characteristic poses of civilians were the most elusive and ambiguous. In a photograph of German civilians viewing corpses at Buchenwald in April 1945 (plate 4), we see the backs of the civilians as they stand in a group organized to face either a horrific pile of dead bodies or a group of liberators and survivors. To judge from the backs of their heads, it seems that very few are looking at the bodies—but their actual line of vision is, perhaps not accidentally, obscured. They exist in a kind of liminal zone of responsibility, and the significance of the zone of autonomy that they are now, as witnesses, at least temporarily being afforded is built into the role of witnessing.

This degree of freedom introduces a strange twist on the act of confession. By confessing to one's own past transgressions, one may transform oneself from a (transgressing) actor into a witness. Salazar finds such speech act switches in the South African Truth and Reconciliation Hearings: "In the TRC's case, criminals come forward as 'witness' of their own transgressions. The criminal is the witness, and often, the only witness, and sometimes to a fact that no one even suspected to have taken place."[37]

Taken together, the "third-party" understanding of a witness and the "bearer of experience" meaning of witness may suggest an internal contradiction or a pull in diverse directions. The former implies an outsider's perspective, the latter that of one who bears the experience deep within the self. This pull ramifies across our examination of the location and actions of witnesses as they are called to witness surrenders.

How might we read the witnesses to the surrender of Breda, as painted by Velázquez? The soldiers may be understood as witnesses first under the *superstes* definition—they bear the experience of the war within themselves—and second under the *terstis* definition—they now act as the historically ratifying third party.[38] In the network of cross-witnessing, we witness their witnessing of the exchange of the key to the city of Breda.

The very presence of the Dutch escort for Justin of Nassau is noteworthy. According to Brown and Elliott in their masterly study of Philip IV's Palace of the Buen Retiro, "A defeated commander customarily would have met his conqueror unescorted."[39] And yet Justin comes with a full, if beleaguered-looking, escort. All these witnesses are there to see the thing resolved. And yet the resolution seems to hang in suspense, as does the key to the city in Justin's hand.

Meanwhile, many of the soldiers seem distracted. They look about, talk to each other, and peer back toward the scene of the anachronistically ongoing war. From one vantage point, this apparent distraction might be said to constitute what I term the network of cross-witnessing, setting up an intricate series of sight lines and visual contacts. And yet it is hard not to feel that many of these witnesses somehow resist their total involvement and alignment toward that neutralizing, flat center space where the two generals meet. So it is just here, in the noticing of all this distraction and disalignment, that it is necessary not to look away ourselves, not to automatically subsume the distraction under an alternative analytical rubric.[40]

The Visual Order of the Witness

Witnesses witness actors engaging in actions. Witnesses also witness others witnessing the action. Second- and third-"generation" witnesses encounter evidence that past actions have been witnessed before by those who have registered their witnessing. All designated witnesses thus variably figure into a networked compositional matrix or field.[41] Describing the shape of that field is a complicated task. For example, Where are the witnesses positioned? Are we likely to find them on the periphery of the composition's center? Are they looking inward or looking outward? Does the compositional structure lead us to follow the gestures of the witnesses, their physical and visual orientations (sight lines), and their stances as they point inward or out? In any of these variable configurations, the scene must cohere around and through a central focal point where the key commitments and performative actions occur.

The witnessing of a coherent scene thus requires a complex perceptual apparatus able to comprehend the alternations of narrative action and moments of suspended time during which the measure of the scene's meaning is gauged. In other words, the relation of the witness to the scene is a function of proximity, point of view, and perception.

The witness is both in and out of the scene. But in order to be witnessed, the scene must be conjured up out of the ongoing movement of social time and must be congealed (however temporarily). Visual theorist Jonathan Crary highlights the critical importance of point of view: "Whether it is a question of the stage, urban design, or visual imagery, the intelligibility of a given site depends on a precisely specified relationship between a delimited point of view and a tableau."[42] The congealed moment is the moment of fate when performatives change the world. Only validated points of view can make the transformations intelligible.

By way of analogy, melodrama—the dramaturgy in nineteenth-century British theater based on combined narrative and pictorial exposition—captures these alignments and their meanings. At key turning points in the melodramas, as the action built toward revelation, the actors on stage would freeze in midgesture, revealing the network of relations just as these relations were on the threshold of transformation. Time was temporarily frozen to allow the spectator's gaze to pan the spatially arrayed matrix of relations. As Martin Meisel writes, "The fullest expression of a pictorial dramaturgy is the tableau where the actors strike an expressive stance in a legible symbolic configuration that crystallizes a stage of the narrative as a situation, or summarizes and punctuates it."[43] In an analogous manner, the witnesses of historical transformations are positioned to observe something that happens in "real time" and yet must also attest to that happening by freezing time. They do this through their acts of notarizing and sanctioning. They are called on to bear witness to a vision of the world that is remade at the very moment when witnessing becomes relevant. In addition, the painter, or photographer, of such scenes is compelled to create a frozen tableau. Performatives, demonstratives, and representations thus differently engage and construe this pulsating rhythm of the ongoing interactions and the crystallized moments. Different kinds of witnesses (proximal or distant, immediate or delayed, notarizing or representing, official or unofficial) who are called on to embody and enact these various tasks confront a very real existential dilemma of knowing where, when, and how to "look."

Movement is hard to see, harder to describe, hardest to ratify and record.[44]

Artists in different cultures and historical periods have grappled with the question of whether, and how, to render movement in painting, poetry, and prose. Some artists have opted to freeze movement (and thus time), some to attempt narrative recapitulation, some to juxtapose different moments in the "same" scene.[45] In her discussion of Renaissance painting, for example, Wendy Steiner claims that the Renaissance instituted a logic that made the image represent the perceiver's vision of the world at a single moment of time, precluding representations of narrativity.[46]

For present purposes, the connection between the complex choices involved in rendering time's ongoingness and stopping points and the complex demands on the witness revolves around the witnesses' position, orientation, and actions. The question is raised, What does it mean to testify to a vision of a world that is simultaneously being remade by (in part) the very testimonial actions of the witness?

We need return to *The Surrender of Breda* and ask why so few of the witnesses appear to be giving the central scene of the transfer of the key much attention. Why are so many distracted? What might it mean for a court painter to portray the moment of surrender of the defeated foe as a moment of distraction?

Art historian Michael Fried took on the complicated and intertwining issues of pictorial absorption and distraction in his study of eighteenth-century French painting in the age of Diderot. Analyzing the great genre paintings of such artists as Jean-Baptiste Greuze and Jean-Baptiste-Siméon Chardin, Fried points to the states of absorption of the figures in these paintings of, for the most part, everyday life. Fried does mention that such seventeenth-century painters as Velázquez can be seen as precursors of this thematic attention to attention. For our purposes, I want specifically to connect my own analysis of attention's opposite, distraction, in *The Surrender of Breda* to Fried's focus—with a twist. For Fried, the clue to these paintings is their approving representation of absorption, as the figures in the paintings are fully caught up in the world of their families, their chores, their thoughts. What Fried notices, but does not dwell on, is that in almost every one of these paintings there is one figure, often a child, who is clearly distracted—who looks away, doesn't pay attention, is not absorbed.[47] How do we read this distraction?

A semiotic analysis keyed to binary opposition would insist that we recognize and feel the full force of absorption only if its opposite, distraction, is also indicated. Thus the distraction is there to set off or highlight the absorption. In the case of *The Surrender of Breda* one might claim that the distraction of the soldiers—looking out, looking back, looking down and across—draws our attention to its opposite, the quietly attentive mien of the two principals, Spinola and Justin, who have eyes only for each other. A more sociological analysis might find the distraction to be a form of resistance to the central authority of the main event. Certainly, for the Dutch soldiers in *The Surrender of Breda* such resistance is logical, and the diverted gazes sustain resistance to a potential moment of shame in defeat. It is hard for the defeated to look the victor squarely in the eye (and perhaps vice versa). It is hard to be asked to bear witness to one's own disbanding, one's own undoing. One Dutch soldier even seems, with his pointing finger, to be admonishing his fellows to direct their gaze toward that center area of the deferred exchange of the key. Such unbearable witnessing might be said to short-circuit the cross-witnessing network. Eyes purposely do not meet each other. Might such deflections and aversions, showing up in a rendering conceived by the victor's court painter, not also be a way of introducing the point of view of the vanquished—a diffused magnanimity reflecting that at the painting's center?[48] The Spanish witnesses in the foreground seem largely to be representatives of the Spanish nobility, made visible in the conventionally self-aggrandizing manner of serial portraits. But in the background we catch a glimpse of the Habsburg foot soldiers, many of them allies of Spain (Italians and Germans), and they seem less involved, literally peripheral. Calderón de la Barca, in his play about the siege of Breda, *El sitio de Breda,* portrays these quasi mercenaries as wanting to sack the besieged town and being prevented from doing so by the magnanimous Spinola.[49] So at least some of their distraction may point to disgruntlement. And then there is the generalized sense of disorientation at a historical vanishing point, in this case for witnesses at the boundary of a city that moves back and forth across shifting national frontiers, between the Dutch and the Spaniards, several times over the course of two decades.

Where Is the Witness?

The city of Breda surrenders to Spinola and the earth figuratively shifts. Dutch Breda is now back within the borders of the Spanish empire. The question of the location of witnesses looms large, particularly when their location is partially a function of their very acts of witnessing (having witnessed the surrender, the soldiers are no longer in Dutch territory). In such shifting terrain, where should the witness be? For example, to what degree does true witnessing require proximity to the central transfers? To what extent do the institutions set up to overcome distance (political institutions, technologies and institutions of communication)[50] mitigate this need for proximity? Does the question of proximity serve to differentiate witnessing from "mere" spectatorship?

If, as Martin Meisel suggests, there is "an interpretive habit of mind that associates proximity with involvement, [and] distance with detachment,"[51] what is the correct distance from the scene for a witness understood as a third party? What is the correct distance for the witness who is a survivor (in which case we might understand the scene as residing inside the witness as opposed to the witness inside the scene)? How do *we*, as second- or third-order witnesses, read the meaning of the literal proximity (both spatial and temporal) of the first-order witnesses, among whom Hermannus Hugo might be singled out?[52] Do we believe their proximity gives them a right to evaluate as well as to ratify the encounter?

Perhaps the doubled meaning (third party and *superstes*) of witness adds to the ambiguity. Proximity gives a kind of epistemological and political purchase on the scene. As John Durham Peters writes, "Singularity is key to the communication economics of witnessing . . . [and] 'being there' matters since it avoids the ontological depreciation of being a copy."[53] But distance creates a kind of zone of autonomy for free recall and chosen combinings of thoughts. Since all witnesses operate under this double vision, albeit to *varying* degrees, they (we) are all both inside and outside an event, both implicated in it and freed from its mandates.

Such complicated understandings point to the signal importance of the modality of witnessing. *How* does the witness perceive the event and perform his or her task? Events can be perceived tactually, visually, aurally, and so forth. Alternatively, things can be "known" in the absence of obvious, examinable evidence.[54] Witnesses can be detailed to perceive events in very specific ways. Their location in relation to the actions to be witnessed thus must provide a vantage point that allows for these ways of knowing. In *Picture Theory*, W. J. T. Mitchell parses these different ways of knowing, thereby suggesting some epistemological dilemmas of witnessing: "The 'differences' between images and language are not merely formal matters: they are, in practice, linked to things like the difference between the (speaking) self and the (seen) other; between telling and showing; between 'hearsay' and 'eyewitness' testimony; between words (heard, quoted, inscribed) and objects or actions (seen, depicted, described); between sensory channels, traditions of representation and modes of experience."[55] For one reading, then, witnesses must be in a position to hear oaths and other speech acts, to see the exchanges of objects and people, to watch the main signatories sign their names. Of course this reading must immediately be confronted with the historical fact of what we might call the commissioned, commemorative witness, such as the painter, who must render the events long after the fact. This witness is often not in the position of presence.[56]

On the one hand, distance creates difficulties for knowing and observing others. Reports on distant conduct, exchanges, and transformations take time and may be lost or distorted. Distance undermines the sense of deeply existential knowing that comes from face-to-face interaction. On the other hand, Hannah Arendt's theory of the political realm rests on a fundamental exigency of, exactly, "distance, the worldly space between men where political matters, the whole realm of human affairs, are located."[57] Political acts are those very acts of crossing distance, of founding institutions that create pathways across the previously unmediated space. Luc Boltanski, in his brilliant reflections on action at a distance, writes in this regard, "In fact, distance is a fundamental dimension of a politics which has the specific task of a unification which overcomes dispersion by setting up the 'durable institutions' needed to establish equivalence between spatially and temporally local situations."[58]

The question then becomes, Under what rubric can we decide if any particular social or political action calls for proximal or distant participation and attention? In the case of the witness, who must perceive, and then sanction, notarize, record, or remember the witnessed actions through the sensory apparatus, how does that proximity relate to the political context? Further, how does such proximal witnessing reverberate outward into more distant concentric circles as second-order witnesses assay the renderings of the first-line witnesses? Finally, what becomes of the essential proximity of witnessing as these subsequent renderings communicate the event to the wider public?[59] The relay of rendering suggests a necessary focus on the diverse media through which the chain of witnesses record what they have seen. Peters provides a typology of four possible temporal and spatial relations to an event, only three of which he recognizes as engaging witnesses: "To be there, present at the event in space and time . . . To be present in time but removed in space is the condition of liveness . . . To be present in space but removed in time is the condition of historical representation . . . [But] to be absent in both space and time but still have access to an event via its traces is the condition of recording: the profane zone in which the attitude of witnessing is hardest to sustain."[60]

Distinguishing between spectators, observers, witnesses, and publics may be one approach to answering these questions. But such distinction proves difficult. Spectatorship has a long philosophical history, perhaps most exhaustively considered and elaborated by Adam Smith in his *Theory of Moral Sentiments* (1759). Such issues as the objectivity of spectators, their ability to see without being seen, and the relation of spectatorship to politics inflected with morality are all taken up by Smith. For later theorists like Arendt and Boltanski, one key question involves ties (or their absence) between spectator and observed, and the assessed credibility of any consequent testimony.[61] Perhaps this dilemma presents a clue for understanding the exigencies of location of the witness.

What Does the Witness Do?

The many possible actions of the witness have already been introduced. Witnesses live through events, they observe them, they escort principals to points where events are transacted (beginnings and endings figure importantly here), and they ratify the transactions that take place. Eventually they record and remember the events and transmit information about them to distant others (distant both in space and in time).

We must consider all these conditions of witnessing through the previously introduced analytic rubric of the performative phase, the demonstrative phase, and the representative phase of action at a moment of transition. Phase switching itself can be viewed as signaling something important about boundaries. In a related manner, Michael Silverstein was among the first to recognize the interdependence of the pragmatic and referential aspects of indexical items of speech (the "shifters," whose referents shift as a function of the speech situation).[62] Thus referentiality gives a minimally secure foundation to pragmatic action as shifters rely on previously agreed-on conventions to intervene in the context, and often to reconfigure it. Silverstein notes that "there is a general creative or performative aspect to the use of pure indexical tokens of certain kinds, which can be said not so much to change the context, as to make explicit and overt the parameters of structure of the ongoing events."[63] I suggest that a similar dynamic is at work in what I am calling "phase shifting" in the acts of witnessing. As in Silverstein's analysis, the importance here comes not so much in the switch itself as in what the shift tells us about the boundaries of the event's context and progress.

Thus, in the shift from a demonstrative to a performative engagement, witnesses are called on to perform their witnessing selves through taking oaths, giving testimony, and appending their signatures. In doing so they make most obvious their move across the boundary separating insiders from outsiders, actors from observers. These witness actions ineluctably combine the performative (taking oaths, appending signatures), the demonstrative (giving testimony, indicating the scene to others from a specified vantage point), and the representational (recollecting the event for chains of third parties, rendering the event in textual or pictorial media).

But highlighting the unique actions of individual witnesses raises another conceptual issue: Do witnesses signify and perform differently when they are constituted as collective rather than individual entities? The Greek chorus may be said to derive its voice from its nature as an assembly. This collective entity comments on the world of men and gods, laments the fates of men, but cannot enter the fray (perhaps because it *is* a collectivity). Scenes of historical transformation seem to draw crowds of witnesses. As the ceremonial moments of exchange and ratification do temporarily stop the flow of action

in their tableaulike suspended moments, these crowds cease their own movements to attend to the scene (plate 5). In this photograph of U.S. servicemen
on board the USS *Missouri,* the clusters of men proliferate, seeming to make
the ship itself a witness to the signing of the surrender documents at the end
of World War II. Of course, the mood of the crowd of witnesses will be differently inflected in different scenes of transformative entrances and exits.
This crowd's mood seems informal and comradely, in distinct contrast to the
formality and hierarchy expressed by conventional military gatherings and by
the stiff and top-hatted Japanese delegation. For the moment of victorious
display, the American troops are not subject to formal military discipline.[64]

The degree of anxiety on the occasion of surrender will be relatively
greater or more diminished. But even in the most uncontentious and predictable of occasions, the collectivity of witnesses will demonstrate the
edgy quality of a boundary event. Writing about the painting by John Trumbull, *The Resignation of General Washington* (plate 6), Ann Abrams notes that
"to illustrate the pacifism of Washington's choice, Trumbull pictured a
tranquil assembly crammed with an orderly assortment of dignitaries and
family members."[65] The word "crammed" begins to give a clue that the witnesses to Washington's resignation were not merely a tranquil assembly but
were a somewhat nervous, somewhat awestruck group of congressional
delegates, concerned to effect a transfer of honor and glory from Washington to Congress.[66]

Collective witnessing has a certain power. It is literally a public reckoning
by a collectivity. And from this perspective, an understanding of society as
comprising authoritative and authorizing institutions is central. The servicemen on the USS *Missouri* bear witness as representatives of the various
branches of the military. The "tranquil assembly" witnessing Washington's
resignation comprises representatives of the newly minted Congress. These
"crowds" are already differentiated and specialized witnesses. But for witnessing to be ultimately responsible and competent, it appears that it must
take a singular, individual form. Individual witnesses are asked to commit
themselves to a singular event by way of a performative act. While performative acts can be accomplished by a group of individuals acting in tandem,
it is as individuals that they record and swear and sign.

Signatories to the Scene

It was J. L. Austin who, in his mapping of how to do things with words, drew
attention to the way the signature acts as a tether, linking the written document to its source (something not so obviously necessary in the case of the

speaker of an utterance).[67] But the signature's relation to its source is complex and contingent.

Signatures are powerful—conventional and explosive at the same time. Signatures are both unique (only one original signature in each signatory space of each document) and repeatable (each signer must be thought capable of generating unlimited "identical" future signatures), both autonomous and linked to all other signatures of all other real and potential signatories, present, past, and future. "Put your John Hancock here" links us and our contemporary mundane signings to John Hancock and other historically significant signings. We become like John Hancock when we sign our names. Signatures create as much as authenticate the self.[68] Further, the ontological status of the signature itself is complex and multilayered. It is both an object and an event, which already marks it as special. It emerges out of a culture of alphabets, a culture of genealogy, and a culture of literacy. It constitutes a text of sorts. It also has elements of the pictorial and the iconic, with its distinctive loops and flourishes and its signal occupancy of very particular areas of papers and paintings. Finally, like the fingerprint (a stand-in for a signature on occasion), the signature metonymically contains and leaves traces of the body on the page. "*I* am here," it says, or raising the issue of intersecting or confusingly cohabiting time frames, "I *was* here."

The "I" of the signature is a unique actant, and each incidence of a signature must be recognized as uniquely belonging to that actant. Each signature is a unique event asserting its own authority, and yet each is necessarily dependent on other signatures that act as countersignatures vouching for the identity and legitimacy of the first. Signatures thus operate in a system of signatures linked to selves, witnesses, and countersigners.[69] Derrida notes that "the effects of the signature are the most ordinary thing in the world . . . In order to function, that is, in order to be legible, a signature must have a repeatable, iterable, imitable form; it must be able to detach itself from the present and singular intention of its production."[70] In a related way, signatures act as a kind of an ontological break. Their appearance announces their quality of being flung onto a surface from another dimension. They are often scrawled across the bottoms of documents that are otherwise orderly, prescribed, and based on formal scripts. They also signal a social commitment, breaking forth to take a stand.[71] In the case of witnesses, the witnesses commit themselves to the event, to a certain vision of the event, and to their role in the event through their signatures. They perform their witnessing through their signatures.

As signatures tether written documents and painted scenes to their sources, they are in the business of buttressing and deploying identities. They link the world outside selves to selves. But how do we understand signatures that commit themselves to a kind of disappearance, sometimes (in the case of principal, vanquished parties and to these parties' witnesses) to a disappearance of the self? How do we understand a signature that undoes itself in the act of its signing?

Witness to a Disappearance

Surrenders are perilous and dramatic transformations that must be witnessed. Both the victor and the vanquished must perform the surrender by appending their signatures to the official documents. In surrender agreements, the victors sign and the vanquished resign, respectively claiming and relinquishing their sovereignty rights. These two sets of signatures of the opposing parties appear to be identical acts, yet they are radically different in their performative force and in their manner of construing identity. The act of surrendering might itself be viewed as a (paradoxical) form of countersigning, the vanquished ratifying the ultimate authority of the victor's signature by rendering his own.

Witnesses must also sign the surrender documents. Typically, theirs are second-order signatures, vouchsafing the identity and power claims of the primary signatories. They literally subscribe to, or underwrite, the agreement. Thus surrender treaty agreements typically include a space at the bottom where the official witnesses add their signatures to those of the victor and the vanquished.[72]

Because the signature is so complexly tied to the identity of the signer, the signer's sovereignty over himself or herself becomes central. As such, the signing of a document with a recognizable signature seems to be an act of unqualified sovereignty over the self. And yet such an understanding does not pay adequate attention to the *forced* nature of the signing on the part of the vanquished and its *enforcing* nature on the part of the victor. For it is through this act of signing that the former enemies and the countersigning witnesses are deictically directed to the transformed relations of sovereign subjects and nations as all are reoriented in time and space. What was "ours" is now "yours." What was *our* "here" is now *your* "here." I am here, but I would rather not be here in this condition. The signature is a conduit for shifting pronouns of power and adverbs of territory where the vanquished is being asked to be a kind of witness—against himself.

Given the enormous weight of the signature (part demonstrative, part performative, part representational), we should not be surprised to find a fetishistic attachment to the actual instruments of signing. Indeed, pens and pencils and royal stamps often become souvenirs in surrender ceremonies. After Lieutenant Horace Porter, an aide to General Grant at Appomattox, lent

General Lee his pencil so Lee could write his response to Grant's offer of surrender terms, Porter recorded the following emotional reminiscence:"When
[Lee] handed it back it was carefully treasured by me as a memento of the occasion."[73] Some eighty years later, a vindicated United States general, Jonathan Wainwright, released and now victorious after several years in Japanese
prison camps, witnessed and recorded General Douglas MacArthur's signing
of the Japanese surrender documents at the end of World War II. Once again,
pens played an important role in the scene:"Then [MacArthur] sat down at
the table to sign as Supreme Allied Commander. He took five fountain pens
out of his pocket and placed them on the table. Then he began to write his
name. When halfway through it he stopped, turned to me and asked me to
step forward. He gave me the pen, a wholly unexpected and very great gift.
He picked up another pen, wrote a bit more, and gave that to General Percival. The next three he set aside to be given to various organizations in the
US. Then he took a small red fountain pen out of his pocket—it was Mrs.
MacArthur's pen—and finished signing the document . . . a stunning flight
of American warplanes thundered overhead."[74] This fragmentation of the
signature into separable parts, each part inscribed by a different instrument,
suggests something interesting about the partitioning of the apparently coherent self. By giving the pens to designated recipients, MacArthur gives a
part of himself, his authority, his historical trace to witnesses, who then share
in the "body" of the signing sovereign.

Of course, the pens and other machinery of surrender are saved when one
is the victor, when one's signature renders one's power, not when it erases
one's power. I argue that for the vanquished to sign his name to a document
that says "I surrender" means paradoxically to assert and erase his power in a
single act. For while one must have signatory power to pen an official signature, that very power is activated in such a case precisely in order to undo it.
As Shakespeare's Richard II rages in undoing himself, "Now, mark me how
I will undo myself," he acknowledges the irony that only he can undo himself. And he also acknowledges the crucial presence of those witnesses who
will literally and figuratively "mark" him. To say "I surrender" is to perform
(in the sense of Austin's performatives) a speech act of a very peculiar sort. It
is an ironic exercise of power that erases its source of authority in the very
moment of its utterance.

The recognition of this has made for some extremely complicated instruments of surrender. The Japanese government's acceptance of the Potsdam
Declaration's ultimatum of *unconditional* surrender at the end of World War II
did, nevertheless, come with a condition. As I noted in chapter 1, Japan's
Emperor Hirohito and the imperial dynasty would be allowed to continue in
its existence and reign. However, the imperial authority would be highly
qualified and supervised: "From the moment of surrender the authority of

the Emperor and the Japanese Government shall be subject to the Supreme Commander of the Allied Powers [General Douglas MacArthur]."[75] Sustaining authority and sovereignty in this intricately contradictory manner required many layers of signatures and countersignatures. Before the official signing of the Instrument of Surrender to the Allies, the foreign minister of Japan, Mamoru Shigemitsu, was presented with the credentials he required to sign the surrender agreement by the emperor, who wrote, "By the Grace of Heaven, Emperor of Japan, seated on the Throne, occupied by the same Dynasty changeless through ages eternal . . . We do hereby authorise Mamoru Shigemitsu . . . to attach his signature by command and in behalf of Ourselves and Our Government unto the Instrument of Surrender . . . In witness whereof, We have hereunto set Our signature and caused the Great Seal of the Empire to be affixed."[76] Undone, but not so completely that the formal first-person plural pronouns would be denied him, the emperor sustains his sovereignty by the fragile thread of a signature and a seal.[77]

In general, surrendering signers will be deeply ambivalent about such acts and may indeed see them as just barely within their control. When General Wainwright was forced in May 1942 to sign a surrender document drawn up by his Japanese military captors, he writes, "It was just midnight when I *scrawled* my signature across the bottom."[78] At this existential level, the identity of the individual performing the surrender is undone in the act. Thus, since surrenders are dangerous in the practical sense of waiting to see if weapons really will be laid down, if peace really will be concluded, they are also dangerous to the sense of the self in that they require that the defeated make a contradictory assertion/negation of identity. For the vanquished, then, the signature on the surrender document acts as a very real vanishing point.

Looking at the Vanishing Point

In the case of the flung-ink painting, Ch'an's solution is to disfigure the image, the bipolar view, by opening on to the whole force of randomness. As the ink is cast, it flies out of the enclosure or tunnel of the frame, and opens the image on to the field of material transformations that constitutes the universal surround. The flinging ink marks the surrender of the fixed form of the image to the global configuration of force that subtends it.[79]

There is something instinctively right about the connection between surrender and the vanishing point. Surrenders entail a kind of vanishing—the vanishing of power or territory or autonomy in the submission to another.

The exchanges necessary to transact the surrender bring the parties together at an actual *point* of demarcation and disembarkation. As one of the parties to the surrender, the vanquished does, in a deeply existential way, vanish, only to reemerge under a different indexical sign. This notion of vanishing at the vanishing point of historical transformation, a vanishing that is both material and metaphorical, may be productively linked to the vanishing point in paintings painted under the Renaissance optic of perspective.[80] For such a linking demonstrates the working out of the subjecthood of participant-witnesses in moments of social transformation.

Although differing in their emphases, theorists of the visual sign called the "vanishing point" or "point of flight," including Norman Bryson, Martin Jay, Brian Rotman, and Louis Marin, agree that this sign acts to position the viewer in front of the painted image, to organize the visual field for the viewer. Of course, the crucial and original viewer is the artist himself or herself: "Thus, the vanishing point, by marking the artist's horizon point, that is the spot he faces on the horizon of the scene he depicts, becomes the mark of the spectator's horizon point. The spectator sees from the artist's point of view."[81] Yet for all its organizational capacity, the vanishing point is also ultimately unsettling, pointing to infinity, suggesting an escape hatch or a leak that the scene slides through. Looking at Raphael's painting *The Marriage of the Virgin* (plate 7), with its Renaissance piazza in the background and its cluster of figures in the center foreground, Bryson writes: "The lines of the piazza race away towards this drain or black hole of otherness placed at the horizon, in a decentering that destroys the subject's unitary self-possession. The viewpoint and the vanishing point are inseparable: there is no viewpoint without vanishing point and no vanishing point without viewing point. The self-possession of the viewing subject has built into it, therefore, the principle of its own abolition: annihilatio of the subject as center is a condition of the very moment of the look."[82] Bryson is correct in two senses here. He catches the contingent and dependent subjecthood of viewers outside the painting, who are forced to get their "bearings" from a *vanishing* point. But he misses the decentering and disorientation of the viewers *inside* the painting; that is, the witnesses whose own identities are contingent and dependent on a different order of vanishing point—the vanishing at the center of the scene.

Raphael's painting may indeed be viewed as a scene of surrender as the Virgin surrenders to her husband, to the authority of the religious official, and to God. Of the five Laudable Conditions of the Blessed Virgin, named the Angelic Colloquy, the first three (Conturbatio—Disquiet; Cogitato—Reflection; Interrogatio—Inquiry) can be read as precursors to the fourth (Humiliatio—Submission). All lead ultimately to Meritatio, or Merit.[83] Thus surrender is the path to merit. Simultaneously, the unsuccessful former suitors surrender their claim to the Virgin. These suitors undergo a swift role transformation as they must now perform the ambivalent act of witnessing their own defeat. Thus the witnesses to this marriage or betrothal (art historians disagree on this point) must bear witness to several orders of vanishings, and in doing so they lose themselves as centered subjects.

In a larger sense then, two vanishing points coexist in the same painting. One establishes and positions the viewer of the painting itself (including, most importantly, the commissioning sovereign and the actual painter), and the other establishes and positions the viewers *in* the painting, the witnesses to the deictical vanishings and reappearances in the center of the scene. Such considerations direct our attention to the image and actions of exchange. In the painting by Raphael, it is the ring that is launched across the gap of the social vanishings, the ring that hangs suspended at that point in the middle. Some art historians have suggested that the ring operates as a second visual vanishing point in the painting (the first and primary one being the open doorway in the temple). It also operates as a historical vanishing point that orients the viewer outside the painting not only in physical space but in historical space as well. The particular, historical ring that Raphael paints was considered a divine relic. This ring had been stolen by the city of Perugia from the city of Chiusi only thirty years before the painting was commissioned. The ring was thus the subject of fierce political conflict, and as a close ally of Perugia, the painting's commissioning city, Città del Castello, would have been understood to be asserting the authority of Perugia's claim on the ring by having Raphael showcase it. Yet in drawing attention to itself as it is caught in a frozen moment of exchange (it is not yet on the Virgin's finger), the ring and the political controversy in which it is enmeshed are as incompletely contained as the former suitors' disgruntlement.[84]

Here is a fundamental insight that connects visual theory, the theory of the witness, and scenes and ceremonies of surrender: there is no way to really look into the vanishing point (configured either literally or metaphorically). While it acts as a point of organization with almost alchemical energy, it is also a point of danger, flight, and mutability. Apprehending the horizon in a gaze, like capturing the vanishing moment (of transformation, of founding, of surrendering), turns out to be difficult if not impossible. Freezing the moment in a tableaulike suspended pause is one strategy for engaging what it is so hard to engage.

Witnesses in every dimension (in the scene/outside the scene; in the painting/outside the painting; during the event/after the event) and witnesses performing a variety of tasks (observing, signing, pointing, painting) create a system of cross-witnessing. The witness-painter invokes the Albertian witness-figure of the history painting who, in turn, gazes out at the witness-viewer and directs the viewer's attention to the focal point of the *istoria*.[85] In this way, sight lines are deflected and recast as the vanishing point loosens its organizational hold. The witness need not actually look at the scene; looking out at the painter or at the camera can constitute witnessing as well. This system thus creates a relay that moves across both space and time and returns us to questions about the responsibility and legitimating power of witnesses as they lock eyes with each other. Such considerations have important consequences for the underlying systems of authority that subtend this network of cross-witnessing. Relations of interdependence are established and articulated between the subtending authority and the witnesses, who both demonstrate their authority and reauthorize it (through their performative actions).

Another marriage scene provides an example of witnesses caught up in the double movement of asserting their authority to sanction a contract and demonstrating the authority of those for whom they countersign. The marriage contract drawn up to formalize the betrothal of Louis XIII, king of France, and the "most Serene Lady Anne of Austria, Infanta of Spain," in Madrid in 1612, devotes its first three pages to listing witnesses. These include religious figures (e.g., the Illustrious Don Anthony Cayetan, archbishop of Capua), figures of the nobility (Lord Count Orfo Delzi, ambassador from the Great Duke of Tuscany, the Duke of Villa-Hermosa, the Duke of Veraguas, Henry of Lorain—Duke of Mayenne and Esquillon, and so forth), and the royal secretary. After listing all names of witnesses, the contract states: "And that [the betrothals] may have their full and entire Effect, the foresaid Lords Commissioners, in the abovesaid Names, in what concerns the Marriage of the most Christian king with the most Serene Infanta, Lady Anne, have capitulated and consented to what follows."[86] This veritable pantheon of witnesses authorizes the marriage and in so doing both reconstitutes and defers to the authority of the royals.

In the moment that witnesses perform their testimony through taking oaths or appending signatures, they stake out a terrain of contingent stability amid the disorienting subject positions of scenes of transformation. I think that Hannah Arendt's acts of promising, the "little islands of stability," serve as refuges located by the relevant performative gestures and temporarily halt the flight of identity and orientation out of the vanishing point of history. More than any other, the artist is the witness with the greatest representational burden. The artist must find a way to reproduce the network of cross-witnessing (cosigners and countersigners) that escorts an event across the threshold of history. And it is the artist who might best capture and reveal the dilemmas associated with witnessing in general and with witnessing surrenders in particular.

Paper and Responsibility

Those who have viewed *The Surrender of Breda,* from Philip IV in his Palace of the Buen Retiro to us here today, must somehow follow the *istoria* of the painting. We must figure out where to look. In bipolar compositions like this one, our attention is inevitably drawn to that center space where the bridging element of the key aims to pull the sides together. There we also see the dancelike gestures of the two main characters. Spinola seems to be both supporting and blocking Justin, as his outstretched arm prevents Justin from kneeling. Justin attempts to pass the key to the city of Breda over to Spinola with his own outstretched hand. Dyadic compositions are notoriously unstable—particularly, one might assume, dyadic compositions that emerge out of the realm of dyadic conflict. Thus, in Velázquez's brilliant rendering the dyadic instability of the central figures of Spinola and Justin is compositionally righted by the painting's two most marginal figures, the soldiers on the periphery looking at us. These two look out of the scene at the painting's spectators, not just to draw us in, but to stabilize the scene by locating and locking in the necessary third party. So while it is critical that the two figures at the center be absorbed in the transaction of surrender exchange, and in each other, it is also critical that they be anchored by the expanded network of witnesses.[87] Some figures turn toward the middle (the moment of the present), some turn toward the background (the past), and some turn toward us outside the frame (the future). These gestures of support or prevention of movement, along with the incomplete genuflection—the slight bows, the outstretched hand with the key, the mutual orientation on the flat plain in the middle of the painting—all suggest a hybrid form of gesture—part practical, part mythical—as the moment of surrender is commenced, deflected, deferred, and ultimately transcended in its very *incompletion.*

The proffered key lives forever in this painting in a state of suspense and suspension. As our eyes follow the arrow/key to the city of Breda, as Justin of Nassau extends it to Ambrogio Spinola and from there find the baton in Spinola's hand (reflecting royal authority), we spot a small piece of unfolded paper at the bottom right corner of the painting, blown in, as it were, from a world outside the canvas. A strange intruder, the paper is blank, and its presence (though not without painterly precedent) is intriguing.

In several of his other paintings, Velázquez carries forward the late fifteenth-century convention of painting his signature onto some piece of "reality" of the scenes—a book or paper held by the subject of a portrait or a piece of stray masonry.[88] But in only two of Velázquez's other paintings, both of them equestrian portraits of nobility and monarchy, does a similarly detached piece of paper appear in the lower corner of the canvas, the fairly new traditional space of the artist's signature—and in all cases the paper appears to be blank.

How are we to conceptualize these blank white sheets of paper that flutter into scenes of empire, force, and sovereignty? Despite their conventionality, there is an uncanniness in their appearance. Like all things uncanny, they are familiar and strange at the same time. In the seventeenth century paper suggests authority, literacy, and developing bureaucracies, but it also suggests something fragile, something the wind might blow away.

To my mind, the paper is the spectator's own point of entry to this painting and to the challenge of "reading" scenes of historical surrender. Let us pause to consider this blank piece of paper, an expectant space on the canvas, a representational conundrum, a grace note of uncertainty about how, exactly, to represent violence in its redirection. One might say that *even* Velázquez, court painter to Philip IV, aspirant to the noble Order of Santiago himself, official witness to sovereignty, empire, and victory (but also imminent defeat on the verge of the Dutch retaking of Breda as he painted his canvas), communicates his preoccupation with representation. With the paper, he inserts a crucial question about genres and their displacement. What genre is adequate to the task of representing the space of violence? Does he (do we) need to consider the different visions of maps, of history paintings, of statues, of military codes, of bureaucratic forms? Are the spaces created by representation in the business of generic displacement, as violence moves from bodies and gestures to images and codes?

The paper in the corner is matter out of place and time. One (admittedly anachronistic) way of conceptualizing that paper in *The Surrender of Breda* is as a kind of hypertext link, a point not only of entry but of exit as well, one that serves as a portal from a space of siege warfare with its bombardments and privations to the realm of a paper-driven burgeoning Habsburg monarchy back in Madrid. It is a portal from war to bureaucracy to art, suggesting displacement in space and in genre and reminding us of the very artifactual nature of war and politics.

A different angle on that paper raises the question of the identity and power of the renderer of the surrender scene and the *signature* status of the artist. In the historical context of the seventeenth century, painters—even court painters like Velázquez—were considered fairly low in status. Painting was considered a craft rather than an art like poetry. Despite this, as I noted above, Velázquez spent years maneuvering to become a member of the Order of Santiago (a military order that was the Spanish equivalent of knighthood) and finally was so designated in 1659 (the red cross painted on Velázquez's self-portrait in his most famous painting, *Las Meninas* [1656], was affixed anachronistically, probably by another hand). Thus, in the larger narrative that each new document or picture tells of the surrender of Breda, the artist who renders the scene can also be understood to point to himself through the piece of paper (which perhaps also summons up the documents relevant to the surrender as they travel back to Madrid).

There appears to be no signature on the piece of paper. There may, however, be a portrait of Velázquez inserted into the scene of the surrender. Some have claimed that the man directly behind the horse, on the far right of the canvas, is Velázquez himself. As in the giant canvas of *Las Meninas,* the horse has its back to us, the viewers, and the painter looks out at us from behind this shield (horse or canvas in the respective paintings); this view we cannot see. Thus, in this complex rendering, the monarch, the bureaucrat, the general, and the artist all participate in a kind of claiming and handing off of the responsibility for forcing, accepting, and effecting the surrender of the vanquished. Protagonists and witnesses all, they do so by appearing in or controlling representations of the signal moment of transfer.

CHAPTER 3

The Exchanges of Surrender

IN A COMPETITIVE encounter such as war, the conclusion will be judged differently according to the opposed points of view of the winner and the loser. In the preface, I claimed that a goal of this book on surrender was to regard winning through the lens of defeat. Such a perspective allows for a more sociologically complex analysis of the surrender configurations. It also provides for a purchase on those extraordinarily widespread, yet understudied, phenomena of defeat, loss, disorientation, and alienation. Nevertheless, even this revised point of view is limited. What is needed is an analysis of surrender that views it as an interaction between winning and losing. The focus on the exchanges of surrender in this chapter is one singularly equipped to perform just such an analysis.

Surrenders demand convergence as the warring sovereigns (or their military proxies) meet to communicate and perform the giving up and giving over. The exchanges of surrender *perform, demonstrate,* and *represent* the realignments of power, hierarchy, and control when one party surrenders to another. Their circuitry establishes a metathreshold: of time, of space, of relationships, and of sovereign power. Exchanges are key to surrender as they effect both a transfer of power and a transformation of identity.

Surrenders may appear to be unilateral in their actions, with the vanquished giving up or returning to the victor all powers and, in the words of Carl von Clausewitz, "trophies of victory."[1] But somewhat counterintuitively, surrender is a deliberately two-sided transaction, as this chapter seeks to demonstrate.

Convergence without transaction and exchange simply recapitulates a siege or a standoff. Some gesture must bridge the gap. Conversely, separate transactions without convergence cannot cauterize a conflict, and a crucial moment of recognition and definition is denied.[2] One of Robert E. Lee's generals, E. P. Alexander, recalled that Lee considered ordering his troops to disperse rather than formally surrender to General Grant. Lee ultimately rejected that option. According to Alexander, Lee stated, "If I should order this army to disperse, the men with their arms, but without organization or control, and without provisions or money, would soon be wandering through every State in the confederacy, some seeking to get to their homes and some with no homes to go to. Many would be compelled to rob and plunder as they went to save themselves from starvation, and the enemy's cavalry would pursue in small detachments."[3]

As such theorists of exchange as Marcel Mauss and Peter Blau have taught us, all exchanges look toward the future, a future in which the parties to the exchange are expected to carry through with relations of reciprocity. In this regard, it is important to distinguish surrender from annihilation. In other words, some aspect of the presurrender autonomy of the vanquished must remain (even if it is simply bare life) to carry out this giving and receiving. Short of total annihilation, no vanquished party can render up absolutely everything to the victor and still be imagined as human. As Rudolf Arnheim writes: "Neither total self-centeredness nor total surrender to outer powers can make for an acceptable image of human motivation."[4] Surrenders' motivations must stop short of annihilation.

Thus the exchanges of surrender are crucial mechanisms by which surrender takes place. But they are peculiar exchanges. Much exchange theory in the social sciences emphasizes that exchanges do not so much reflect or build on preexisting relationships as actually constitute them. I argue that a theory of exchange is needed that identifies not just the way exchange constitutes identities and relationships but the way it can also *deconstitute* these states. In other words, there is a deconstitutive moment in the work of exchange, one in which extant identities and relationships must be unmade in order to be remade. Thus, even with all of their constitutive force, the exchanges of surrender are, in fact, doubly deconstitutive. They undo the binary relationships of belligerence (for even a belligerent relationship is still a relationship) between the two opposing sides, and they unmake identities. In surrender, a self (which can be either singular or collective in nature) is undone and given over. In that interstitial *moment* of undoing, the requisite exchanges deconstitute identities. This *deconstitutive moment* is one that, in spite of being embedded in a temporally extended project of *reconstitution,* deserves its own analytic recognition. How might one do this?

At the conclusion of the peace, armies, weapons, treasures, symbols and speech acts are exchanged across (former) enemy lines. Analysis of these exchanges must identify their interactional aspects, their material aspects, and their symbolic aspects. Turning over the key to a city, for example, may be viewed as an interaction between the giver and the receiver, as a material exchange of a concrete object (heavy or light, functional or not, old or newly minted) at a particular time and place, and as a symbolic gesture regarding accessiblity and control. In all these incarnations, the exchanges involved in the termination of conflict create what Lewis Coser, following Georg Simmel, claimed was "a social process dependent upon, but not directly deducible from its pursuits."[5] Thus, also following Simmel, the actions of termination of a conflict have their own logic and meaning beyond that of simply ending the conflict. In taking its own particular shape (or shapes), this moment of transition retains a significant element of ambiguity. This chapter will demonstrate that even where the victor and the vanquished are clearly identified, there are important variations in the way this identification is marked and its consequences are made apparent.

The Dangers of Surrender

Any exchange that is simultaneously in the business of cauterizing violence, confirming asymmetries of power, deconstituting identities, and reworking relationships must be understood as fundamentally dangerous and suspenseful. Thus the analysis must draw on the important variations (both empirical and theoretical) in the ways victor and vanquished transact the exchanges of surrender, as variables are balanced between withholding and giving over.

Something essential about the critical ambiguity in surrender exchanges is bound up in this balancing of variables. There is the palpable sense of both functional and semiotic danger in the actions associated with surrender in war. Having reached the point where the nearly defeated party's desire to surrender meets the imminent victor's willingness to grant or accept surrender terms, the parties must still bring the fighting to a halt and cross the threshold to peace. Analysts of war note the particular dangers of such transactions and their on-the-ground contingencies and interpretations. Randall Collins notes that "surrendering in the midst of combat conditions can be a physically very dangerous act, since it requires communicating to enemy soldiers, who are still expecting to be menaced, and getting the signal accepted. Given the victory frenzy that frequently occurs among the conquering side, many troops are killed in the action of surrender, or even shortly thereafter."[6] This most dangerous moment of a conflict is far from straightforward. For combatants to go from a condition of attack (or readiness to attack) to a condition of retreat or cease-fire involves physical and existential circuit switching of the most extreme nature. Armies that have maintained discipline in the ranks during the fighting may indeed experience the kind of release Collins identifies. This release may derail the anticipated conclusion of the fighting itself, instigating renewed hostilities. Historians of early modern armies and soldiers recount just such cases. In early modern Spain, for example, "there was a similar danger of the collapse of discipline after a battle, even with the victorious army. In 1644, after overpowering the Portuguese army at the battle of Montijo, the troops of the Castilian army immediately dispersed in search of booty from the fleeing enemy. The resulting widespread disorder in the Castilian army provided the Portuguese commander with an opportunity to regroup several squadrons, retrieve his army's artillery and baggage train, and subsequently claim victory on the battlefield."[7] The disorganization of the victor thus undoes the surrender and reignites the fighting.

In his analysis of the United States Military Code statute "Misbehavior Before the Enemy" (10 USCS 899 [1977] Art. 99), William Ian Miller reflects on the way soldiers' running away from the battlefield can be variably interpreted and responded to. The consequences of such actions can be radically diverse. Single soldiers engaged in abandoning the field or their place of duty may indeed be accused of misbehavior. But large numbers of soldiers who panic simultaneously seem to give the acknowledgment of defeat a collective credibility (reminding us of the way participants can effectively transmute into evaluating witnesses).[8]

The perils associated with moments of surrender highlight the important work of the attendant promises, oaths, demonstrations, gestures, and representations. These actions attempt to fix the event, align its meaning for all participants, and ensure its trajectory. But disalignments and uncertainty are always present: different genres of action may signal differently and set off diverse interpretations; strategic actors may see arrangements as either temporary or permanent, as it suits them; surprise attacks when the enemy's guard is down may give the lie to promises to desist. And the perils are not only logistical and physical. There are also existential perils to be navigated, and they are most obvious in the more *ceremonial* moments of surrender.

If, as political scientist Marc Ross claims, all surrender ceremonies contain elements of both recognition and degradation (with attendant ambiguities about the consequences),[9] the sequence of exchanges will tend to be highly structured. The debate about the emblematic source of the central image in *The Surrender of Breda,* the attempt of the Dutch general Justin of Nassau to hand over the key to the city to the Spanish general Ambrogio Spinola, illuminates the existential tensions of this act that contains both recognition and degradation.

Art historians have identified the popular book of emblems by Andrea Alciati, the *Liber emblemata* (1531), as a probable source for the two figures and their mutually aligned stances at the center of Velázquez's painting (plate 1). In particular, the emblem named *Concordia* (plate 8) is said to provide the main model. Here two soldiers in armor face each other in the foreground of a scene of a field in which battle camps have been set up. We see tents and spear bearers in the background. Although both soldiers carry swords, their right hands are clasped in a handshake of concord and reconciliation. Such an attribution would be in harmony with the reading of the painting's central motif as magnanimity—after a siege, concord is established through the magnanimity of the victor. Yet such an attribution does not gather in the fullness of the story of Breda, particularly the back-and-forth of the city over the course of the sixteenth and seventeenth centuries. It also does not reflect the subterranean etymology of surrender, detailed in chapter 1, in which the notion of return is built into the transactional program. Accordingly, John Moffitt points out a different emblem from Alciati's book as another probable source. The emblem titled *In dona hostium* (Against Gifts from Enemies) (plate 9) is compositionally similar to *Concordia*. Two armed warriors face each other in the foreground. But in this illustration the focal point of contact and exchange is an upright sword and a sword belt, instruments of war. This wary exchange of sword and belt portends a bad end. This emblem was based on the scene from *The Iliad* in which Ajax and Priam exchanged sword and sword belt after calling a truce in their initial encounter. Both sword and sword belt would later be implicated in the deaths of their recipients. Based on his reading of the extended commentaries on the emblems illustrated in Alciati's book, Moffitt argues that the distrust of "gifts" from the (former) antagonist best expressed by *In dona hostium* better captures the mood in Madrid, and Velázquez's own stance, at the time of the painting of *The Surrender of Breda*. Depending on the dating of the painting,[10] the city of Breda would have been either on the verge of being retaken by the Dutch or already retaken when the painting was finally hung in the Hall of Realms. Such a historical turn would have indeed given a different retrospective inflection to the magnanimous surrender terms Spinola provided. Thus the gift of the key in the painting, analogous to the gift of the sword in *In dona hostium,* portended false reconciliation and ultimate revenge on the part of the Dutch. Most important, perhaps, it is the contradictory combination of *Concordia* and *In dona hostium* that best expresses the ambiguities in the central transfers and exchanges of surrenders. Reconciliation yes, but for how long and how truly?

As the case recounted above makes clear, the exchanges of surrender are indeed existentially and semiotically ambiguous. One way to deal with such ambiguities is to establish rules to conventionalize the transactions. In early modern Europe, the "consciously cultivated and painstakingly perfected art of war"[11] involved the development of conventions of warfare generally and the conventions of surrenders specifically. As I noted previously, siege warfare became the norm as important towns and forts, defended by increasingly sophisticated guns and cannons, reworked the moral and strategic landscape of emergent absolutism.[12] Surrenders after a siege were among the most highly conventionalized transactions ending a war. For example, a large breach in the wall of a town or fortress signified that defeat was imminent, and the defending commander was both forced and allowed to surrender at that point (with dire consequences for refusing): "It was a law of war that if a place refused to surrender when a practicable breach had been made in the body of the works, when there remained no hope of succor, and the attack was compelled to have recourse to the assault, the garrison was granted no quarter, the place was open to sack and the commander hanged."[13] Other norms concerned the way the defeated troops might exit, the positions in which they might carry their weapons and flags, and the fate of deserters. Several of these conventions will be discussed in detail below. Here it is important to note that even within these rules, there were contradictions. One rule called for a garrison to surrender when it still had at least two days' rations and ammunition. Another rule called for the fortress to hold out until all stores had been exhausted. Actions that might be interpreted as heroism could alternatively be interpreted as foolhardiness. Thus, even within this highly conventionalized context, the meaning and consequences of surrendering exchanges were contingent on interpretation.

The Case of the Unconditional Surrender

One analytic strategy for investigating a historically evolved system of social conventions is to locate its most extreme variant, that variant that pushes against and thus reveals the parameters of the system itself. In this case the proposition and working out of the "unconditional surrender" can reveal much about the conditions of possible conventionalized surrenders. The most explicit formulation of the "unconditional surrender" demand in modern warfare was that developed during World War II by Franklin Delano Roosevelt at the January 24, 1943, press conference at Casablanca. Certain "unconditional surrender" precedents did exist in the history of warfare, but most often in regard to the surrender of a specific fort or garrison. Such a formulation meant that "the military personnel of the captured fort [would] be taken prisoner and confined under the rules of war until the end of hostilities."[14] Application of these terms to larger social and political entities, such as cities or states, was more problematic. The uncertain meaning of the modern referent of "unconditional surrender" was reflected in a February 1945 Gallup Poll in the United States that asked a series of questions about public attitudes toward the policy as the end of the European theater of World War II seemed imminent.

Tellingly, the poll began the series of questions with "Will you tell me what the term 'unconditional surrender' means to you?" Here the possibilities were numerous and highly detailed. They ranged from (1) "Complete surrender—surrender without any provisions; surrender with no advance peace terms; acceptance of the dictated peace terms of the Allies; no compromise; no clauses," to (2) "Surrender—end of fighting; whole place gives up," to (5) "Change form of government, get rid of Nazis," to (7) "Take everything away from them, give up everything, no longer exists as a nation," to (8) "No future wars, permanent peace," to (10) "Fight until the last man; kill them all."[15]

In these proffered responses the line between unconditional surrender and total destruction or annihilation is revealed to be a confusing one. The redundancies ("whole place gives up," "take everything away") may reflect the psychological and political nervousness of a war-weary public. The slight but crucial variations of both tone and signification engage discourses of revenge, hegemonic control, or targeted destruction. Looking for meaning in historical precedents would not have been entirely fruitful. One example, Rome's ultimately *unmet* demand for the unconditional surrender of Carthage in the Third Punic War (149–146 BCE), entailing the surrender of territory, cities, and populace, did lead to the eventual sacking and destruction of all of Carthage in 146 BCE. One of the questions this chapter will address is how far the kinds of identity and fealty transformations involved in such demands for "unconditional" turning over, in themselves, are interpreted as being synonymous with annihilation. Historically, outright refusal of surrender by the incipiently vanquished, whether of the negotiated or unconditional kind, could indeed lead to sacking and destruction.[16]

In the modern epoch, in accord with evolving international law, wars often ended with negotiations and a peace treaty between the belligerents. Thus Roosevelt's demand for "unconditional surrender" had no modern precedent. This was so even though Roosevelt himself claimed to have come up with the term while thinking about Ulysses S. Grant's nickname: "We had so much trouble getting those two French generals [de Gaulle and Giraud] together that I thought to myself that this was as difficult as arranging the meeting of Grant and Lee—and then suddenly the press conference was on and Winston [Churchill] and I had had no time to prepare for it, and the thought popped into my mind that they had called Grant 'Old Unconditional Surrender' and the next thing I knew I had said it."[17]

The actual details of the conditions of Robert E. Lee's surrender to Grant during the American Civil War will be described below. Here it is important to highlight the convention-breaking nature of Roosevelt's declaration. For one thing, the combining of *political* and *military* surrender in the eventually codified policy was historically remarkable.[18] Justification by the Allies for the demand of "unconditional surrender" involved indexing the enemies as similarly unprecedented in nature. Thus the Allies termed the Axis powers "not normal belligerents" and the war they had initiated "aggressive."[19]

And then there was the fact that the very process by which Germany might be brought to a state of unconditional surrender would probably entail the collapse of any authority capable of performing the surrender (performatives of such nature requiring the authority to be authorized, viz. felicitous, in carrying out the surrender). Thus, "Towards the end of March 1945, the British government became convinced that once Germany had been completely overpowered, there would in all probability no longer be any military or civil authority capable of signing such an instrument of surrender. As a consequence, the victors would have to resort to a different procedure and unilaterally proclaim total German defeat and their assumption of supreme authority in Germany. Accordingly, the surrender document was redrafted by the European Advisory Commission into the form of a declaration."[20] Ultimately, the members of the German High Command did sign the military surrender instrument at General Dwight D. Eisenhower's headquarters in Reims. But it is analytically interesting that in the case of Germany, it was provisionally understood that the *unconditional* nature of the demand coincided with the *absence* of any sovereign authority it would be possible to negotiate with.

Such problems of authority and recognition find partial solutions in the decoupling of military and political authority, as I noted earlier. If the victor pronounces no recognizable political authority with which to negotiate the surrender, it might accept a military authority as a kind of signing proxy. Such was also the case in the American Civil War, as General Grant and General Lee signed a surrender instrument in their capacities as military officials, and as General William T. Sherman and General Joseph E. Johnston attempted to sign a surrender instrument in similar capacities. Just after the signing of Grant and Lee's surrender instrument at Appomattox, President Lincoln made a speech in which he clarified the nature of these negotiations: "Unlike the case of a war between independent nations, there is no authorized organ for us to treat with . . . We simply must begin with, and mould from, disorganized and discordant elements."[21]

The delicate navigation of the boundary between military and political authority in the attempts to end the Civil War was evident in certain missteps and reconfigurings. For example, during the Sherman-Johnston meeting, a Confederate cabinet member, Secretary of War John C. Breckinridge, was initially rejected as a participant by Sherman, who would not recognize or negotiate with a Confederate politician. Sherman changed his mind when "Johnston explained that Breckinridge was also a major general."[22] Ultimately Sherman himself, a military man, would be accused by newly inaugurated President Andrew Johnson and his cabinet of overstepping his boundaries in his attempt to forge a much more political manifesto out of his negotiations with Johnston. General Grant was sent by the president to meet with Sherman and arrange to terminate and nullify Sherman's surrender "memorandum."

The final conceptual conundrum presented by the "unconditional surrender" formula is bound up with the semiotic phases of surrender designated by this book: the performative, the demonstrative, and the representational. In order for transformations and exchanges like surrenders to be successful, specified actions and renderings must be generated, witnessed, and accepted. The very blankness of the "unconditional" formulation seems self-annihilating. The practical and the phenomenological coincide here. As historian Raymond O'Connor writes about the application of the doctrine to the surrender of Italy during World War II, "The presence of numerous 'conditions' in both the long and short-term documents . . . revealed a disposition toward flexibility in interpreting and applying the doctrine." Lest one think this was the case only with belligerents who were soon to be transmuted into allies, O'Connor goes on to write, "What the formula could not eliminate was the necessity for specific terms in any armistice or surrender document. Essential items . . . the disarmament and disposition of troops, the release of prisoners, the administration of internal affairs."[23]

The sheer fact of the existence of specified agents, times, and places for the performance of the speech acts associated with surrendering made the unconditionality of the surrender reachable only asymptotically. Beyond that, a more generalized "sense" of the surrender might stand in for specified conditions when complicated messages were entailed. A director of the Overseas Branch of the United States Office of War Information during World War II quoted an anonymous source talking about precisely the sense that Roosevelt wanted to convey to the citizens in the Axis coalition at war's end: "[Roosevelt] wanted to rule out any pledge or offer like the Fourteen Points and still convey to the enemy peoples the idea that they would be treated generously by the Allies. He thought that the story of Grant and Lee at Appomattox would convey this idea . . . what he especially wanted to bring out was Grant's gesture in letting the confederates keep their horses. The President felt that this incident from American history would help the enemy peoples to realize that they were facing chivalrous foes who did not desire to impoverish them or humiliate then but who would treat them with magnanimity."[24]

Here the allegorical power of the Grant-Lee reference was meant to reassure the *people* of the Axis countries, while the "unconditional surrender" demands were directed toward the soon-to-be former *authorities*. Such historical analogies and policy genealogies relied on what I am terming the network of cross-witnessing. The nature of this network is to be constantly augmented and revised. In this case, the conditions and exchanges of World War II were brought into alignment with those of Appomattox as chains of actors and their interpreting witnesses pointed contemporary audiences in the right direction, toward the right interpretation.

The "Potsdam Declaration," the ultimatum demanding Japan's "unconditional surrender" issued at the conclusion of the meeting in Potsdam in July 1945, took a different form from the ultimatum issued to Germany. One significant difference hinged on the recognition of the continuation of the imperial dynasty under Emperor Hirohito. Such a recognition was complicated: How could surrender be unconditional when the vanquished could successfully demand, as the Japanese did, a condition that went to the heart of their own *endogenous* authority? The mechanism by which such a nuanced navigation of the questions of conditionality and authority proceeded comprised nearly coterminous "lumpings and splittings."[25] Thus the concept of unconditional surrender was alternatively targeted at the military forces, at the Japanese government, at the emperor, and at the whole entity named "Japan." These associations came in and out of focus in the various documents generated over the waning days of the war, sometimes even in the same document. For example, Point Thirteen of the Potsdam Declaration said, "We call upon the Government of Japan to proclaim now the unconditional surrender of all Japanese armed forces . . . The alternative for Japan is prompt and utter destruction."[26]

However, the Japanese acceptance of this declaration sought to insert its own condition into unconditionality: "The Japanese Government is ready to accept the terms enumerated on July 26, 1945 . . . with the understanding that the said declaration does not comprise any demand which prejudices the prerogatives of His Majesty as Sovereign Ruler."[27] And the complications of balancing what I will term the "compositional system" of surrender become most clear in the American response to this *conditional* acceptance: "From the moment of surrender the authority of the Emperor and the Japanese Government to rule the state shall be subject to the Supreme Commander of the Allied Powers who will take such steps as he [General Douglas MacArthur] deems proper to effectuate the surrender terms. The Emperor will be required to authorize and ensure the signature by the Government of Japan and the Japanese Imperial General Headquarters of the surrender terms necessary to carry out the provisions of the Potsdam Declaration."[28]

This exchange of messages thus culminates in an American response that enumerates and demands a series of embedded actions of authorization. On the one hand, it functions as a performative speech act, *ordering* the emperor and the Japanese government to subject themselves to the supreme commander of the Allied powers. At the same time, it *demonstrates* or indexes a series of embedded authority structures that must authorize each other in order for the surrender to proceed. The emperor is positioned as the authorizing institution that must guarantee the signature of the government of Japan and the Japanese Imperial General Headquarters. That signature, in turn, will perform the surrender. In J. L. Austin's terms, the chain of constative and performative speech acts are deployed in overt fashion, with a kind of fabulous simultaneous constitution and recognition of subsidiary authority structures. The emperor's role retains its singularity in some important authorizing sense. And yet he must submit himself in turn to the supreme commander of the Allied powers: "The Emperor will be *required* to authorize and ensure the signature." This hierarchical and nested construction allowed for the insertion of a condition into the unconditional, that being the retention of the imperial sovereign in Japan.[29]

Ultimately, "unconditional surrender" operates as a kind of theoretical ground zero of surrenders generally, a conceptual vanishing point that keeps disappearing (Is it all territory, is it all sovereign authority, is it all armaments, is it the entire nation and its people?) as the transactions of surrender work themselves out.

The Nature of the Surrendering Exchange

At the conclusion of the peace, people, objects, and speech acts are exchanged across (former) enemy lines. But are these inaugural acts, or must they be interpreted as acts of recompense and return? Giving back, the idea of a return, recalls the etymological origins of "surrender," in which what is rendered to the victor is thus designated as "always having been" the victor's. And when the category of victor extends to include the victims of the vanquished, as it did after World War II, the "gift" of reparations is explicitly restorative: *Wiedergutmachung* was Germany's term for the reparations, literally meaning "to make good again," that is, "to return to former conditions."[30] Following Germany's unconditional surrender, these reparations signify that the former conditions were the proper conditions. Unconditional surrender and reparations combine to heighten the normative inflection of the embedded idea of "return" in surrender.

Such exchanges reveal how extraordinarily complex is the temporal looping involved in surrender accords and exchanges. Postwar reparations of the sort that Germany was compelled to pay after World Wars I and II have, according to legal scholar Ruti Teitel, a hybrid temporal extension. They assist in the suturing work of the transactions in the present, they restore and thus revive the past, and they point toward a new equilibrium in the future.[31]

But equilibrium is not always the goal or the outcome of surrender exchanges. A survey of surrenders reveals a high degree of contingency in these transactions. What gets exchanged? Who gets to keep what?[32] Who must give what to whom? These contingent arrangements deliver a tone and a sense to individual surrenders that then take shape as essentially in the business of, alternatively, humiliation or reequilibrium or magnanimity.[33]

But even within the highly contingent situation of specific wars and their endings, there are formal models of exchange relationships that each case may, more or less, resemble and embody. These models include the gift, the contract, and the debt, among others, and it is possible to analyze the exchanges of surrender as variously approximating these forms. Each of these models assumes an extant *system* of exchange and relies on it for its functioning. And thus the question of the first mover (or first transfer) is raised once again, as it was in chapter 1's discussion of the etymology of surrender. Georg Simmel's attempt to theorize the physiognomy of exchange, in his essay "Exchange," circles in on his own sense of a first mover. Simmel writes, "I hold it to be completely possible that the forerunner of socially fixed exchange was not individual exchange, but a form of transfer of possessions that was not exchange at all—[rather] something like robbery. Interindividual exchange would then have been nothing other than a peace treaty."[34] Thus does Simmel tie the origins of a system of exchange to an extrasystemic act of physical coercion. He charts the evolution of social exchange from originary acts of alienation to conflict-ending peace treaties. Given this, it is not surprising either that exchanges constitute the basic building blocks of surrenders or that we seem to hear the echo of surrender in every social exchange.

But what of the various codified systems of exchange that surrender transactions may mirror? We begin with the gift, one among several media by which social relations are organized and reorganized.[35] Many of the objects exchanged during surrender ceremonies can be understood as types of gifts—keys, swords, supplies, freedom from captivity, and so forth, as I will describe below. As a fundamental social form of exchange, the gift has been analyzed by social theorists from Marcel Mauss, Pierre Bourdieu, Jacques Derrida, and Maurice Godelier to Viviana Zelizer. On one thing all these theorists agree: gifts are paradoxical objects of exchange. Of the many paradoxes of the gift, a central one relates to its ontological claim—the gift claims to be, as Pierre Bourdieu put it, "an inaugural act of generosity."[36] Yet there are certain clear systemic expectations for gift giving and repaying. Gifts need to be appropriate to the situation; they need to be proportional to expectations that involve, among other things, restitution; and they imply time limits or terms: "The difference between the gift and every other operation of pure and simple exchange is that the gift gives time . . . but this gift of time is also a demand of time. The thing must not be restituted immediately and right away . . . there must be waiting—without forgetting."[37] And it is just this delay between occasions of gift giving and counter gift giving that allows each gift to appear "inaugural" and that creates the generalized sense of indebtedness.

The significance of this "inaugural" appearance lies in the gift's self-representation as uncoerced, voluntary, or unmotivated. A *free* giving over has nothing to do with force or violence. Yet exchanges in surrender are not thereby inappropriately interpreted within the paradigm of the gift, as one might assume given surrenders' forced nature and violent backdrop. For gifts, according to their many analysts, are never inaugural, never unmotivated, never without a history, and never completely uncoerced, regardless of their idealization. Here is the link between gifts and violence. We might recall Simmel's speculative understanding of the evolutionary origins of codified exchange—from robbery to peace treaty to exchange. The exchange may be said to domesticate the violence that, under another name, set off the series of transfers in the first place. But domestication may also be a form of mis-recognition. And the confusion about the nature of gifts given in ceremonies of surrender has to do with just what Bourdieu terms "symbolic violence": "the gentle, invisible form of violence which is never recognized as such, and is not so much undergone as chosen, the violence of credit, confidence . . . gifts, gratitude . . . all the virtues honored by the code of honor—cannot fail to be seen as the most economical mode of domination."[38] Surrenders are principally about the cauterization of violence. But if the exchanges that are the medium of surrenders' taking place (here read through the gift paradigm) are really violence under a different, symbolic rubric, then violence itself survives the acts of surrender.

What kind of gifts are these? What is their directionality? Who is giving what to whom? Are there simultaneous or coinciding gifts and repayment of gifts? Are there different orders of gifts (e.g., symbolic objects and freedom)? Finally, is there a kind of poison infused in the gifts that the vanquished give to the victor, the expectation of return in the future metamorphosing into the dream of revenge? These questions reveal how complicated and how dependent on point of view is the analysis of the mechanisms of exchange in surrender.

Taking one example, one might view the victor's giving the vanquished permission to surrender as a kind of gift. It may be a gift of life (as opposed to annihilation) or of partial autonomy or of freedom from slavery. Alternatively, looked at from the agentic vantage point of the vanquished, the act of surrender itself may be viewed as a gift to the victor: "Victory . . . involves yielding of the vanquished. By the very act of declaring himself beaten, he achieves a last assertion of his power. With this act, as Georg Simmel has said, 'he actually makes a gift to the victor.' The capacity of making gifts is a measure of autonomy."[39]

Regardless of the point of view, the exchange of gifts of a variety of types and orders during ceremonies of surrender works to bind the giver and the receiver together in the temporally extensive way that Teitel articulates in her analysis of the meaning of reparations. This binding is, and must be to varying degrees, always tainted and dangerous. The scene it emerges from is one of violence, enmity, and destruction. And the undeniable (however temporary) asymmetry of the victor and the vanquished foregrounds the symbolic violence of gifts given in surrender. Even in the text beneath the apparently pacific emblem *Concordia* in Alciati's *Liber emblemata,* one senses the anxiety of the emergent asymmetries after conflict:

> When Rome shall drive leaders of equal rank into war;
> And Mars will come to earth with his forces:
> The custom has been after dreadful slaughter on both sides;
> To give gifts to each other having joined their right hands;
> This is the manner of the treaty;
> That peace may be known, so:
> That love and their own hands; Join them.[40]

Here an initial situation of equality has ended with mutual destruction and, most likely, a reconfigured world. The mandate is to reconcile, but the repetition in the text, amplifying the insistence on the mechanics and meaning of reunion, along with the final performative order, "Join them," belies the emblem's serenity: the joining, or shaking, of hands may more readily suggest a contractual exchange than a gift.

But even as *Concordia* may have served as a source for the two central figures in Velázquez's *Surrender of Breda,* there is no manifest handshake in that painting. In fact, I have yet to encounter a representation of surrender that features an actual handshake at the essential moment of exchange between victor and vanquished. Near handshakes, demurred handshakes, or handshakes in the prelude to the surrender are more the norm and suggest, as the following section on objects and gestures of exchange will demonstrate, that the surrender handshake can be approached only asymptotically. Most typically, figures of the vanquished kneel or bow or stand at attention as they face the victor and their fates. Nevertheless, certain aspects of surrender exchanges may evoke the legal contract paradigm of exchange (as defined by the *Oxford English Dictionary:* "In a legal sense: An agreement enforceable by law. a. An accepted promise to do or forbear; b. An agreement which effects a transfer of property; a conveyance").

That the surrender terms must, to varying degrees, be a function of collaboration of both parties to a conflict helps make surrenders contractlike.[41] This is so even if the only acts of collaboration are when the vanquished signs the signature and desists from fighting. Inevitably, copies of the surrender instrument and terms are distributed to both sides, such copies acting as a kind of written "contract" and record of what happened at the surrender ceremony. Yet contractual compatibility and coordination of the actions and exchanges at the point of surrender do not imply symmetry or mutual satisfaction. The defeated party may attempt to translate surrender agreements into more symmetrical programs and pledges than they actually prescribe. Linguistic translations provide a flexible medium for such attempts, as a bilingual thirteenth-century surrender pact between the Muslim al-Azraq and the Christian King James of Aragon reveals. Alternating lines of Arabic and Castilian text demonstrate variant interpretations: "The Christian text makes al-Azraq a vassal and partner, while the Arabic text merely agrees to a three-year truce . . . and implies no real subordination to the infidel."[42]

Other attempts fail even to be translated (literally and metaphorically) and make it into the historical record. At the end of World War II, the German general Alfred Jodl made an apparently impromptu hortatory speech immediately after signing the surrender documents in May 1945 in Eisenhower's Reims headquarters. In this speech he attempted to reequilibrate the outcome of the surrender by making maximalist claims about Germany's war experiences. Speaking in German, Jodl declaimed, "With this signature the German people and the German armed forces are, for better or worse, delivered into the victor's hands. In this war, which has lasted more than five years, both have achieved and suffered more than perhaps any other people in the world. In this hour I can only express the hope that the victor will treat them with generosity." As Douglas Botting recounts, "Complete silence greeted this plea from Jodl. No written translation was made of it."[43] The very absence of any translation of this unprogrammed intervention reveals the importance of the scribe's role in codifying the meaning of such transactions. The clear decision not to officially witness this speech meant that it would have virtually no temporal, archival, or legal extension and consequence.

Finally, the vectors of the exchanges of surrender may be understood as demonstrations of agency and responsibility. The compositional system that emerges out of the transfers highlights the ultimate ground of legitimacy. First movers and final arbiters are located via actions that are both practically effective and symbolically exemplary. In one of the letters that Ulysses S. Grant sent to Robert E. Lee in the complicated prelude to the surrender of the Lee's Army of Northern Virginia, he wrote, "The results of the last week must convince you of the hopelessness of further resistance on the part of the Army of Northern Virginia in this struggle. I feel that it is so, and regard it as my duty to shift from myself the responsibility of any further effusion of blood, by asking of you the surrender of that portion of the Confederate States army, known as the Army of Northern Virginia."[44] In the matter of ultimate responsibility, then, Grant implies that inasmuch as both parties had engaged in armed conflict, both generals had some responsibility for the "effusion of blood." But inasmuch as the outcome of further fighting, after great Confederate losses at Petersburg and Richmond, was destined to favor the Union, Grant was taking it upon himself to "shift from myself the responsibility" in exchange for the Confederates' surrender. Responsibility is effectively transferred in this communication—although not, interestingly, authority. Grant designates himself the arbiter of the course of the war and gives himself the autonomy either to maintain responsibility for its ongoingness or to divest himself of it. But the transaction must take the form of an exchange—responsibility is *transferred* to Lee, who must in turn divest himself of it by the only option available to him, surrender.

The Objects of Exchange

What kinds of things are exchanged in surrender transactions, as victor and vanquished reconstitute their worlds? The actions and objects of surrender exchanges can be divided into four categories: originary objects of contention in the conflict; secondary objects of contention that emerge during the conflict or opportunistically present themselves at the point of surrender; objects and actions that comprise the mechanics of surrender exchanges; and symbolic objects of authority and solidarity.

Originary and Secondary Objects of Contention

> Not the act of tracing boundaries, but their cancellation or negation is the constituting act of the city.[45]

Simultaneous and conflicting claims of ownership, jurisdiction, control, or authority over people, territory, resources, sacred objects, or worldviews form the background of many wars. The relevant objects of contention may indeed contingently ignite a conflict, and they may remain in the sights of the antagonists over the course of the conflict to become the focus of its termination. As Lewis Coser writes, "The more restricted the object of contention and the more visible for both parties the clues to victory, the higher the chances that the conflict be limited in time and extension."[46]

These originary objects of contention may be said to have the imprint of the "inalienable." They are the focal points of conflict exactly because they are experienced as essential to the identity of the regime or the collective entity claiming possession of them. In this regard it is useful to think about the distinction made by Marcel Mauss between alienable things that are part of the ongoing systems of exchange across social groups and those that are kept out of exchange. Commenting on Mauss's distinction, Maurice Godelier notes that it is this inalienable core that allows the system of exchange to be set into motion.[47]

These objects may have variable physical and symbolic physiognomies. They may be crucial towns or forts or other military units, they may be borders themselves or national capitals.[48] They may also be sacred relics or objects of traditional authority, whose alienation is tantamount to a loss of essence.[49] Thus it is not surprising that many of these original objects of threatened or forced alienation appear as central figures in the ceremonies and transactions of surrender. Nor is it surprising that similar objects emerge over the course of a conflict as focal points for exchange at the conclusion of the peace, taking on something of the essential or of an identity-articulating or reinforcing quality. They include territory, legal rights and responsibilities, warriors and populations, and flags, gems, medals, and emblems.

One method by which historians have come to identify war "in a legal sense" is the degree to which conflicts "led to important legal results, such as creation of a state, territorial transfers, or changes of government."[50] Such obvious reconstitutions of territory and social organization can be most actively worked out during surrender negotiations. Once again, the apparent subordination of the vanquished and the superiority of the victor provide only the first approximation for predicting what the reconfigured landscape (both literal and figurative) will look like after the transactions. New, expanded borders can represent a real challenge to the victors: "On the one hand, terms of settlement that include giving up territory will increase the relative strength of the winner in the current war. On the other hand, by withdrawal the loser may gain more defensible borders."[51]

Jurisdiction over territory must be further analyzed into several types of control: military, political, economic, legal, religious. These different kinds of rights do not necessarily all align, as cities or castles or garrisons move back and forth across the antagonists' divide. Defeated residents or citizens, variably configured, might be left with economic autonomy but some religious restrictions (Breda); traditional authority but political and military strictures (Japan after World War II); modulated political subjugation but military and traditional hierarchies intact (Játiva, 1245); and so forth.[52] Further complicating these variable formulations is the possibility of alternative interpretations of the "same" surrender treaty, as I have already demonstrated. Language is key here, as is the relative weight given to different channels of performative action. Which, for example, becomes more meaningful and binding—what is agreed to in speech or in writing? Discussing the case of the 1840 Treaty of Waitangi in New Zealand, when forty-six Maori chiefs surrendered sovereignty over their territories to the queen of England, Roger

Chartier notes that "for the English, the Maori chieftains' signing of the text ceding 'to Her Majesty the Queen of England, absolutely and without reservation, all the rights and powers of sovereignty' was an unambiguous recognition of the colonizers' political domination. This was not the case with the Maori. First the term translating 'sovereignty' in the vernacular version of the treaty (*kawnatanga*) meant only acceptance of British administration, not the abandonment of power over the land; second, the fact of signing the treaty had no particular value for the Maori, since what they considered essential were spoken words and promises made orally."[53]

Surrender treaties may also engage a dual-action mechanism whereby territory is theoretically alienated from the vanquished upon defeat and surrender and then immediately "given back" in a gesture of magnanimity. Thus, in the thirteenth-century Christian-Muslim surrender agreement signed by Prince Alfonso and King James of Aragon and by al-Azraq, "The [victorious] prince *confers* the two main castles on the Muslim's family 'to give, sell, pledge' or use entirely according to al-Azraq's wishes."[54] These gestures are as practical as they are symbolic, with calculations about the feasibility of territorial alienation *in the long run*. Thus when Louis XIV returned Franche-Comté to the Spanish in 1668, after dismantling its fortress, he noted that "Franche-Comté, which I handed back, could be reduced to such a state that I could be its master at any time, and my new conquests, firmly established, would open a more certain entry into the rest of the Low Countries."[55]

A Note on the Work of Maps

The role of maps in the transfers of territory in surrenders became particularly important in the historical epoch of the formation of the modern state.[56] The codification of the conventions of mapmaking in the development of cartography was, according to scholars, complexly bound up with the making of war: "Cartography became an instrument of rule in the 16th century [as] it was initially adopted for war. Around 1495, the first map commissioned by a king of France showed the Italian peninsula along with Alpine passes suitable for an invading army . . . Conversely, fear of invasion led Henry VIII of England to commission maps of the coastline in the 1530s."[57] The knowing and the ruling of territory developed in tandem.

Historians convincingly claim that the very process of mapping a territory in a particular way participated in the creation of the state that the map pretended to represent. As the motivations, techniques, and conventions of mapmaking changed over time, there was a dynamic relation between the political entity and its cartographic representation. Maps thus served to both record and constitute the shift from empires to states during the sixteenth and seventeenth centuries. As Chandra Mukerji writes, "If the land of empires was known by its power centers and expansiveness, the land of the state was known by its boundaries; it was the product of a kind of political 'enclosure' movement that identified a particular, marked part of the European continent with the state. Any ambiguity about the placement of its boundaries was welcomed as an opportunity to go to war . . . Old maps were marked with castles and towns, centers of commerce and social action, and with the rivers, roads and seas along which one could pass from center to center. The newer maps of the 16th and 17th centuries . . . started to mark boundaries with clear lines."[58]

Nevertheless, as early as the Renaissance, princes hung maps on walls as emblems of power and stateliness. And by the time of the seventeenth century, the displayed map appeared in many allegorical paintings in which "dream states" alternated with real states in situations of flux. Jan Vermeer's famous *Art of Painting* features a mythical map in its prominent background. This map fantastically portrays the Netherlands as one united political territory rather than as divided into the northern Dutch United Provinces and the Spanish Habsburg south.[59] It should not be surprising, then, that among the cases of surrender under examination in this book, one stands out for its preoccupation with maps and their rendering of the site of battle and surrender. That is the seventeenth-century siege and surrender of Breda. The monumental map drawn by Jacques Callot was a marked point of reference for, among others, Isabella, the infanta of Spain and Phillip IV's royal representative to Breda. Isabella refers specifically to Callot's map in her letters to General Ambrogio Spinola, a reference that places Callot's map "within the realm of courtly diplomacy and military propaganda."[60] Beyond this map, Spinola's Jesuit confessor presents literally dozens of diagrams and maps of the fortifications at and around Breda in his *Obsidio Bredana,* a journal of the siege and surrender. These etchings by Theodore Galle are detailed and precise. They demonstrate a literally on-the-ground knowledge of the city and surrounding countryside and pictorially describe Spinola's gradual acquisition of control over it.

Civil War Territory

In civil wars, territory becomes particularly charged, since secession presents unique challenges. As an object of exchange during surrender procedures, the territory that seceded and must now be reabsorbed (if the victor is the original sovereign entity) is a conceptual conundrum. How ought this territory, which the victor always still considered present during the civil war, now be re-presented by the rendering foe? Civil war thus takes to an expressive extreme the etymological deep structure of the notion of return in surrender—to render back what the victor always, really, rightfully possessed. In the case of the American Civil War, these complex conceptualizations and administrations were given further resonance by the historically extant tension between regionalism and federalism in that country. On the occasion of his Farewell Address, President George Washington himself felt compelled to weigh in on this tension: "The name of American, which belongs to you in your national capacity, must always exalt the just pride of patriotism more than any appellation derived from local discriminations."[61] Almost seventy years later, General Robert E. Lee makes the following intervention during the Appomattox surrender meeting with General Ulysses S. Grant: "There is one thing I would like to mention," Lee replied: "The cavalrymen and artillerists own their own horses in our army. Its organization in this respect differs from that of the United States." A participant of this meeting, Lieutenant Colonel Horace Porter of the Union delegation, noted that "this expression attracted the notice of our officers present as showing how firmly the conviction was ground in his mind that we were two distinct countries."[62]

The legal entity of the Confederacy, never recognized by the Union in any case, was nevertheless decomposed by the surrenders of the Southern generals. Beyond the simple paradox of how one undoes something whose existence was never recognized, questions were raised as to how to reinvoke recognition of the Southern states whose status as states reemerged at the end of the war. Lincoln's approach was pretty straightforward and had everything to do with the varieties and predictability of exchange relationships with these states. Objects and agents would go from the North, and especially from Washington, to the South, and objects and agents (representatives, population, taxes, commercial products, mail) would come from the South to the North: "Once the war is over, Lincoln wants to establish normal commercial relations with the former Confederate states as soon as possible. The cabinet agrees. The executive agencies should resume their traditional functions in the South: the Treasury Department would proceed to collect revenues; the Interior Department would set its surveyors and land and pension agents to work; the Postmaster General would reestablish mail routes."[63] The very objects of contention acted to reconstitute the country through being reinserted in a system of *ongoing* normalized exchange.

The Fates of Warriors and Civilians

Along with territory and rights of residents or citizens, the actual status of entire populations and military forces is bound up in the contentious competition of wars. The fate of soldiers is often decisively decided during negotiations of surrender. Will they be captured, arrested, and tried for various crimes, including (in civil wars) treason or the more recent "crimes against humanity"? Will they be allowed to return to their homes and take up civilian life? Will they be conscripted or enslaved by the victorious forces?

Even with the codification of conventions of war in the seventeenth and eighteenth centuries, there were variations on a theme of soldier exchange. Of the early modern Spanish soldier, historian Lorraine White notes, "Unlike men in England's armies who swore to do 'loyall true and fythefull service' to Queen Elizabeth I, there is no evidence that common soldiers who enlisted in Spain's royal armies actually swore an oath. Given the multinational, not to mention multi-confessional composition of many of Spain's armies, along with the presence of mercenaries, perhaps this is not surprising . . . Transfers of allegiance were frequent after major defeat, though this was perhaps truer of foreign soldiers in Spain's peninsular armies in the 17th c."[64] Thus was allegiance to one or another monarchy and army a highly contingent thing, and thus were armies and monarchs or governments not entirely in control of their military forces. Another significant thing about such shifting of allegiance is that it demonstrates the willingness of antagonists to absorb rather than prosecute former enemy soldiers. In addition, victorious forces might allow deserters or traitorous soldiers who had gone over to the enemy lines to escape unharmed when exiting the defeated forces' strongholds.[65]

Retreating and surrendering soldiers were of course always in a certain amount of danger. Even when it appeared that provisions had been made to protect the defeated forces, as they were exchanged they might instead be attacked. In the surrender of the parliamentary foot at Lostwithiel in England in 1644, "the parliamentary army was to have a convoy of a hundred royalist horse, which in turn was to be safely convoyed back to the king." Instead, the Cornish people attacked the Parliamentarians on their way.[66] Often it has mattered to whom soldiers, and civilians, would be permitted to surrender. In World War II, the German admiral Karl Dönitz kept up the fighting in the east even as it was clear that the Allies were definitively victorious, in order to allow German soldiers and civilians to escape to the west and surrender to the British and Americans rather than to the more volatile and punitive Soviet troops.

Civilian populations have experienced varied fates after surrender agreements, from enslavement to exile to freedom. In the *Obsidio Bredana,* for example, map 11, etched by the artist Theodore Galle, reveals thousands of refugees fleeing, on foot and in carriages: "Etiquette required that the defeated should leave through a breach in the city wall."[67] Buttressing this pictorial image is Hermannus Hugo's transcription of the "Articles of Surrender" at Breda, which included number 3, "Freedom of movement and belongings to citizens and inhabitants," and number 5, "It shall be granted to the [Protestant] preachers of the word to depart freely with their wives, children, family goods and movables, without all offence or damage."[68] In all cases, the movement of populations within and across reconstituted borders is an essential part of the pacification and remaking of the world.

Finally, beyond the territory, population, and military forces that ignite or emerge over the course of conflicts, there are objects of great symbolic value to the contending parties that are exchanged at the conclusion of the peace. These include flags, medals, emblems, and gems. The focused attention given to such objects serves several purposes. Within the press and chaos of battle itself, they can function to draw psychic attention of the warriors and mitigate the natural fear. Randall Collins writes in this regard about the capture and carrying off of symbolic tokens by medieval knights and theorizes about the power of such concentration on specific objects: "The individual overcomes fear by displacing his attention to symbolic tokens which structure the perceptual field among the chaos of the battlefield."[69]

These symbolic tokens often are flags, and their flying tracks and maps the territorial shifts at stake in the conflict. To see the work of flags, one need only look at the fresco of Guidoriccio da Fogliano, probably painted by the Sienese painter Simone Martini in the fourteenth century (plate 10).[70] Guidoriccio, a condottiere hired by Siena to recapture (note the theme of return) two nearby hill towns from the Pisans, is portrayed on horseback moving from right to left on the fresco, from a town he has successfully retaken (now flying the flags of Siena) to the still alienated town that waits, silent and unadorned with flags, for him to arrive and take it over. His troops are encamped on the far right of the painting, and he traverses this empty space of historical expectancy in the middle alone. With the precedent of the other town's surrender, there is the expectation that the second town will follow suit. Yet we do not see either town in the act of surrendering; one already has, the other will. No actors are visible in and around these towns. Only towers and walls are visible, with or without flags. The motif of the flags is recapitulated in the garments of both soldier and horse. We see Guidoriccio, literally one with his magnificently vested horse, as their garments blend seamlessly into each other, insisting on a symbolic standard that does the work of staking claims. As he moves across the empty space of the middle, we notice that the barren landscape between the two hill towns participates in the narrative of history. On the right, where the already reconquered town sits adorned with flags, the land has settled down. On the left, where the next conquest waits, the land roils and undulates with the shock waves of transformative energy.

The painting of Guidoriccio, whether painted by Simone Martini or not, was one of a group of castle paintings, beginning in the early fourteenth century, that covered the walls of the main council room of the Palazzo Pubblico in Siena. The takings and retakings of these feudal castles were considered important enough to be represented publicly, a way of metonymically charting the territory of the city of Siena during a period of expansion.[71] The political universe of Siena is reproduced within the walls—actually on the walls—of the government's seat of power. The surrendered castles are literally worn, like emblems, by the victor.

Hundreds of years later, during the surrender ceremony on board the USS *Missouri* in Tokyo Bay on September 2, 1945, another emblematic, historic flag would announce victory and possession. The American flag originally flown by Admiral Matthew Perry when he entered Tokyo Bay ninety-two years earlier had been brought to Japan especially for this ceremony and mounted on a bulkhead of the ship. Where these symbolic objects are focused on as proof of ownership and authority, their metonymic power is magnified. These are flags that have literally lived through and survived encounters and battles. The traces of their histories remain on them as they are caught up in the transactional systems of surrender.

Like flags, other objects present a complex essence—part object of contention, part symbol of reconstituting relations, part booty. Such objects as precious gems get caught up in the ceremonies and performances of ownership, power, identity, and fealty that flow through surrendering exchanges. The fascinating case of the famous jewel the Koh-i-nor, handed over to Queen Victoria's representative Governor General Dalhousie during the surrender of the maharaja of Lahore in 1849, demonstrates this complex of transactional meanings. Years after the gem was taken from him, Queen Victoria herself met the maharaja Dalip Singh, brought him to live temporarily in one of her own residences, and commissioned a portrait of him. As recounted in anthropologist Brian Axel's study of the Sikh diaspora, a strange and powerful scene occurs during one of the sittings for the portrait. Queen Victoria instructs a lady of the court to ask if the maharaja would like to see the Koh-i-nor once again after so many years. His reply reveals much about the power and symbolism of objects in surrendering exchanges:

> "Yes indeed I would! I would give a good deal to hold it again in my hand! Why? Because I was but a child, an infant, when forced to surrender it by treaty; but now I am a man, I should like to have it in my power to place it myself in her [Queen Victoria's] hand". . . . After a quarter of an hour examining the gem, Duleep moved deliberately to where her Majesty was standing, and, with a deferential reverence, placed in her hand the famous diamond, with the words: "It is to me,

Ma'am, the greatest pleasure thus to have the opportunity as a loyal subject, of myself tendering to my Sovereign the Koh-I-noor!" Whereupon he quietly resumed his place on the dais, and the artist continued his work.[72]

The Koh-i-nor is thus worked and reworked in a performed cycle of possession, dispossession, repossession, and "voluntary" alienation. The coercive nature of gifts, their sublimated violence, and the many-layered system of relations they constitute and reflect are all exposed in the maharaja's rendering up, for the second time, the famous jewel.

Transactional Objects of the Process of Surrender

Surrenders need to be managed as a series of decisions, and actions must occur at certain times and places. At the most basic, existential level, food and provisions must begin to flow across the enemy divide. The halting of the fighting and the restructuring of relations between human agents and between collective entities and authority structures must all be accomplished through contingent negotiations. Terms are proffered, debated, and rejected or accepted. Credentials authorizing representation of collectivities and sovereignties are presented. Letters cross antagonists' lines. Oaths are then taken, promises and pledges are made, orders are given—a whole series of performative speech acts constitute the very stuff of the surrender. The mechanical aspects of these features do not thereby make them less resonant and meaningful. These are legal and moral and military and political acts.

Most surrenders are preceded by a chain of letters and documents that flow back and forth across the conflict's divides. In the three main case studies of this investigation of surrender—at Breda in 1625, at Appomattox in 1865, and in Tokyo Bay in 1945—these missives hammered out the terms of the surrender instruments and authorized the eventual signers of these terms. Before the performative act of signing could occur, the authority and legitimacy of the signer needed to be assured. As always, the legal and political force of such transactions relies on the tricky dialectic between the performative and the constative. This dialectic is often exposed for its logical and practical complexity when there is disalignment or potential disalignment. Two cases of such awkward fitting are especially clear here (and they will be described below): the case of General Sherman's thwarted surrender memorandum with the Southern general Johnston and the case, already introduced, of the Japanese emperor's authorization of the signers of the World War II Instrument of the Surrender of Japan.

When the course of the conflict begins to become clear, the imminent victor will usually proffer terms to the soon-to-be-defeated group. Toward the end of the siege at Breda, initial terms were indeed offered by the Spanish general Spinola to Justin of Nassau, the Dutch general defending the town. As recorded by Hermannus Hugo, Spinola's Jesuit chaplain and memoirist, "Spinola confirmed once again by these letters [that were intercepted from the Dutch] of the penury of their provision, and advertised of the slow coming of their help . . . thought good to try Justin's mind, by demanding of him to render it up. For this purpose he sends the Trumpeter of Count Salazarius with his letters privily . . . that he would make him offer of reasonable conditions, if he would treat with him of a composition."[73] Ultimately, the Dutch would come to accept to "treat with him of a composition," and terms of the surrender agreement were copied and sent back and forth for the signatures of both generals.

In the case of Appomattox a series of letters between Grant and Lee circled in on the surrender of Lee's Army of Northern Virginia and the provisional terms of the surrender. The terms derived from President Lincoln's magnanimous stance, codified as the River Queen Doctrine, toward a South he greatly desired to be reconciled with: "To get the deluded men of the rebel armies disarmed and back to their homes . . . let them once surrender and reach their homes, [and] they won't take up arms again . . . Let them all go, officers and all, I want submission and no more bloodshed . . . I want no one punished; treat them liberally all around. We want those people to return to their allegiance to the Union and submit to the laws."[74] But it was left to the two generals to maneuver their way to a time and a place of meeting and exchanging documents and signing on to the agreed terms. Grant writes about this correspondence at some length in his *Memoirs,* reproducing the letters and recalling the terrible headache he suffered during the several days leading up to final acceptance. Lee's final letter read, "I received your note of this morning on the picketline whither I had come to meet you and ascertain definitely what terms were embraced in your proposal of yesterday with reference to the surrender of this army. I now request an interview in accordance with the offer contained in your letter of yesterday for that purpose." On receiving this letter, Grant writes in his *Memoirs,* "When the officer reached me I was still suffering with the sick headache; but the instant I saw the contents of the note I was cured."[75]

Approximately a week after Grant and Lee signed the surrender instrument at Appomattox, General Sherman was to meet with General Johnston to perform a similar operation for all remaining active troops. Over the course of some ten days, these two men hammered out a "Memorandum, or Basis of Agreement" that was sweeping in its reach. It called for Confederate armies to be "disbanded and conducted to their . . . state capitols, there to deposit their arms and public property in the state arsenals"; for Federal courts to be reestablished throughout the land; for the United States president to recognize existing state governments as soon as their officials took loyalty oaths to the Union, and for all citizens to be guaranteed "their political rights and franchises . . . as defined by their constitution."[76] In spite of, or perhaps because of, its grandeur and sweep, this memorandum was, as I noted above, rejected by President Johnson. Sherman's lack of civil political authority made his autonomous decision to go beyond the terms laid out at Appomattox illegitimate. He was, in brief, not authorized to sign the document he forged (note the double entendre embedded in that word).

Finally, in the case of the surrender of the Japanese to the Allies at the end of World War II, much of the work of the letters that prepared the way for the surrender focused on the status of the emperor and the imperial monarchy in Japan. The "unconditional surrender" of Japan made obviously problematic the maintenance of the imperial dynasty as authoritative. The conditional recognition of the emperor's authority was nested in the overarching authority of the supreme commander for the Allied powers. Yet in a fantastical performative looping mechanism, only the emperor could authorize the Japanese foreign minister to sign the Instrument of Surrender: "By the Grace of Heaven, Emperor of Japan, seated on the Throne occupied by the same Dynasty changeless through ages eternal, To all to whom these Presents shall come, Greeting! We do hereby authorise Mamoru Shigemitsu, Zyosanmi, First Class of the Imperial Order of the Rising Sun to attach his signature by command and in behalf of Ourselves and Our Government unto the Instrument of Surrender which is required by the Supreme Commander for the Allied Powers to be signed."[77]

It was powerfully clear that Douglas MacArthur was indeed the supreme authority and that the emperor could not act autonomously to make policy or direct the fate of Japan. Nevertheless, it is interesting to analyze the beginnings of the eight paragraphs of the Instrument of Surrender (in the English version) for what they reveal about this complex and internally cross-referencing system of authorizing. The first paragraph begins: "We, acting by command of and in behalf of the Emperor of Japan, the Japanese Government and the Japanese Imperial General Headquarters, hereby accept the provisions." The second paragraph starts with: "We hereby proclaim the unconditional surrender to the Allied Powers." The next three paragraphs "hereby command" Japanese forces to cease hostilities and surrender. But then there is the strangely worded sixth paragraph that begins: "We hereby *undertake for* the Emperor, the Japanese Government and their successors to carry out the provisions of the Potsdam Declaration." These words, "undertake for," are confusing in their forcefulness and the directionality of their agency. Finally, the last paragraph reasserts MacArthur's command status:

"The authority of the Emperor and the Japanese Government to rule the state shall be subject to the Supreme Commander for the Allied Powers." Thus the Instrument begins with the "command of" the emperor of Japan and ends with the subjection of this same commanding authority. This document and the debates about the agents responsible for it, on both sides of the completed war, demonstrate just how complicated the credentializing process can be—those credentials that authorize, those that undo authority, and those that authorize a redoing or shifting of authority.

Surrenders call forth the world-changing *final* commands and orders that definitively end a conflict. These are orders that stand literally on the brink of their own mortality. This aspect may be what gives them a kind of poetic, elegiac quality. They have the *authority* to undo, but the *pathos* of self-immolation. The speeches in which these last orders are given by the defeated commanders contain a mixture of reflection, description, hortatory words, admonitions, and performative speech acts. They thus constitute intricately hybrid documents. All of these things are obvious in Robert E. Lee's "General Orders Number 9":

> After four years of arduous service, marked by unsurpassed courage and fortitude, the Army of Northern Virginia has been compelled to yield to overwhelming numbers and resources. I need not tell the brave survivors of so many hard fought battles, who have remained steadfast to the last, that I have consented to the result from no distrust of them. But feeling that valor and devotion could accomplish nothing that would compensate for the loss that must have attended the continuance of the contest, I determined to avoid the useless sacrifice of those whose past services have endeared them to their countrymen. By the terms of the agreement officers and men can return to their homes and remain until exchanged. You will take with you the satisfaction that proceeds from the consciousness of duty faithfully performed, and I earnestly pray that a Merciful God will extend to you His blessing and protection. With an increasing admiration of your constancy and devotion to your country, and a grateful remembrance of your kind and generous considerations for myself, I bid you all an affectionate farewell.[78]

Lee has crafted his "order" from the verbs "compelled," "consented," "determined," and "prayed." His order emerges out of the sentiment of affection and his description of brave service rendered by his troops. Such a document raises important questions about how one recognizes an order, a command. A speech act full of indexical expressions locating the war and the soldiers in time and in place (including the words with the still unresolved territorial and legal referent "countrymen" and "your country") functions, in fact, as an order.

The terms of the surrender agreement are embedded, almost hidden, in the middle of the text, not quite an afterthought but not the main message. Lee's own authority to order the soldiers to surrender appears to need no external legitimation—he does not refer to the government of the Confederacy, and his reference to God is aimed only at auguring God's protection of the soldiers. This is thus a very personal and deliberately military (that is, apolitical) speech. The foe, perhaps now a countryman once again, is never mentioned, even with his "overwhelming numbers and resources." The world conjured up in this speech is one that exists only between Lee and his men.

Pledges, Oaths, Promises, and Pardons

Along with the presentation of credentials and letters of agreement and instruments of surrender, there are other processual objects and speech acts that make surrenders happen. These include pledges, oaths, promises, and pardons. They are often embedded in the formal documents and speeches that constitute the surrenders and carry them forward. Sometimes they appear in the preludes, sometimes in the aftermaths, doing the work of preparation or solidification.

This class of speech acts can either refer to the past or point to the future. They are in the business of normalizing postconflict relations and reorganizing ties of fealty. Together they form a class of guarantees—guarantees that the fighting will actually stop, that those who surrender will not be arrested or enslaved or killed, that those who surrender will not reactivate their animosity and violence before (or after) being exchanged, that those who are victorious will accept the redefinitions of the political selves of the vanquished, and so forth. As I noted in chapter 1, citizens of the United States have had a recent experience of a political surrender replete with promises and oaths. Presidential candidate Albert Gore, grudgingly acknowledging his defeat more than a month after the election was held in 2000, gave a nationally broadcast speech in which he referred to an exchange he had just had with his opponent George W. Bush: "Just moments ago I spoke with George W. Bush and congratulated him on becoming the 43rd president of the United States. And I promised him that I wouldn't call him back this time."[79] The promise not to call back after acknowledging defeat is a powerful and necessary mechanism of this transactional apparatus, especially since it undoes a previous "call back."

Pledges or promises occur on both sides of the victory divide and can in-

voke future behavior and relations to deal with past offenses. They participate in the attempt to suture the world torn by war and bind parties together
in recognizable, predictable ways. They also reveal the nuances of the power
dynamics in the conditions of the exchanges. In these acts, the victor may be
obliged to promise the vanquished certain conditions in exchange for surrender. Hermannus Hugo transcribed the instruments of surrender at Breda
in his *Obsidio Bredana* (two such instruments were drawn up, one for the governor and garrison, one for the magistrates and burgers). Exhausted by the
long and arduous siege, with Spain's military resources already stretched thin,
Ambrogio Spinola had been anxious to extract a surrender agreement from
the Dutch. He was thus willing to accede to many of their demands, including "that *pardon* and *forgetfulness* be both *promised* and *performed,* of all those
things which were committed by the citizens and inhabitants of Breda . . .
whether committed before, or after the recovery of the city in the year
1590."[80]

This first of fifteen articles of surrender insists explicitly on its pledge to
pardon "all things" done by all people in Breda during the period 1590-1625
(the most recent period of Dutch control). It is sweeping in its concrete (unconditional) referent and in its temporal demarcation. It is not enough that
the pardon will be promised and *performed* (a proto-Austinian parsing of the
performative); the crucial element of forgetfulness powerfully responds to
the inherent cyclical element of surrender. Forgetfulness invokes a break from
the past, a linear orientation to time, an escape from the deep structure of
such exchange systems as the gift.

The exact nature of such speech acts as pledges is contingent and shifting,
as befits the liminality of the situation of surrenders. When embedded in an
instrument of surrender or a newly revised constitution, they take on a
clearly legal imprint. When inserted into the text accompanying a magazine's
lithograph, as was the case after the surrender at Appomattox in the American Civil War, the pledge may act more as a religious or moral assurance. On
Palm Sunday, 1865, *Harper's Weekly* published a double-page spread by
Thomas Nast (plate 11). In the print, two scenes are displayed side by side.
On the left is a drawing labeled "The Savior's Entry into Jerusalem," and on
the right is a rendering titled "The Surrender of Gen. Lee and His Army to
Lieut. Gen. Grant." The analogy-making work of this print is stunning in its
explicit yoking of salvation, religious revelation, and the surrender of the
Confederacy to the Union. I will discuss the thematic nature of the print in
chapter 4. Here I want to focus on the caption under "The Savior's Entry into
Jerusalem." In this caption, Nast assumes the reconciling voice of the North:
"We hold out the olive branch to our erring and misguided brethren of the
Southern states and pledge to all of them who are loyal a hearty welcome to
all the benefits of our free Republic."[81] The Confederate soldiers are thus

described as erring and misguided, not criminal or traitorous, but the pledge is quite specifically directed only to those who are now loyal.

In some cases the victors may refuse to make legally binding pledges to the vanquished, preferring to have the freedom to deal with the defeated in an unfettered manner. It was with the precedent of Wilson's World War I fourteen-point pledge in mind that the Western Allies in World War II and Roosevelt in particular explicitly ruled out such pledges.[82] However, as we have seen, it was by deploying the Appomattox example that Roosevelt wanted to make the indirect, *moral* pledge to the people of Germany that the Allies would treat them fairly.

The foundational logic of symmetry in exchange transactions often requires oaths and pledges from the vanquished to match the pledges of the victors. But what if the vanquished refuse to swear oaths of loyalty to the victors? This dilemma was confronted toward the end of the Civil War when very few of the many thousands of captured Confederate soldiers would swear an oath of allegiance to the Union.[83] Brigadier General Joshua Lawrence Chamberlain, the Union officer designated to organize the ceremony of the surrender of the Confederate troops, recalled a rebel officer who articulated this resistance: "Chamberlain recalled telling a Rebel officer that the good will that soldiers from both armies exhibited at Appomattox augured well for the future . . . 'You're mistaken sir,' the Confederate replied with undisguised bitterness. 'You may forgive us but we won't be forgiven. There is rancor in our hearts . . . which you little dream of. We hate you sir.'"[84]

An oath of loyalty may indeed incorporate an acceptance of the pardon tendered by the victor. In that sense it refers not just to a past that is cauterized through the swearing of the oath but to the future as an assurance of future conduct. Legal scholar Ruti Teitel usefully differentiates between Abraham Lincoln's proposal of eliciting loyalty oaths from former supporters of the Confederacy, which were largely prospective and solidarity making in their orientation, and what were termed the "iron-clad oaths," "whereby deponents would attest to past allegiance to the Union as a condition for future public service. Anyone who had broken his oath to support the Constitution would be disqualified from public service."[85] The iron-clad oath announced a consistency of identity and fealty across time and was therefore nonfoundational (perhaps almost antifoundational) in its impact and motivation.

Instruments and Weapons of War

In his incisive *Strategic Surrender,* Paul Kecskemeti discusses the multiple steps in the process of surrender. He defines "strategic surrender" as the "orderly capitulation of the loser's remaining forces" and focuses his analysis on the actions and motivations around the hinge movements that transform violent interactions into nonviolent dealings. Significantly, he is sensitive to the transformation in identities, status, and relations as winner and loser are decided. And the act of disarming troops materially and symbolically participates in these transformations. Thus, Kecskemeti writes, "The disarming of troops is merely one phase of a more comprehensive act by which a sovereign abandons or loses belligerent status. Thus strategic surrender is a political act as well as a military act."[86] The implications of the sovereign's abandonment of belligerent status in surrender will be discussed at length in chapter 5. Here I want to stress that, as a practical matter, the vanquished must relinquish the weapons and instruments of war and turn them over to the control of the victors (or destroy them before the moment of surrender).[87] This action ensures the inoperability of these weapons in any potential reinvigorated violent conflict between the antagonists. Of course, the way the armaments of war are exchanged bespeaks the symbolic potency attached to machines of destruction and their handling. The symbolic variations on a theme of laying down arms are taken up below. But is important to note how very critical the exchange of weapons is for the actual halting of violence.

The fact of disarming an eventually defeated foe was very much on Roosevelt's mind early on in the progress of World War II. In a speech delivered in October 1942, he contemplated the war's end, declaring that "it is clear to us that if Germany and Italy and Japan—or any of them—remain armed at the end of this war, or are permitted to rearm, they will again, and inevitably, embark upon an ambitious career of world conquest. They must be disarmed and kept disarmed."[88] In fact, as the formula for unconditional surrender came to be codified and communicated to the Axis forces, it was decided, in mid-1944, to use the term *Bedingungslose Waffenniederlegung* (laying down of weapons) in American propaganda broadcast to the enemy. As Michael Balfour wrote about this decision, "Once a government's armed forces have laid down their weapons, the government becomes powerless to resist—except passively—any orders which the conqueror may choose to give, while the 'conditions' presented to it or to its armed forces are better described as 'requirements,' since little or no argument is possible about them."[89]

Sometimes the apparently practical difference between self-disarmament and disarmament before the victor becomes symbolically critical. The Japanese military reluctance about accepting the concept of "surrender" itself led General Yoshijirō Umezu to argue for self-disarmament at the moment of Japan's imminent defeat to the Allies: "Up to now the Japanese military has not permitted open surrender. The word 'surrender' is not in the Japanese military lexicon. In military education, if you lose your weapons, you fight with your bare hands. When your hands are no longer any good, you fight with your legs. When you can no longer use your hands and legs, you bite with your teeth. Finally, when you can no longer fight, you bite off your tongue and commit suicide. That is what we have been teaching. I do not think that it will go smoothly to order such an army to abandon its weapons and surrender . . . We ourselves will collect the weapons in those designated places and the units also will gather there to hand over their weapons."[90]

General Umezu's speech also has uncanny echoes of Richard II's soliloquy of self-undoing. Only the sovereign self has the power and the authority to undo itself—and it does so in graphic, physical modalities of self-consumption.

Symbolic Objects of Authority and Solidarity

The same weapons and instruments of war that are laid down for the purpose of cauterizing the violence are also laid down (or not) for symbolic purposes. The line between the practical and the symbolic in these exchanges is permeable. This is clear in the famous case of Grant's decision to allow the Confederate officers to keep their swords and to let the officers and troops keep their horses and their baggage. In this decision, the identity of these items was conceptually and legally altered. After the surrender agreement was signed and ratified, they were no longer instruments of war. They were instantly domesticated by Grant: "I take it that most of the men in the ranks are small farmers, and as the country has been so raided by the two armies, it is doubtful whether they will be able to put in a crop to carry themselves and their families through the next winter without the aid of the horses they are now riding, and I will instruct the officers I shall appoint to receive the paroles to let all the men who claim to own a horse or mule to take the animals home with them to work their little farms."[91] As long as the farmers are "small" and as long as the farms are "little," the fairy-tale metamorphosis of the identity of the horses could proceed.

On the other hand, Grant's own magnanimity was apparently prompted by a bit of humiliation on his own part. General Lee had come to the meeting at Appomattox dressed in a new uniform and wearing a beautiful sword. Grant writes in his *Memoirs*: "In my rough traveling suit, the uniform of a private with the straps of a lieutenant-general, I must have contrasted very strangely with [Lee]."[92] And Grant's aide, Horace Porter, wrote that it was the very sight of this sword hanging at Lee's side that inspired Grant to reject the "unnecessary humiliation" of requiring the officers of the Confederacy to surrender their swords. A strange and not entirely predictable exchange network of honor and humiliation thus emerged: Lee bedecked in a most honorable military attire and Grant in his scruffy, literally degrading private's uniform. Lee claiming, as he did, that he wore this uniform because he thought he would be taken prisoner by Grant and wanted to do so honorably. Grant using the occasion of his own humiliation to avert the humiliation of the vanquished.

Beyond the practical and the sociologically symbolic nature of the exchanges or giving back of such weapons as swords in the modern era, there is the powerful psychoanalytic potency of these exchanges. Much of Porter's recollections about Lee's sword and much of Grant's own *Memoirs* concern the focus on this sword by the two protagonists of surrender during the Appomattox discussions. A shining, hanging synecdoche, the sword caught everyone's attention, called forth a series of myths about its fate, and personified participation in the event. According to Porter, Grant's attention is drawn to the handsome sword, and he subsequently concocts his remanding plan for the Confederate officers. But then, unable to let go of the topic, Grant apparently is compelled to explain to Lee the absence of his own sword: "I started out from my camp several days ago without my sword . . . I have generally worn a sword, however, as little as possible, only during the actual operations of a campaign." Lee responds: "I am in the habit of wearing mine most of the time. I wear it invariably when I am among my troops, moving about through the army."[93] A story developed and spread throughout the country that Lee actually surrendered his sword to Grant and that Grant then handed it back. Grant's refutation of this story in his *Memoirs* is itself noteworthy, but the protest goes beyond clarification. "The much talked of surrendering of Lee's sword and my handing it back, this and much more that has been said about it is the purest romance. The word sword or side arms was not mentioned by either of us until I wrote it in the terms."[94] Romance indeed. A mythical exchange of masculinity, of potency, of the unacknowledgable (it "was not mentioned by either of us") aspect of war and of surrender of man to man.

Tributes, Demonstrations, and Gestures

Weapons figure importantly in the ceremonies, tributes, and demonstrations of surrender. The conventions of warcraft determined specific positions of honor or dishonor on exiting a garrison or town in a posture of surrender. Swords worn at the side were honorable, swords carried under the arm and pointing to the rear were dishonorable. Sabers drawn and resting on the shoulder pointing upward, or muskets pointing upward, were honorable. Sabers in their scabbards were dishonorable.[95]

But there were several other channels and media of communication and identity reconstituting involved in these ceremonies: "To march with drums beating, trumpets sounding, and colors flying was a distinction; flags furled and the drums and trumpets silent was humiliating."[96] As noted, General Grant assigned to Joshua Chamberlain the task of planning a formal day of surrender for the Army of Northern Virginia, April 12, 1865. Chamberlain arranged for the Union soldiers to "carry arms" and raise their muskets in a salute to the surrendering foe. Grant himself admonished the troops not to engage in "demonstrations [cheers] in the field."[97]

Art historians Jonathan Brown and J. H. Elliott maintain that the conventional manner of depicting surrender in paintings is as a "pageant of triumph and humiliation" in which the victor is either positioned above the vanquished or sitting while the vanquished kneels in abjection.[98] In the three principal cases of this book, the surrenders at Breda, Appomattox, and Tokyo Bay, such traditional demonstrations of the asymmetry of power at conflict's end either are specifically rejected or are much muted. And it is in the bodily gestures of orientation and extension at the center of the compositional field of exchange that these variations are expressed.

In chapter 2, the unstable representability of surrender was demonstrated through an analysis of the complications of the witness. Here the liminal situation and siting of surrender exchanges can best be interpreted by attention to the body and its gestures as they work to indicate and constitute new relations. Anthropologist William Hanks writes that "in many . . . cases of demonstrative reference, a crucial role is also played by the execution of bodily gestures simultaneous with the utterance, such as pointing, directed gaze, handing the object over, cocking the head, or pursing the lips."[99] Certainly in the network of cross-witnessing these gestures play a crucial role in directing attention to the focal point of commitment and exchange. But the lion's share of gestural deixis is formulated and expressed by the central protagonists at the signing of the surrender agreements and the surrounding ceremonies. Liminal moments such as these know themselves to be critical and transformative. They are all about directionality—literal physical directionality as de facto territorial realignments are made law, historical directionality as the past is both negated and recovered and the future prescribed, social and political directionality as relations of power and solidarity are rerouted. A certain predictable quotient of ambivalence and contradiction is necessarily present.

This ambivalence and contradiction are evident in posture, orientation, and gesture. It is as if the entire conflict and its trajectory are condensed in the central site and acts of exchange. Art historian Rudolf Arnheim discerns such a central condensation in works of art, which he terms the "microtheme": "The microtheme presents at some prominent center of the work, usually in the middle, a small, concentrated version of the subject that is played out in the composition as a whole . . . Such microthemes can be discerned remarkably often, especially in the action of hands, whose expressive behavior finds its place quite frequently in the middle of a work."[100] The relevant composition here is the structured series of actions that draw antagonists together to "compose" a surrender. The theme may be the expression of hierarchy, or of magnanimity, or of loyalty, or of humiliation. Or, more complexly, it may be a combination of these things as victor and vanquished must work in tandem and must demonstrate clear distinctions. The actual signers of the agreements, the bearers and deliverers of the keys, the swords, the weapons, the flags, and so forth, present the concentrated microtheme at the center of this world.

Certainly the actions of hands and other parts of the body caught up into the gestural praxis (as A. J. Greimas terms it)[101] are key and necessarily draw the attention of the cross-witnessing network. Handshakes, both those that are offered and performed and those that are anticipated but refused, figure prominently in this program. Both historically and semiotically, the handshake enjoys a close proximity to violence (deferred or anticipated). Handshakes operate as proxies for violent interaction. For example, what is really interesting about the interpretation of the handshake as a demonstration that one's hands are empty of weapons is that it acknowledges the latent social expectation of violent encounters, particularly true following a war.

In his positioning of the Spanish and Dutch generals in *The Surrender of Breda,* Court painter Velázquez may be referencing either the *actual* handshake of former enemies in the emblem *Concordia* or the *deflected* handshake (actually it would be a kind of mutual handclasp around a sword) in *In dona hostium.* The contradictory quality of the doubled source for this painting revolves specifically around the question of joining hands or not joining hands. In the center of the Breda painting by Velázquez hangs the key that the Dutch general is attempting to hand over to Ambrogio Spinola.[102] The actual breach in the wall that makes a surrender feasible in the seventeenth and eighteenth centuries ironically makes the possession of the key to the city literally irrelevant but symbolically essential. Its unrepresentable but inevitable grasping by Spinola stands in, conceptually, for a handshake.[103]

In the case of Appomattox, Grant and Lee did shake hands in the preliminary moments of the surrender talks, but this gesture gets confused and fragmented in the many prints and reproductions made after the fact. Most often the hands of the two generals are portrayed signing a document or, in the case of Lee, holding on to his sword. But in the Nast print in *Harper's Weekly,* Grant is drawn tentatively extending his hand to Lee, while Lee stands staunchly self-contained, left hand on his sword, right hand not shown but most likely on his hip.

Finally, during the period of preparing and transporting the Japanese surrender delegation at the end of World War II, the American colonel Craig Mashbir was confronted with the head of the Japanese surrender delegation,

General Masakazu Kawabe, en route to the Philippines: "Looking casual in suntans and no tie, Mashbir said in fluent Japanese, 'I have come to meet you.' Kawabe saluted and Mashbir returned it. Then the Japanese [general] put out his hand to Mashbir, who instinctively brought his own forward. At the last second, [Mashbir] realized that such a greeting was inappropriate, and jerked his hand back as though it were burned."[104]

Swords, muskets, horses, soldiers, letters, memoranda, handshakes, keys, pens, turbans,[105] and so forth transmute into a whole series of transitional objects that constitute the flow of exchange across the borders of surrender. They are absolutely crucial, and the various ways they are directed and received give particular shape and meaning to the event. Together they participate in giving the act of surrender the force of law.

Sites of Exchange

In order for all these exchanges and demonstrations to occur, the principals to concluding the peace must come together at a point of contact and convergence. They must focus on each other and on the artifacts of the surrender agreement. They need, in other words, a site of surrender. This space, however it is selected, is itself transformed by its designation as the surrender site. As it is readied for the surrender, it must empty itself out of a fixed identity and nature. I argue that this space must become liminal, even empty (sometimes literally; souvenir hunters ransacked poor Mr. Wilmer McLean's home after the Appomattox agreement was signed there), a context for metaphysical transformations. War is to be displaced by peace; instruments of death are to be transmuted into tools of domesticity (swords into plowshares). In this it shares something with the emptiness of "spaces" of founding. Working through the writings of Hannah Arendt and Jacques Derrida on the acts of founding a republic, Bonnie Honig refers to each theorist's articulation of this necessary, though problematic, blank space. For Arendt, she writes, "Political action has no anchor . . . ; [it] has as it were nothing to hold on to; it is as though it came out of nowhere in either time or space." From Derrida she takes the idea that "God is the name Derrida gives to whatever is used to hold the place of the last instance, the place that is the inevitable aporia of founding."[106] In a manner both analogous and obverse, I am making such a claim for the emptiness of the "space" of surrender. But as foundings emerge *out of* their originary aporia, or break, from what is known or what is past, surrenders may be understood to disappear *into* an aporia, or vanishing point, of dissolution, of undoing,[107] after which the world is made anew. I will return to this most difficult of existential issues related to surrender in both chapter 4

("Sovereignty and Its Afterlife") and chapter 5 ("The Deep Structure of Surrender").

The (former) schoolhouse (scene of the surrender of the German military to Eisenhower in May 1945), the (former) siege perimeter (site of the surrender of Justin of Nassau to Ambrogio Spinola in June 1625), the (former) farmhouse (site of the surrender of Lee to Grant in April 1865), the (former) battlefield (site of the surrender of Cornwallis's proxy to the American general Benjamin Lincoln, Washington's proxy, in October 1781) all transmute from sites experiencing the trauma of war into sites that, as Thomas Dumm claimed for the analogous contexts of letters of resignation, "contribute to bringing a traumatic experience to a conclusion . . . to contain it and to remove its effects."[108] They are to be the first of an outwardly expanding circle of "pacified social spaces," as Norbert Elias described the civilizing consequences of the emergence of a monopoly of force.[109] And they are positioned as a provisional, conceptual borderland between the past and the future, the former territorial alignments and the reconstituted ones. However pacified, they are also the space of power, as Jorge Arditi conceptualizes power in early modernity: "I refer here not to power in itself, power as a mere resource, decomposed to its fractional dimensions, but to a social space (in the case of the res civile, a space structured around the figure of the king) that enabled power, symbolic and otherwise, to be organized and exerted and a culture to be formed."[110]

The space of surrender must also be empty because it functions as a medium, a host for actions that are undertaken in extremis and under duress. Its image is as meaningful as its practical and strategic location. Similar to Barthes's idea of the "somehow empty image [of a city's center] needed for the organization of the rest of the city," the "emptiness" of the site of surrender is directly related to the reorganized world that it anchors.[111] This is not to say that some surrender sites are not tendentious. The main deck of the battleship USS *Missouri,* with its powerful guns much in evidence, appears to deviate from this rule. Nevertheless, sights such as American soldiers and sailors casually draping themselves over these guns to get a better look at the proceedings and the actual construction off the main deck of an elaborate platform for newsreel cameramen and newspaper photographers reveal a temporary domestication of the space of the battleship in the service of establishing it as a site of surrender, momentarily emptying it of its violent essence.[112]

As always, the choice of the site of surrender itself reflected the renegotiated power dynamics occurring at conflict's end. This includes power dynamics within one party's forces as well as between the opposed parties. For example, according to William Craig, "the choice of the *Missouri* as the surrender site had its origins in Washington and reflected the intense rivalry between Army and Navy."[113] Thus, from one point of view the army wins as Supreme Allied Commander Douglas MacArthur conducts the ceremony instead of Admiral Chester W. Nimitz (although Nimitz does sign), but the navy also wins with the location of the ceremony, the battleship USS *Missouri* anchored in Tokyo Bay.

In surrenders oriented to magnanimity toward the defeated foe, choosing a setting for surrender is overtly a process of negotiation and attempted symmetry. Thus does Ambrogio Spinola send a message to Justin of Nassau via the offices of a mediator (Henry of Bergues, a blood relative of the house of Nassau and familiar with the language and customs of the United Provinces): "Wherefore that he should the next day come to meet them out of the city halfway and declare what conditions he required, to be put in writing and our guards standing near adjoining."[114] The prescription of meeting halfway reflects more than a predictable mandate for caution (no one ventures too far into the field) in an ongoing battle. It is clearly metaphorical in its meaning as well. By the same token, in one of the last of the surrender-prelude letters between Grant and Lee, Grant wrote: "I am at this writing about four miles West of Walker's Church and will push forward to the front for the purpose of meeting you. Notice sent to me on this road where you wish the interview to take place."[115] Generosity and magnanimity thus flow in a synchronic manner through the many media that converge to deliver the peace.

Convergence and Divergence

The parties' drawing together at a physical point of exchange for the surrender suggests a connection between physical space and mental space. In order for the antagonists to conceptualize and attend to the varied performative, demonstrative, and representational matter that must materialize and flow in the event, continuity and convergence seem imperative. Perception requires this kind of point of focus.[116]

The burden on perception is even greater because of the complex existential tasks involved in surrendering. A nation, a political party, a juridical territory, a royal line—any or all of these may stand on the brink of disappearance on such occasions. The vanishing point of history cannot be entered easily. Thus the perception and structuring of the "spatial field," as Hanks terms it, is exceptionally marked. This is why gestures—such as handshakes or bows or salutes—or signatures come to matter so much. An analysis sensitive to the political semiotic of these interactions can illuminate how they gather together to assume the force of law. This is a *social* world in the unmaking and the making. Hanks insists on this point: "The spatial field of deictic reference is not simply egocentric but sociocentric, mediated by the socially defined physical configuration of the participants."[117]

It is through the aegis of the exchanges of surrender that the new social, political, and legal relations are forged and codified. The vectors of these exchanges are imbued with the political attitudes and emotional stances of both the giver and the receiver in any particular case. They also, themselves, set off new chains of probable future relations. Sworn oaths can lead to solidarity; the giving over of a precious gem can foster a sense of indebtedness or resentment; the disarming of a nation can lead to an assumed obligation to take control of that nation's entire operation; the return of a horse and a sidearm can recapitulate and revive an idea of individual autonomy against that of collective enthusiasm.[118] As these items and gestures and identities disappear into the historical vanishing point of surrender, they must reappear under a different paradigm. In this way the compositional apparatus of the actual ceremony of surrender can perhaps be best understood via the analysis of the vanishing points in Renaissance paintings. But such an analysis would be extended in its reach to incorporate not just the spectator but the participants as well, as they attempt to gain a perceptual purchase on the proceedings. Thus Louis Marin writes, "We may theoretically consider that in the vanishing point, in its hole, the things represented gradually disappear . . . or that from the viewpoint [of the spectator] they gradually appear to be distributed in the represented space."[119] The redistribution of things represented emerges out of the agreements, exchanges, and instruments of surrender and demonstrates a new world. The exchanges of surrender thus suture the ruptured historical narrative while they also provide the perceptual and conceptual apparatus to stare into the breach.

Sovereignty and Its Afterlife

THE SPECTACLE of surrender, with its transactions of exchange and its networks of cross-witnessing, does more than contemplate and manage the end of a conflict. It invokes a *system* of sovereignty and power. In its very undoing of specific sovereigns and sovereign claims, the spectacle of surrender exposes the machinery of that system. There is a danger in exposure that cannot be underestimated. When gestures, speech acts, exchanges, and images work to formalize defeat, the vanquished may not be the only sovereign power to feel the undertow. The victor may also experience its menace. Exposing the mechanisms of power showcases their maneuverability. The spectacle of surrender thus shoulders the double burden of decomposing sovereignty and reiterating it at the same time. This chapter will examine how such a seemingly paradoxical commission is accomplished.

The painting in plate 12 is Charles Le Brun's *The Queens of Persia at the Feet of Alexander* (ca. 1661). In it, the mother, wife, and children of the defeated and killed Darius surrender and submit themselves before Alexander the Great, offering obeisance after the Battle of Issus—or at least they think they do. In a powerful case of sovereign misrecognition, Sysigambis, the mother of Darius, has actually thrown herself on the mercy of Hephaestion, Alexander's general, rather than Alexander. Alexander and Hephaestion stand side by side in the painting, and in fact both are tall and striking in appearance, gloriously outfitted for war and ceremony. The misrecognition of a sovereign is a terrible mistake, yet understandable, and Alexander magnanimously forgives it. Here is how André Felibien, the *historiograph des bâtiments* (official descriptor) for Louis XIV renders the scene: "The painter has chosen the moment in which Sysigambis, who was mistaken in addressing Hephaestion, throws herself at the feet of Alexander and prays for his pardon . . . Alexander extends a hand toward that princess to raise her up, and with the other he holds Hephaestion by the arm and seems to say to Sysigambis that she has actually not really been mistaken, because Hephaestion is another Alexander."[1]

Alexander is the true sovereign who thus manages to appear and disappear and reappear in this scene of surrender. His doubling, through his accidental stand-in Hephaestion, pulls off a variation on the concept of the king's two bodies.[2] It traffics in a fiction of a plurality of sovereignty that is manifest in space (as opposed to the more frequently theorized dimension of time).[3] In Felibien's interpretation, Alexander cannot be either misrecognized or definitively located because his sovereignty is ubiquitous and is necessarily present in his proxy, the general Hephaestion. The emperor lives in all his subjects. Yet his actual presence at the submission of his defeated enemy's family seems problematic in ways that are useful to examine. He, like all sovereigns in this situation, *accepts* the submission in a manner more passive than active. The infusion of superior passivity into a transaction between a superior and an inferior is both necessary and problematic. As Georg Simmel wrote, "Each individual is at the same time an active and a passive agent in a transaction."[4] But it seems logical that the passivity of the superior who is on the receiving end of the inferior's offerings must be muted in representations of the superior's superiority. What is being asked of Alexander? Will he spare the lives of Darius's family members after defeating Darius? Will he even, in a demonstration of surplus magnanimity, spare the lives of those who did not *recognize* him as their conqueror? Here Felibien, writing a long description of the painting for his own latter-day sovereign, Louis XIV, takes the concept of sovereignty to a level at once sublime and didactic: "The painter could not have exposed to the eyes of the greatest king in the world an action more celebrated or [significant]. Because history records [this action] as one of the most glorious that Alexander had ever undertaken, owing to the clemency and moderation that the prince extended in this encounter. In overcoming himself, he overcame not the savage peoples, but the vanquisher of all nations."[5]

Meanwhile, the viewer of the painting puzzles over exactly who is Hephaestion and who is Alexander. The shifting back and forth of the two male figures from sovereign to subject-witness blurs the distinctness of these roles in the scene. According to classics scholars, the story of Darius's family's mistake in submission is mythical. It became inflated and elaborated only during the medieval period, carrying enough appeal to be painted by several painters and entering the mythos of stories about Alexander.[6] One understands this appeal. The Alexander of this story does seem to demonstrate and perform the general themes and dilemmas of sovereign identity in the moments of conflict's end: magnanimity in victory, recognition, representability, and repetition. It turns out that it is not just difficult but complicated and dangerous for both the victorious and the vanquished sovereigns to appear at scenes of surrender. One of the difficult tasks for the victor may be to overcome himself and his own impulses of pride or revenge. But the co-appearance of the two sovereigns raises even greater dangers. The victor's task is to avoid an unnecessary and dangerous leveling with the undone, vanquished sovereign. The vanquished, meanwhile, must undo himself, a most unbecoming act of unbecoming. Without sovereignty there can be no surrender, and without surrender there can be no sovereignty (since subjects must surrender themselves to the one recognized as sovereign). Yet the relations between these terms are anything but symmetrical on the ground. In this chapter I explore the historical management of the dangers of surrender and their political significance for relations among sovereigns by identifying the semiotic and cultural processes that have done this work.

What Is Sovereignty?

The term "sovereign" has multiple meanings. With broad applicability it is "one who has supremacy or rank above, or authority over, others; a superior; ruler, governor, lord, or master (of persons, etc.). Freq. applied to the Deity in relation to created things; The recognized supreme ruler of a people or country under monarchical government; a monarch; a king or queen; A gold coin minted in England from the time of Henry VII to Charles I; and, Of persons: Standing out above others or excelling in some respect."[7]

The sovereign stands out, stands over, and stands for. But he or she (most often he) does not simply stand; he also circulates and rules. It must signify that a gold coin named a "sovereign" circulated in England from the early to the mid-seventeenth century, the period of the consolidation of the system of absolutist states in Europe. It is in the nature of the sovereign essence to circulate, the nature of its image to be exchanged, reproduced, and recognized. Its value, in fact, derives from its circulation, the way it makes a relay from one subject to another, linking them to each other and to itself.

These circulations and recognitions of sovereignty suggest an important set of conceptual relationships. There is the connection between sovereignty and knowledge. The body of the king and the regnant body of knowledge (what is accepted as true) reinforce each other, as scholars such as Michel Foucault and Jens Bartelson have noted. And there is the connection between sovereignty and territory, since the power of the sovereign to be recognized as such reaches over a given territorial space. So that we can understand the semiotic conditions and mechanisms of the *surrender* of sovereignty, sovereignty's links to knowledge and to territory need to be highlighted.

In his genealogical study of sovereignty, Jens Bartelson examines these connections by pausing to consider the distinction between domestic and international politics: "So long as humanity has not achieved unification into a universal state, an essential difference will exist between internal politics and foreign politics. The former tends to reserve the monopoly of violence to those wielding legitimate authority, the latter accepts the plurality of centers of armed force."[8] Thus this emergent spatial system of political power necessarily identifies an inside and an outside, with different rules for domination and reactions to attempts at domination. For our purposes this difference can illuminate the semiotic stakes for sovereignty in moments of surrender, as the actual line dividing the inside and the outside keeps expanding and contracting. What was yours is now ours, and vice versa. Recalling the concept of return embedded in Western terms for surrender, what was temporarily (and wrongly) yours is now ours, and vice versa. Thus the outside was really inside. This liminal assertion and recognition reveal that the acceptance of plurality of centers of armed force was only provisional—conceptually logical, empirically unstable. How does sovereignty navigate in such an ultimately contested territorial and semiotic space? It constantly seeks its acknowledgment by subjects within and competitors without. And in its own policing of borders, it anticipates the collapse, one way or another, of the subjects and the competitors. These questions reveal how vexed the issue of the source and scope of sovereignty can become. And Bartelson claims that each new historical age of sovereignty takes up this task of staking its own foundations.

As there are conceptual contradictions of sovereignty, there are also distinct historical types of sovereigns. Sometimes in the transactions of surrender there is a confusion and combining of these types—a collective sovereignty is undone by means of a singular sovereign's decision and act. A singular sovereign thus may hold a collectivity's identity in his hands. Nevertheless, a typology of types of sovereignty is useful in sorting out the stakes of surrender for the parties involved.

Types of Sovereignty

Singular Rulers

Most cultures are habituated to the idea and image of the individual ruler. Whether identified and installed by means of lineage, charisma, sheer physical strength, or persuasive rhetoric, the singular sovereign is the focus of attention and deference. The sovereign makes claims. He can claim territory, loyalty, faith, and riches. In this the sovereign is exceptional. No one else can make these claims or, better (in the spirit of Max Weber), make them stick. Authority and a monopoly of violence are so intricately entangled in the essence of the sovereign claim that theorists from Hobbes to Weber to Schmitt to Foucault and Agamben have struggled to merely *analytically* circumscribe it. Does the violence "back up" the claims to authority? Does the violence of the sovereign differ existentially from that of pretenders or challengers or mere lawbreakers? How and why does a monopoly of violence translate into legitimacy? Does the violence of foundings differ from that of established political entities? What makes the sovereign's exceptionalism recognizable and palatable, at least for a while?

In spite of his singularity (or perhaps because of it), the sovereign is ubiquitous. He is now at the center of the realm, giving law and upholding it. He is now at the realm's periphery (literal or figurative), indifferent to the law, suspending it, flouting it, reconstituting it. As Giorgio Agamben writes, "Just as sovereign power presupposes itself as the state of nature, which is thus maintained in a relation of ban with the state of law, so the sovereign power divides itself into constituting power and constituted power and maintains itself in relation to both, positioning itself at their point of indistinction."[9] Sovereign power thrives in this charged zone where a kind of wild, breakthrough constituting power and a legislated constituted power are confused. The state of nature is both located in the lawless wild beyond the periphery and, in the figure of sovereign, smuggled into its very domestic core.[10]

The sovereign is thus exceptional and representative at the same time.[11] Such a being is recognized as having qualities that are superhuman, as having an ability to be part of everything that occurs in the realm, an immortality just short of deity (yet sometimes assessed as deity). Mechanisms by which to explain and understand these qualities have been developed by theologians, logicians, jurists, and court followers. They include the medieval notion of the king's two bodies, with all of its complexities. They include the development, in such contexts as France in the fifteenth century, of the idea of successive kingship and its transformation into the system of quasi-hereditary monarchy. They combine ideas about the immortality of the king himself and the perpetuity of his dynastic lineage. Ernst Kantorowicz's magnum opus explicates many of these aspects of sovereignty in all their particularity: "The perpetuity of the head of the realm and the concept of a *rex qui nunquam moritur,* a 'king that never dies,' depended mainly on the interplay of three factors: the perpetuity of the Dynasty, the corporate character of the Crown, and the immortality of the royal Dignity."[12]

The existential transcendence and multiplication of the sovereign across time and space are central concepts for analyzing the fate of the sovereign in surrender. They link directly to all the cases of sovereign doubles, proxies, portraits, appearances, and disappearances encountered in the charged environment of this act. They are also important in delineating the connection between the singular sovereign and that of a collectivity, the way the sovereign is "incorporated."

The Commonweal

As has already been evinced, the cases of war and surrender under analysis in this book, even those more mythical than real, reflect Western social and military forms and conventions as these were consolidated during the early modern period. They traverse the road from ancient Rome, through dynastic feudalism to the absolutist state and, finally, to the international system of sovereign nations. Conceptions of the relation between sovereign and collectivity obviously have varied. God-chosen lords, kings, and emperors ruled realms that identified themselves with their own person; rulers of realms with developing political state structures and homogenizing languages experienced more diffuse and contested legitimacy; elected officials of constitutional states recognized that their own temporary authority derived from the forthrightly collective sovereignty.[13]

Of course, the modern idea of the nation stresses the collective nature of sovereignty, what Benedict Anderson famously termed an "imagined community."[14] This idea actually dates back to the early modern period. Quoting the fourteenth-century Baldus de Ubaldis, Kantorowicz locates early linkings of ideas of territorial boundaries and monarchical subjecthood to ideas of the temporal transcendence of the collectivity as a sovereign realm: "A realm contains not only the material territory, but also the people of the realm because those peoples collectively are the realm . . . And the totality or commonweal of the realm does not die, because a commonweal continues to exist even after the kings have been driven away. For the commonweal cannot die [non enim potest respublica mori]; and for that reason it is said that the commonweal has no heir because in itself it lives for ever."[15]

Nearly five centuries later, the didactic import of the resignation of the first president of the United States, George Washington, is clear in this regard. Washington's voluntary and adamant surrender to the constitutional ideal of democratic elections foregrounds a concept of temporary individual sovereignty in a context of a permanently sovereign citizenry. He manages to make the intricate complex of patriotism, leadership, politics, and process clear in his resignation speech when he reiterates his decision to retire, "satisfied that if any circumstances have given peculiar value to my services, they were temporary. I have the consolation to believe that, while choice and prudence invite me to quit the political scene, patriotism does not forbid it."[16]

The relations between the authority and power of individual sovereigns and those of bounded collectivities have thus been various and complicated.

This variability certainly affects the roles and powers of individual sovereigns and their proxies as they navigate the perilous waters of war and its conclusion. They even affect the very classification of the conflicts and wars themselves, with the emergent categories reflecting shifting concepts of territorial boundaries and their prerogatives. As Quincy Wright puts it, "From the point of view of the society of sovereign states which emerged in Europe after the Renaissance and gradually spread to the rest of the world by recognition and annexation, wars were classified as 'balance of power' wars (between members of an international society), civil wars (within sovereign states), defensive wars (a member of that society against an outside state), and imperial wars (a member of that society attacked and often annexed an outside state or people, thus expanding the Society of Nations)."[17]

In critical moments of making and unmaking, it is surely the contingent (and often contested) identification of the individual sovereign's sovereignty with that of the collectivity of the realm that is cast in high relief. Does the surrender of the sovereign, or his refusal, necessarily drag his subjects along with him? Might they choose different trajectories if given the chance? Or might their identities be differentiated at this juncture? Paul Kecskemeti explores these conundrums of surrender and sovereignty in the context of the surrender of Germany at the end of World War II: "[Hitler] ruled out the possibility of capitulation. He adopted the position that the German people, having suffered defeat, no longer had the right to exist. The only alternative to complete victory was complete annihilation."[18] Here Hitler is seen to conflate his own refusal to surrender, and his ultimate suicide, with that of the German people—the sovereign vanishes and so do his subjects.

Since the territorial borders and political boundaries of sovereign realms (both internal and external) were fixed and challenged largely through war, the endings of these wars did often transform identities and loyalties. Even before the Enlightenment's declarations of individual rights, individuals experienced the ground of their existence as singular subjects of religious or imperial or monarchical dynasties. They did so largely through linguistic and other semiotic conventions that were as syntactic as they were semantic. Human temporality itself depends on this.[19] Human sociality does too, as certain orientations to place, institutions, and other people provide temporarily fixed viewpoints and relations.

Thus, when exploring sovereignty and the challenges to it during scenes of surrender, it is important to connect the macro (even transcendent) level of the sovereign to the micro level of the individually sovereign subject. The question thus shifts slightly: What happens to the sovereignty of the sovereign and his subjects when that selfhood is undone in surrender? The work of language and of the bodily scheme (*schéma corporel*) in providing orientation proves crucial in deciphering the fate of sovereignty in these scenes. A focus on the body in and of surrender suggests an examination of the political marriages of monarchical states.

Erotic Exchange and Vicarious Surrender

In 1612 Marie de Médicis, Florentine-born wife of Henry IV of France and mother of Louis XIII, brokered a politically strategic set of marriages. The double marriage that Marie arranged while queen regent was metaphorically to be a marriage of France and Spain. The consecration of this alliance, and its actual conduit, was the marriage of Anne of Austria (sister of the future Philip IV of Spain) to Louis XIII, a marriage already introduced in chapter 2, and simultaneously that of Elizabeth of France (Louis XIII's sister) to the future Philip IV. Marie de Médicis had herself negotiated the treaty with King Philip III, and this exchange of sisters was programmed to take place in 1615.

The famous artist and diplomat Peter Paul Rubens was commissioned in 1620 to paint a cycle of paintings recounting the story of Marie's life, including the minor civil war between Marie and her son Louis XIII. Art scholars have interpreted two of these paintings, *The Conclusion of the Peace* and *The Final Reconciliation* (both ca. 1622), as essentially scenes of Marie's reconciling herself to her son (who had gone so far as to place her under what was essentially house arrest), and thus as scenes of Marie's surrender. In a larger sense, one might say that the entire cycle has surrender as a dominant theme. The life of Marie de Médicis as portrayed by Rubens (closely overseen by Marie herself) was a long series of provisional triumphs, humiliating surrenders, and attempts at enduring reconciliations, both literal and psychological. But I am interested here in another of the cycle's paintings, the single one of the series from which Marie is herself absent:[20] *The Exchange of Princesses at Hendaye* (plate 13).

In this painting an allegorical figure representing France renders up Elizabeth to marry Philip IV of Spain. Simultaneously, Philip IV's sister Anne is exchanged for her marriage to Louis XIII by an allegorical figure of Spain. Contemporary interpreters understood that the dual marriage was anticipated to assist in transforming the relationship between the two countries from one of almost constant war to one of peace. However, more relevant here, the art historian Margaret D. Carroll reads this surrendering exchange of the sisters of the two princes as accomplishing a reconciling of the nations through a sexualized back door.[21] Carroll goes much further with this analysis in positing a representationally realized relation between sexual violence and absolutism. She analyzes another of Rubens's paintings, *The Rape of the Daughters of Leucippus,* as an allegory of international submissions and exchanges. Carroll claims that Castor and Pollux stand in for Philip and Louis and that the kidnapping scene of that painting celebrates the forcible subjugation of women by men as both a real and an allegorical mode for forming political alliances. And the mechanism by which these alliances are forged might be best understood as vicarious surrender. One conceives of the political marriage as voluntary in the same way that surrenders are voluntary, incorporating both privilege and constraint.

Key to the Rubens *Exchange of Princesses* is the space of the meeting and exchange of the very young women, on a pontoon in the middle of the Bidassoa River on the literal border between France and Spain. As I noted earlier, as the European system of absolutist states developed and crystallized over the course of the sixteenth and seventeenth centuries, the emphasis on boundaries became more pronounced, both in the drawing up of maps and in the conceptualizing of national territory.[22] Thus there is a striking logic to the symbolism of this river-crossing exchange on the border. The neutralizing mutual exchange marks the open space of surrender even as it simultaneously erases it. For the exchange only changes the incumbents of the original brother-sister pairings and thus reestablishes the initial equilibrium state.[23] But what of the sovereignty (small *s*) of the girls themselves? How does Rubens portray them as individuals and simultaneously as royal currency? The two soon to be sisters-in-law hold hands in the middle of the painting as a golden shower falls on them from an opening in the curtain/sky above. They do not exactly face each other—in fact, their bodies and their faces are in various states of disalignment, both within themselves and toward each other. And they seem to be pushed and pulled by the allegorical figures of Spain and France toward each other and thus toward their new national territories and, ultimately, their new (and markedly absent) husbands. In a series of transactional relays involving both real and allegorical figures, Marie de Médici orchestrates the hand-offs from sovereigns to noble surrogates (the duc de Guise escorting Elizabeth to the river and the Spanish ducque de Uceda escorting Anne) to allegorical escorts (France and Spain) in Rubens's painting. The young women are passed along this chain of proxies. Even as they themselves are surrendered to the project of political alliance building, the performance of the act works hard to be demonstrably symmetrical. In this way, a gendered form of sexual surrender is embedded in a form of peace accord. The ways the figures of Spain and France hold and grasp the sisters-in-law (to be) is ambiguous and charged. Does it constitute support, or does it propel them away? In Greimas's terms, we need to ask if the figures in the representational space are being *supported* or *displaced* as their orientation takes on an ambiguous directionality. The only eye contact being made in the scene is between these two allegorical figures, highlighting the true meaning of the exchange—this is a scene about political competitions and alliances, not about love. While the princesses' expressions are pleasant, or distracted, enough, their faces are strangely vacant, there on the limen of their new lives.

This is a picture of surrender, at once erotic and political. Note—and here we recall the intricate network of witnesses signing on to the deal of one half of this royal pairing described in chapter 2—that both the literal absence of the two princes and the figurative absentmindedness of the two princesses can be understood to reflect the greater absence of the very source of power behind the surrender exchange (whatever it may be in any particular case) that is always necessarily outside the system itself and may best be captured in an only partially metaphorized notion of the sovereign exception.

Finally, lest such complex erotic-political machines of surrender and re-composition of sovereignty be understood as exclusive to the era of absolutism in the West, it is useful to summon another scene of sovereign surrender from the twentieth century. In some ways the obverse of *The Exchange of Princesses,* in which sexual surrender does the work of geopolitics, this scene has geopolitics refer itself to sexual surrender and marriage. A famous photograph of the diminutive and formally attired emperor of Japan and the casually dominating General Douglas MacArthur, standing together some weeks after Japan's surrender to the Allied forces in September 1945, is strikingly characterized by acute scholarly observers. As Yoshikuni Igarashi writes, "In the sexualized power relations of the two countries it is only appropriate for [political scientist] Douglas Lummis to call this picture their 'wedding photo.'"[24] Douglas MacArthur's own description, in his book *Reminiscences,* of his first meeting with the emperor on September 27, 1945, at the United States embassy conjures a scene that is similarly charged. The highly erotic gesture of lighting a cigarette for someone, which in the cinema usually involves a man's lighting a woman's cigarette, is put to the service of a political exchange between a military victor and a vanquished sovereign: "I noticed how his hands shook as I lighted it for him [an American cigarette]. I tried to make it as easy for him as I could, but I know how deep and dreadful must be his agony of humiliation."[25]

Actions of the Sovereign

According to Hannah Arendt, sovereignty is often spurious and, at its best, tenuous. The minimalist program she allows, as seen earlier, relies on "many men mutually bound by promises." And it is minimalist precisely because of the incalculability of the future, an incalculability slightly modified by promises that are made and kept.[26] This is an ideal vision of a collective sovereignty that wields the *promise* against the vicissitudes of time. Alternative theories of sovereignty, described above, focus on the sovereign's move outside time.

These theories read the sovereign as one who both gives law and forgoes law, uniquely capable of actions (even violent actions) under the rubric of the sovereign exception. Thus, in declaring a state of emergency, the sovereign suspends time—that is, the time of law.[27]

It is not law that compels warring sovereigns to agree to a surrender; calculations about waning force or political support or exhausted provisions do that. The moment of law's (re)introduction here is always extralegitimate. The alegality of superior might in battle that translates into norms and law becomes legitimate only after it finds its shape in the process of codification. Law is present at the point of its convening. The parties to a surrender must invoke or must generate rules of conduct that are authorized by law (either codified or customary or some combination). If the parties share a common worldview, they can more easily depend on traditional notions of authority and rule-bound process. But in any event, the previous enmity means that any law accepted by both must be, to a significant extent, emergent. On the other hand, the radical suspendings and undoings of surrender are the work of a sovereign power that operates (through its forceful dominance) outside the sphere of law while deposing a sovereign power that surrenders. So perhaps the zone of surrender is best described as one in which overt, illegitimate violence hands off to the realm of covert or legitimate violence that is, precisely, law.[28] The terms of surrender and the reconfigured power relations that are engendered through the performative acts of the victorious and the vanquished are best understood as temporary suspensions of bellicose violence.

Performatives seem to be speech acts par excellence of the sovereign. In Austinian terms, the most typical are verdictives (casting judgments) and exercitives (ordering and appointing).[29] These performatives appear to take center stage in the statecraft of the sovereign, often outpacing Arendt's favored performative type, the commissive (promises, espousals). The sovereign declares a state of emergency, a state of war, a state of peace. The sovereign decrees taxes, claims territory, and makes treaties. The sovereign declares amnesties as well as punishes and banishes. The singular nature of the sovereign role is most evident in moments of transition and transformation, moments when responsibility or its divestment are accentuated. Legal theorist Ruti Teitel assesses the linked acts of punishment and amnesty as both signaling sovereignty: "Ultimately, amnesties and punishment are but two sides of the same coin: legal rites that visibly and forcefully demonstrate the change in sovereignty that makes for political transition . . . These transitional practices play the role of defining political time: the discontinuity of transition—its before and after—as well as their related role in defining the continuity of transition."[30]

Ultimately, the task here is to locate and track sovereign power in its making, sustaining, and unmaking. As I suggested above, the role of force, the role of law, and the role of performative speech acts with perlocutionary force begin to account for sovereign power. In accounting for the variable interactions among these conditions, we will come to focus on the hard and dangerous work of sovereign unbecoming.

Assumption and Divestment of Responsibility

It is fascinating to catch sovereign authority in its self-articulation. There is a magisterial grandness in these pronouncements, however modest the concrete action, and even when that action is actually in the service of divestment of responsibility for an ongoing situation. In the critical transitional moments that end conflicts, the sovereign self-articulation of responsibility becomes singularly charged. Pronouns and other deictical markers play a major role here, as do appeals to logic and higher powers.

The question of responsibility often elicits appeals to a deity or to the godlike quality of earthly rulers (Louis XIV as the Sun King, Emperor Hirohito as a god). In the case of a victory the appeal is obvious, as when, having conquered Breda, Archduchess Isabella of Spain forbade "bonfires or any other public show of joy to be made, in respect of the reverence she bore to God, till first she had caused Sacrifice to be offered to him the day following in the great Church, as to the chief Author of the victory."[31]

In the case of defeat and surrender, the subjects of a deified sovereign are baffled and disoriented by an incomprehensible, impossible responsibility. When Hirohito broke with his own tradition of maintaining an apolitical reign and made the decision to accept the Allies' Potsdam Declaration that Japan must surrender unconditionally at the end of World War II, many Japanese citizens and military personnel simply did not believe it. A rebel group of military officers at Atsugi Airbase dropped leaflets over Tokyo announcing this impossibility: "Government officials and senior statesmen who were caught in an enemy trap have enticed the Emperor to issue the message ending the war. It was a terrible thing to do. The Emperor is a God. There is no such thing as surrender in Japan. There is no surrender in the Imperial forces. We, as members of the Air Force, are sure of victory."[32]

The discourse of responsibility taking leans heavily on pronouns and their referents as performative speech acts reshape the world.[33] To what extent can responsibility be diffuse and shared when specific individuals are positioned to command armies to fight or to desist from fighting? To what extent do collective bodies of soldiers or politicians assume responsibility when one or two individuals must actually sign a surrender document? When it was clear that the Germans could no longer hold out in the west against the Allied forces at the end of World War II, German general Alfred Jodl sent a coded signal to Admiral Karl Dönitz, who, for a very brief period after Hitler's suicide, ruled Germany as führer: "General Eisenhower insists that we sign today . . . I see no alternative—chaos or signature. I ask you to confirm immediately by radio that I have full powers to sign capitulation. Hostilities will then cease at midnight German summer time, May 8."[34]

Beyond the telling deictical switching from "we" to "I," Jodl solicits from Dönitz a complicated weave of constative statements (of the type, "you have full powers to sign") and performative speech acts (of the type, "I confirm that you have full powers to sign"). Confirmation is much more here than a simple clarification of the chain of command or division of labor. Meanwhile, responsibility for the decision to sign is found in the appeal to order as contrasted with chaos. Chaos here is the unthinkable alternative to surrender. Jodl's authority is tenuous not solely as a consequence of who he is in the military chain of command (and whether this position has a certain sovereign agency). It is also tenuous because it is an authority that is both singular and collective simultaneously and because it stands, as all surrendering authorities do, at the crossroads of its own undoing.

The case of Jodl's borrowed or proxied authority to sign the surrender document highlights the complexity of authority and responsibility shared between civilian and military authorities during the prosecution of a war. Ultimate authority must be referred to the sovereign, whether that is a feudal lord, a divinely chosen monarch, or an elected president. But battles are fought on the ground, and surrenders are, as we have seen, often signed by the military official who actually led the charge or the retreat. This occurs for both practical and symbolic reasons, reasons that go to the heart of the issues of recognition and responsibility as well as the avoidance of shameful encounters.

Another case highlights the charged quality of either sustaining or suspending the distinction between political and military officials in surrender transactions. In mid-April 1865, after the surrender of Lee's army at Appomattox and after Lincoln's assassination, General Sherman of the Union army and General Johnston of the Confederacy attempted to conclude the war by signing a surrender "Memorandum" of their own. As I noted in chapter 3, on the morning of the first meeting to come to terms, Johnston invited the Confederate secretary of war John C. Breckinridge to join them, and Sherman objected to the inclusion of a politician in the discussion. However, Johnston changed his mind on learning that Breckinridge was also a major general in the Confederate army, and thus a fellow soldier. But the matter of overlapping or crosscutting authority between military and civil matters did not end there. When the "Memorandum" was sent to General Grant, "He was thunderstruck by the 'Memorandum' and cover letter from Sherman.

Although he agreed with the military aims, he was dismayed to see that his friend Sherman had gone far beyond his authority by addressing civil as well as military matters."[35] Under President Johnson's orders, Grant quickly rescinded the "Memorandum."

Proximal responsibility and authority and ultimate responsibility and authority are often only situationally distinguished in spite of social-structural hierarchies and emerge clearly only out of the demonstrations and performative actions of specific encounters. Military authority and civil authority are likewise variously combined and separated. The president of the United States is, after all, also the commander in chief. Nevertheless, it is important to highlight the special role that these differentiations and chains of command play in liminal moments like those of surrender. The deflection or transmission of sovereign authority through military officials makes it unnecessary for the sovereign to be present at the moment of the undoing (his own or another's). The military men are often left to do the dirty work. I will take up the question of the sovereign's presence or absence from the scene of surrender more fully at the conclusion of this chapter.

The Itinerant Sovereign

It is true that the success of the sovereign *performatives* must ultimately derive, in the reductio ad absurdum of the dialectic between force and legitimacy, from the acquiescence or consent of the subject-witnesses to the sovereign's power. Here the power of *demonstration* is foregrounded as witnesses, cosigners, and countersigners (recall chapter 2's discussion) observe and authorize these performative acts. Accomplishing the necessary visual and discursive exegeses of demonstration requires that the sovereign, his representatives and proxies, and his image (highlighting the importance of the third aspect of the analytic rubric of this book, *representation*) circulate among his subjects. Even when not physically on site, the sovereign must make his presence felt. At the same time, an idea of centrality and concentrated power must create a certain tension between a circulating, itinerant sovereign and one situated in what Rudolf Arnheim calls a "dynamic center." The link between the work of pictorial composition and the work of sovereign political power is obvious in Arnheim's analysis of the visual field: "A dynamic center is invariably present in any visual field. It may be explicitly marked or created only indirectly by perceptual induction."[36]

In a classic essay, "Centers, Kings, and Charisma: Reflections on the Symbolics of Power," Clifford Geertz compared the symbolic machinery of the reigns of three historically and culturally diverse sovereigns: Elizabeth I of England (sixteenth century), Hayam Wuruk of Java (fourteenth century), and Mulay Hasan of Morocco (nineteenth century). As different as these reigns and realms were in conceptions of sovereignty and in religious ideology, each sovereign responded to a felt need to circulate in variable modalities of "the progress," the highly ceremonial form in which a sovereign travels throughout his realm. However it is organized, the progress is essentially demonstrative. The sovereign shows and is shown. Whether the progress is allegorical (as in the case of Elizabeth), analogical (as in the case of Hayam Wuruk), or agonistic (as in the case of Mulay Hasan), the idea is to map out an itinerary of sovereign symbolic reiteration. Geertz contrasts his three ideal-typical examples:

> In 16th century England, the political center of society was the point at which the tension between the passions that power excited and the ideals it was supposed to serve was screwed to its highest pitch; and the symbolism of the progress was, consequently, admonitory and covenantal . . . In fourteenth century Java, the center was the point at which such tension disappeared in a blaze of cosmic symmetry; and the symbolism was, consequently, exemplary and mimetic . . . [In traditional Morocco] society was agonistic—a tournament of wills; so then was kingship and the symbolism exalting it. Progresses here were not always easy to tell from raids . . . even Mulay Hasan (d. 1894) the last of the old-regime kings of Morocco, normally spent six months of the year on the move, demonstrating sovereignty to skeptics.[37]

Historians of early modern Europe have noted that the itinerancy of feudal lords and monarchs was as practical as it was symbolic. The difficulties of moving large quantities of goods for consumption by royal courts and the necessity of overseeing acquired lands and landlords (often warriors newly provided with land) contributed to the semiconstant movement of the sovereign.[38] In eras when territory was often contested and largely noncontiguous, feudal kingdoms were, as Michael Biggs remarks, "neither centered nor unified. The state was a 'mobile camp.' King and household were peripatetic, ceaselessly traveling from place to place."[39]

Reflecting the itinerary of the sovereign, the slow process of disentangling worldly power and its territorial purview from its theological roots, and the rudimentary state of cartography, feudal realms were mapped in accordance with courtly itineraries. Pathways and progresses (including the time it took to travel between locations) rather than bounded entities with central locations provided the mental schemata. Nevertheless, the exceptional and ultimately mysterious nature of the sovereign requires an element to balance the hypervisibility of the progress: an element of invisibility. Here is the need for a center that is powerful in its generation of energy and that is occupied by an essentially unseen sovereign. This sovereign can send out his image and his proxies in lieu of his sovereign self. Individual sovereigns will vary in the degree to which they withdraw and the degree to which they venture out. Writing about the early modern Spanish monarchs, Lorraine White notes that "in contrast to . . . Ferdinand and Isabella, who traveled the length and breadth of Castile, Spain's Habsburg monarchs had withdrawn into their palaces and the common people saw little or nothing of them . . . but . . . [d]evotion to the monarch was cultivated continually by exposing the populace to festivities, processions and solemn acts marking the birth, marriage and death of members of the royal family."[40] Something of the sovereign essence must thus continue to circulate even as the sovereigns themselves withdraw.

Art historians from the time of Leon Battista Alberti through contemporary scholars such as Rudolf Arnheim and Hubert Damisch echo this intuition about the essential mystery of sovereignty in their characterizations of artistic compositions, the necessity for empty but dynamic centers, and their political lessons. Alberti, for example, criticizes painters who "do not manage to accommodate any empty spaces in their compositions, but instead cram them with so many figures, disposed in such confusion that the istoria, taken over by tumult, no longer possesses the dignity of action."[41]

The stress on "dignity of action," or *dignitas,* is central, and it recalls Kantorowicz's three factors of kingly immortality. Beyond the variability of the grounds for legitimacy, sovereign action must seem both to reflect and to create a transcendent essence, something that, in Durkheimian terms, emerges.

Finally, earthly sovereignty (whether or not of divine imprimatur) requires a territorial base. And the singularity of the sovereign's claim is exactly about territory and its inhabitants.[42] These claims are upheld by the way so many takings are designated as retakings and are the reason so many relinquishments are designated as provisional and rescindable. Here we need only recall the back-and-forth sovereignty of Breda for an empirical example, or the embedded concept of return in the etymology of surrender. Vanquished sovereigns dream of return. Victorious sovereigns may go out of their way to ostentatiously "hand back" freshly conquered territories, often with an explicit proviso that such handing back is provisional. We have encountered such a move in the previous chapter's discussion of Louis XIV's ceding of Franche-Comté back to Spain in 1668 (after dismantling its fortress).[43]

In spite of his apparent magnanimity, Louis doesn't blink at asserting his long-run objective of conquering the Low Countries. A more modern diffidence about announcing imperial aims as pure territorial grab (as opposed to a retaking or a maintaining of what already was claimed) can be heard in the ex post facto justification made by Emperor Hirohito in his famous radio speech declaring Japan's unconditional surrender: "Indeed we declared war on America and Britain out of our sincere desire to ensure Japan's self-preservation and the stabilization of Southeast Asia, it being far from our thought either to infringe upon the sovereignty of other nations or to embark upon territorial aggrandizement."[44]

How to Recognize the Sovereign

The sovereign acts in a variety of areas, demonstrating his authority and powers and transforming the physical and social worlds. But as I noted, the effectiveness and meaning of these actions depend on the relevant subjects' recognizing the sovereign as such, as well as on the complex and contradictory recognition by other, sometimes competing, sovereigns. What are the mechanisms of this recognition, and how is it derailed or rerouted in the surrender of sovereignty?

Clearly, recognition occurs through a sustained series of semiotic cues. The sovereign is above, the sovereign is bigger, the sovereign is in the foreground, the sovereign (or his image) is ubiquitous or, what comes to the same thing, invisible. In the realm of the political semiotic, where the practical meets the symbolic, cues can be linguistic, pictorial, or gestural.

As the crucial relations and transformations are rendered in treaties and proclamations, specific languages, dialects, words, and terms of address become lightning rods for political struggles over recognition. These struggles are particularly evident when the conflicting parties come from different linguistic and religious communities. The case of the thirteenth-century bilingual surrender treaty between al-Azraq and Prince Alfonso, brilliantly translated and analyzed by Robert Burns and Paul Chevedden, provides a transparent view of these recognition mechanisms at work.

Each version of the treaty, one in Castilian and one in Arabic, portrays a different set of postconflict relationships. The Castilian version describes a classic surrender in which the vanquished Muslim proclaims that he is now the vassal of Alfonso. The Arabic version, as I noted earlier, portrays the relationship as more of a partnership or, at most, one of clientage. Here, though, it is important to look at the languages of the treaty in a more detailed manner. The Castilian version is actually written as a recitation in two voices (an act of political ventriloquism by the Castilian scribe on behalf of al-Azraq). In it al-Azraq is heard to declaim, "Let it be known to all present and future: that I Abu ʿAbd Allah ibn Hudhayl, vizier and lord of Alcala, make myself your vassal, lord Don Alfonso the elder son of the king of Aragon, and I give you eight castles—one called Pop and the other Tarbena, and Margarida, Cheroles, Castell, Alcala, Gallinera, and Perpunchent." He is answered by Alfonso: "And I Don Alfonso, by the grace of God prince, elder son of the king of Aragon, receive you Abu ʿAbd Allah ibn Hudhayl vizier and lord of Alcala as my cherished and much esteemed and very honored loyal vassal. And I grant and give you two castles, Alcala and Perpunchent."⁴⁵

So far, so good. There is a clarity to the new relationship established, confirming mutual, if not symmetrical, recognition. And we find the anticipated complex series of givings back (there being no recognition for originary gifts in the return motif of surrender). But the Arabic text is an altogether different document, in the form of a single-voiced decree: "This is a noble decree, enjoined by the Exalted Prince for the Heroic, the Most Fortunate, [he whose beneficence is] hoped for [and] sought, the Infante Don Alfonso, son of the Exalted King, the Divinely Assisted, the ruler of Aragon, upon the Most Illustrious Wazir, the Noble, the Highest, the Most Eminent, the Most Exalted Abu ʿAbd Allah b. Hudhayl—may God honor him! [Wherefore] the above mentioned Exalted Prince makes an agreement with him for three years."⁴⁶

The interlinearity of the surrender document shows up the differences in tone and meaning as the two versions lie cheek by jowl on the same parchment. In the Arabic version, a partnership is described with exclusively third-person pronouns by a deus ex machina proclaiming the terms. Symmetry is more than implied by the emphasis on the temporary nature of the agreement and by the absence of those first- and second-person pronouns found in the Castilian version that would actualize the text (and its communicants) as a unique instance of discourse. Forms of deference do different work when the indexical features that present them shift in this way. The phrase in the Castilian version, "I make myself your vassal," demonstrates all the contradictory imperatives of doing and undoing in surrender. It is personal and immediate in a way that the Arabic proclamation is not.

Is there, then, a correct, consensually recognized interpretation of the meaning of the surrender transaction in this case? And consequently a correct way to recognize the emergent sovereign(ties)? This thirteenth-century bilingual document may be at one end of a continuum of divergent-to-convergent interpretations, with "boundary works" like those sixteenth-century Mayan letters to the Spanish Crown described by William Hanks somewhere in between.⁴⁷ But it is in the essence of surrendering sovereignty to attempt to insinuate the idea of return into the codified agreement and to pin hopes, however inarticulate, on the shifting fortunes of war and politics. Norbert Elias draws on the covenantal quality of the interdependencies of sovereigns in the feudal period to illuminate the circumstantial and shifting quality of the meaning of alliances: "Individual dependencies are established. One warrior enters an alliance with another under oath. The higher-ranking partner with the greater area of land—the two go hand in hand—is the 'liege lord,' the weaker partner the 'vassal.' The latter in turn can, if circumstances so require, take still weaker warriors under his protection in exchange for services. The contracting of such individual alliances is at first the only form in which people can protect themselves from one another."[48]

Even in cases where the ultimate recognition of sovereign powers and their realignments converge, with victor and vanquished both signing on to the same thing, the process by which this interpretation is achieved may be adversarial and rely on linguistic parsing. Recalling and undermining the medieval concept of sovereign *dignitas,* the original American draft (in Japanese) of the surrender proclamation to be read by the Japanese emperor omitted the formal pronouns conventionally applied to the emperor's name in favor of more common terms. William Craig reports that the Japanese representatives viewed this draft as an insult to the imperial throne, and the terms were ultimately replaced with the more traditional ones. Further, in the official surrender document, a strategic mistranslation by the Japanese foreign ministry turned out to be a face-saving device aimed at staving off objections by extremist military commanders opposed to surrender. In English, the most important phrase read: "From the moment of surrender the authority of the Emperor and the Japanese Government to rule the state shall be subject to the Supreme Commander of the Allied Powers who will take such steps as he deems proper to effectuate the surrender terms." Kyoko Inoue writes, "The English phrase 'shall be subject to,' which clearly implies subordination, was translated *seigen-no moto-ni okaruru-mono-to su.* This phrase, which literally means something like 'will be placed under the restraint of,' does not carry the same implication of direct subordination . . . This 'translation' thus made it possible for the military to save face, while enabling the Japanese government to accept the substance of the Allies' terms."[49]

The examples above have dwelled almost exclusively on the linguistic cues to sovereign recognition. But as the case of Alexander and the family of Darius demonstrates, visual cues are equally compelling and at times confounding. The individual sovereign seems to be recognizable from the magnificence of his person or his setting. Philip IV of Spain devised his Hall of Realms specifically to create a setting in which his magnificence was amply reflected in the escutcheons of Habsburg realms on the ceiling and in the paintings of military triumph on the walls, including *The Surrender of Breda.* Louis XIV saw his sovereign power augmented in what Chandra Mukerji terms the "material instantiation of power" (including Versailles and its gardens and various projects of civil and military engineering).[50] And traditional artistic genres of representation, from sculpted busts and statues to portraits and history paintings, most often reflect this keyed magnificence. As noted earlier, in artistic representations of surrender, the transaction between sovereigns (or their proxies) "was almost always represented as a pageant of triumph and humiliation, in which the victor was shown as standing or seated on a throne or horseback and accepting tribute from the kneeling and submissive vanquished general."[51]

Despite these norms and conventions, there is a surfeit of cases in which explicit notice is taken of the unconventional representation of sovereignty: the *antimagnificent*. This can occur in the context of a surreptitious survey of one's subjects' true feelings and loyalties, as when Shakespeare's Henry V walks unrecognized among his troops on the eve of the Battle of Agincourt, or in the context of an exaggerated indifference to finery, as in the case of several sovereign proxies. Amanuenses for both Ambrogio Spinola and Ulysses S. Grant reflected on their notably unkempt vestments. In his *Obsidio Bredana* Hermannus Hugo writes in a puzzled but admiring way about Spinola's appearance: "In his apparel he was negligent of all curious trimming and careless of adorning himself, even in the dignity of a general. Touching the cruelty of the season, and the weather, and whether it rained or snowed, or freezed or blew, or whether it were evening or midnight he cared not."[52]

The suggested link is between true heroism and indifference to appearance, a distilled form of sovereign authority that gets to its essence. The opposite interpretation understands a rough appearance to be the sign of a kind of sovereign amateurism that, while not without its own brand of heroism, is nevertheless not quite up to the professionals. Here are Ulysses S. Grant's own reflections on the difference between his and Robert E. Lee's appearances at Appomattox: "General Lee was dressed in a full uniform which was entirely new, and was wearing a sword of considerable value, very likely the sword which had been presented by the State of Virginia; at all events, it was an entirely different sword from the one that would ordinarily be worn in the field. In my rough traveling suit, the uniform of a private with the straps of a lieutenant-general, I must have contrasted very strangely with a man so handsomely dressed, six feet high and of faultless form. But this was not a matter that I thought of until afterwards."[53]

For his part, the "handsomely dressed" Lee came to the surrender at Appomattox in a formal general's uniform, "including a fine red silk sash, a gleaming jeweled and engraved sword, and a pair of handsome thread gloves. 'I have probably to be General Grant's prisoner today,' he later explained to his men, 'and I thought I must make my best appearance.'"[54]

What is clear from the variations on a theme of visual indexes of authority or sovereignty is that in transitional moments such things are highly significant. Whether an individual divests himself of the raiment of power or dons it in a demonstration of magnificence, sovereignty speaks through its appearance.

Finally, though, recognition must occur through the aegis of *relations*. And here we pick up a major theme from the previous chapter's examination of the exchanges of surrender. Sovereigns and their subjects recognize each other by enacting loyalty, fealty, deference, and interdependency in their mutually aligned behavior. This behavior encompasses the performative, the demonstrative, and the representational actions in all their richness.

Mapping Sovereign Relations

According to historian of cartography Michael Biggs, dynastic monarchs before the sixteenth century (when cartographic maps became instruments of rule) conceived of their realms as a network of relationships: "The geographical extent of entities such as the country or kingdom was in turn defined by tradition and relationships . . . The oldest villagers were asked to whom they owed allegiance, where they paid taxes and bought salt, and which courts judged local disputes. Actual relationships with royal authority thus determined the realm's spatial extent, and not the reverse."[55]

Paying taxes, buying salt, and appealing to certain courts, along with serving in armies and fighting in wars—these are the critical, habitual acts that compose a realm.[56] Some markers of relations were less overtly procedural and practical. Obeisance could be gauged through what Chandra Mukerji calls "the exercise of taste and decorum." Writing about the court of Louis XIV, Mukerji draws attention to the diacritical power of dress: "The courtiers who dressed in appropriate dress, then, not only displayed traditional obedience to the king's will but also made themselves visibly French, using their bodies as markers of their political alignment behind the French state and French commodities."[57] Here is the flip side of the preoccupation with the sovereign's appearance. In its turn, it is the appearance of the *subject* that reinforces the aura of the sovereign.

Thus even before a realm, or a state, could be viewed as a coherent, bounded entity on a map, it was sociologically known through its vectors of relations.

As I noted in chapter 3, it was during the transitional period of the sixteenth and seventeenth centuries that the nature of the knowledge of domains changed. The shift was from a knowledge based on relations as the key diacritical features to one based on the abstract renderings of bounded geographical entities.

In this regard, Jacques Callot's map of the siege and surrender of Breda (plate 2) may be viewed as a transitional object. The figures in the foreground, engraved according to the conventions of Renaissance perspectivalism, are engaged in the activities of life—albeit activities disrupted and shattered by the siege. But there they are in full-bodied action, with their herds of emaciated cattle, their dogs, and their transactions. As our eyes move toward the background, our point of view gets higher and higher until we actually see the defeated troops of Justin of Nassau exiting an almost completely cartographically rendered Breda. The presence of the Habsburg sovereign, Philip IV, is felt in several ways. It is felt in the doubled image of Spinola who, in the background, awaits Justin's exit outside the breached walls of the city and, in the foreground, himself pays obeisance to the arriving Archduchess Isabella. Spinola's image is involved in a relay of giving and getting submission to the power of the sovereign. He accepts the submission of Justin, and he submits to Isabella, who in turn represents and submits both to the Catholic Church (she wears a modest religious habit) and to Philip IV back in Madrid. Callot's vision mirrors that of the victorious sovereign. It is a view from outside, from the siegeworks, to which the central activity is in a sense displaced. It is the distant city of Breda, the prize of the conflict, seen from the bird's-eye view, that seems abstract and empty and the periphery in the foreground that seems teeming with life. Finally, the sovereign hovers over the map in the form of the three royal insignia that appear in the two top corners and in the middle of the base. These insignia provide the most emblematic imprimatur of the sovereign, but they are disjunctive—clearly they do not participate in the gradient movement from foreground to background that puts figures of the realm in relation to the abstract entity that is the realm in the cartographic imagination. This is of a piece with the emergent ontology of the map: "It represented an entity that was impersonal—set apart from the person of the ruler (and even from the character of rulership)—and natural, grounded in physical reality."[58]

Agency without Sovereignty

Intimations that sovereign and realm might be disengaged return us to questions of recognition and misrecognition. We have tracked the linguistic, visual, and relational modalities by which sovereignty is made manifest. The *refusal* to speak to, see, and interact with a sovereign claimant in prescribed ways makes recognition impossible. An existential and political conundrum emerges and must be dealt with at the level of political semiotics: Is it possible to treat with an entity that is not recognized?

When contesting parties both speak the same language (literally and figuratively), conventional modalities of recognition may be explicitly forgone or contested. This is often the case with internal revolts and civil wars, and it introduces the idea of the pretender. A pretender is an impossible double, unlike the sovereign proxies we have thus far examined (Hephaestion and other generals). A pretender can be singular, a claimant to a throne or an office, or collective, a claimant to state or nationhood. In the latter case, negotiations can become impossible when a sovereign entity is not recognized to exist. Generic substitution can help get around this dilemma. Thus it was with Germany at the end of World War II, leading to the reformulation of the demand for unconditional surrender as a proclamation (there being no civilian authority to treat with).[59] It was also the case with negotiations at the end of the American Civil War. We have already seen General Sherman bridle at the idea of admitting a supposed Confederate civilian officeholder to the surrender negotiations on the western front. This diffidence went even further: "Sherman informed Johnston that as he was prepared to grant him the same terms Grant had given Lee, he would be able to surrender with dignity. Johnston interrupted to remind Sherman that the purpose of the meeting was to search for a way to begin negotiations between civil authorities. No, countered Sherman, because the United States did not recognize the Confederacy."[60]

When the conflicting parties speak different languages (again figuratively as well as literally), there can be a kind of coded nonrecognition of sovereignty passing itself off as recognition. Scholars of colonialist encounters between conquering civilizations and those they have subdued have drawn attention to the multivocality of the emergent genres of official discourse on the part of the native population. William Hanks, as noted, has written about sixteenth-century Mayan-Spanish texts as being hybrid in nature. Roger Chartier describes the Treaty of Waitangi, signed by forty-six Maori chiefs in 1840, which appeared to give the queen of England sovereignty over their territories. In reality, according to Chartier, the recognition of England's purview was in no way definitive or sweeping. The Maori still held oral promises to be more compelling than written declarations: "In the twenty years before the Waitangi treaty, the Maori population was subjected to a triple revolution: the indigenous speech was set down as an alphabetical written language; missionaries . . . carried on literacy campaigns in the vernacular . . . ; printing was introduced . . . [yet] the book—the Bible in particular—was a ritual object giving power and protection; reading (or listening to reading aloud) was only a precondition for memorizing and reciting texts learned by heart; the written text was secondary to oral conventions."[61]

How to Represent the Sovereign

The representation of the sovereign and of sovereignty itself is a paradoxical task. To whom is the sovereign being represented, if not to the subjects of his reign?[62] How is it that the subjects have the power to observe, animate, and thus fix the sovereign image? It is through the action of the observer that an image gains its power, its life. Yet subjection implies a process that is the inverse of observation. In subjection one's gaze is cast down and one is observed by others. And what of the creator of the image of sovereignty, the artist? Isn't there a paradox here as well, as the artist composes what is represented? What does it mean to acknowledge that the artist brings the sovereign to life?

Michel Foucault explored many of these questions to great advantage in his analysis of *Las Meninas,* Velázquez's painting about, if not of, the Habsburg monarchs—a painting in which mirrors, deflected visions, reversed canvases, and the like keep the representational conundrums ricocheting in a kind of large-scale firing of synapses. But Foucault's conclusion that the painting participates in freeing representation from its relation to the S/sovereign subject and that it may now "offer itself as representation in its pure form" is too dismissive of the power of the sovereign's imagined emanations.[63]

Of course, there are different types of sovereigns, sovereigns who find and redeem their authority from different sources. In contrast to the popularly ratified leader of a democracy, a deity or a royal monarch *appears* to be self-redeeming, thus literally incapable of requiring an observer's gaze. Discussing a sketch for a painting by Jacques-Louis David of the French revolutionaries taking the Tennis Court Oath, William Kemp notes that the deputy Jean-Sylvain Bailly, who leads the oath standing atop a table, is painted in such a manner as to have his frontward gaze meet that of the painting's observer. However, writes Kemp, "His makeshift position and his gaze really cannot claim what the eye of God and of the king could claim: that they not only see all and everything but give rise to all and everything. The gazes of God and the king have no counterparts that look back. These gazes are directed one way."[64]

Representations of one-way gazes are caught up in an impossible world, then. The sovereign image circulates in an augmentation of its power, yet it cannot be observed by its subjects. They cannot look back. On the other hand, theorists of the dialectic between vision and visuality, image and observer, such as Jonathan Crary, Norman Bryson, and Roger Chartier, emphasize the way the image actually constitutes the person who looks at it, along with the possibilities of vision itself.[65] So, far from authorizing the sovereign image via observation, observers are subjected to, dependent on, the image for their own condition.

This brings us to surrender. It is one thing to be the loyal subject of a sovereign whose image floats by beatifically or magnificently in a progress or a tableau vivant. It is another thing to stand or kneel before the image of a sovereign to whom one has surrendered in subjection. In this case, all the paradoxes and strange interdependencies of the image and the observer seem to multiply. Recalling the painting with which the chapter began, *The Queens of Persia at the Feet of Alexander,* we can see this multiplicity worked out in what Norman Bryson calls "the lexical dimension" of the painting. The various queens, princesses, and retainers of the house of Darius act out a variety of reactions to this seeing double, this confounded vision of their new sovereign. According to Felibien's reading, one in particular, Princess Statira, goes so far as to close her eyes "to escape the sight of the conqueror."[66] In order to get at this complex representational network, it will be useful to revisit several themes related to sovereignty already introduced in this chapter: the theme of visibility, the theme of replicability (doubles and copies), and the theme of substitutability (proxies).

The Multiplicity of Singularity

> For the King has in him two Bodies, viz., a Body natural and a Body politic . . . his Body politic is a Body that cannot be seen or handled, consisting of Policy and Government, and constituted for the Direction of the People and the Management of the public weal . . . and for this Cause, what the King does in his Body politic, cannot be invalidated or frustrated by any Disability in his natural Body.[67]

Historians and theorists of sovereignty since Jean Bodin have dwelled on the premise of the singularity of sovereign power, "that which can neither be delegated nor divided."[68] This theory of absolute sovereignty, supported by the contractual theory of absolute sovereignty of Thomas Hobbes, must nevertheless deal with a historical reality in which even absolutist states were arenas for conflicting claims to power between the monarchy and the aristocracy.[69] It must also deal with the reality of a power that has persistently been delegated to ministers and generals as the work of ruling, taxing, and fighting occurs in a variety of venues and territories and the sovereign cannot be everywhere at once.

The sovereign's image may be ubiquitous. The sovereign himself may try to be ubiquitous through the "progress," but political labor will be divided. As Scott Gordon writes, although "there seems to be nothing in political theory that serves to specify the limit to which the dispersion of political power might be carried, without indivisibility, the whole doctrine of sovereignty is fatally undermined."[70]

Whatever this dispersion does to the doctrine of sovereignty, there is still value in specifying the mechanisms of this dispersion. While singular in essence, the image and agency of the sovereign are nevertheless reproduced and represented through portraits, emblems, and proxies. Perhaps the very proliferation of these symbolic and political representations belies the fact that the sovereign essence, its exceptional quality, is unapproachable. It is difficult indeed to theorize this exceptionalism. Giorgio Agamben puts it most bluntly: "The sovereign exception is thus the figure in which singularity is represented as such, which is to say, insofar as it is unrepresentable."[71] What can one say about the perpetual representation of the unrepresentable?

Once again, it is the claim of this book that theory can leverage such paradoxes by focusing on transitional moments during which the gaps in the weave of the system are momentarily on view. The contrapuntal doings and undoings of sovereign power in surrenders (the demonstrations, the performative acts, the representations) put the mystery and the profanity of sovereignty on a collision course. As I noted at the outset of this chapter, the danger is *exposure*. The collisions and paradoxes are a symptom of the anxiety that accompanies the exposure of the mechanisms of power.[72] When the victorious sovereign's forces showcase the unmaking of the other, there is a danger that the witnessing subjects will extrapolate to their own sovereign. "Ah, this is how it is done!" The performative, demonstrative, and representational acts of the political semiotic thus labor to keep the sovereign intact and singular in the face of such exposure.

Two disparate images of surrender, from historically and culturally separate conflicts, together illustrate the necessity and difficulty of representing the singularity of sovereignty and its dispersion. One comes from seventeenth-century Spain (plate 14). One, already introduced in chapter 3, comes from the nineteenth-century United States (plate 11). They are similar in refracting the problem of fixing or pinpointing the source of authority and power when undoings are the order of the day. In *The Recapture of Bahia* (note the motif of return) by Juan Bautista Maino (ca. 1635), Dutch citizens of Bahia in Brazil genuflect before a multifaceted image of sovereign power. Standing in front of the conquered, those kneeling citizens to the right, is Don Fadrique de Toledo, the victorious commander of the fifty-two Spanish and Portuguese vessels sent to retake Bahia from the Dutch West India Company (which had taken it from the Portuguese inhabitants in 1624, who had no doubt taken it from native peoples). Don Fadrique, in turn, stands in front of a tapestry and gestures toward it. One can simply follow the hands here. There are the upraised supplicating hands of the Dutch, the pointing hand of Don Fadrique, and the clenched hands of those represented *in* the tapestry, who hold the implements of war and peace: Count Olivares, Philip IV's chief minister, Philip IV himself, and Minerva, goddess of war.[73] In the tapestry within the painting, Philip IV stands in the foreground and is flanked by Olivares and Minerva. They together place a wreath of laurel leaves on Philip's head, while Olivares holds an olive branch of peace and Minerva hands Philip the palm of victory. Gods and monarchs and generals form an interacting network of reciprocal sovereignty here. Power on the battleground, power in the heavens, power in the court, all converge around the king, who both is and is not present. The painting within the painting secures his presence at one remove. Of all the paintings of victory and surrender commissioned for Philip's Hall of Realms, this is the only one that features an image of Philip IV himself. And it should not surprise us that his image is an embedded one, a painting within a painting. Doubly framed, with a reality that recedes before the observer's gaze, the painting seems to illustrate the point that sovereignty is approachable only through its mediations.

Gods and generals also figure in the lithograph from the nineteenth century, the double-page spread by the illustrator Thomas Nast that appeared in the May 20, 1865, issue of *Harper's Weekly.* On the left page, Christ is shown entering Jerusalem on a donkey. The people surround him, waving palm branches and reaching out to him. An olive branch lies on the ground in the lower left corner of this drawing. On the right page, Grant and Lee stand in the imagined parlor of the McLean house at Appomattox. Unrealistically, Grant is positioned to appear taller than Lee, and he holds out a hand of reconciliation. Lee stands in the foreground perpendicular to the drawing. We see only one hand, the left, which holds firm to the hilt of his sword (about which we have already heard quite a lot). Here is dignified, resigned humiliation indeed. Two Union soldiers flank the duo in the middle, including one Native American soldier who holds the surrender document. This soldier, Colonel E. S. Parker, was indeed one of Grant's officers at the scene of the Appomattox surrender; known as an excellent penman, he wrote out the final copy of the surrender agreement. He is interestingly mirrored by a dark-skinned individual in the print on the facing page, similarly located on the margin looking toward the center. These two witnesses, for witnesses they are, suggest worlds and selves somewhat oblique to those of the central actors and set off these actors by their differences. There on the limen, they bear the scene both inward and outward.

Self-contained and somewhat compositionally abandoned in the foreground stands Robert E. Lee. He gives no indication that he will accept Grant's hand. It is almost as if he had entered the scene from and on a different plane and resists being fully a part of it. The scene portrays the moment of his surrender—or right before, or right after. Perhaps it is this uncertainty that makes him also seem to be out of time, not just from another place but from another era.[74] His likeness has something of the nested portrait quality about it, as he appears to look across the page, out of the McLean parlor and into the scene in Jerusalem. Who will deliver him from his own liminality?

In the middle of the two tableaus, a female allegorical figure in classical dress both wears and carries wreaths of laurel leaves. She also holds a dove with an olive branch in its mouth. Framing the two high arches of these connected scenes are the words *Palm* and *Sunday,* and branches of the various symbolic trees are garlanded around, thus recapitulating all the conventional emblems found in *The Recapture of Bahia.* Appearing a month and a half after the surrender at Appomattox, a surrender whose actual scene was not reproduced in firsthand witness drawings or photographs, and more than a month after the assassination of President Lincoln, the linkages suggested between Grant and Christ are compositionally unavoidable. They both face the same direction, they both hold out their hands. Deliverance and sacrifice are obvious themes here; Christ's self-sacrifice for humanity is clear on Palm Sunday. But the obvious parallel figure, Abraham Lincoln,[75] is absent from the adjoining scene. Lincoln's absence is overdetermined: he is the sovereign who cannot easily appear at scenes of surrender; he is the dead sovereign who lives on only in memory; he is the democratic sovereign who can be unproblematically likened to a deity only after he is dead. The absence of Lincoln is palpable. Christian symbols, classical symbols, and military icons attempt to pull together the two scenes, but something seems to be missing to make this more than a sum of its parts.

The sovereign is missing, missing in his exceptional, invisible singularity. And yet he had actually been present in a mediation available to sovereigns reticent about exposure; he had been present via reproduction, in a photograph (plate 15). The contradictory imperative on sovereignty, to be ubiquitous and to be unlocatable, attempts to find its resolution in representations. On the very day that the surrender at Appomattox took place, April 9, 1865, President Abraham Lincoln went to have his photograph taken at a photographer's studio in Washington, DC. In the multivolume work *The Civil War through the Camera* (1912), where this photograph appears, Henry Elson describes it in the following way: "As [Lincoln] sits in simple fashion sharpening his pencil, the man of sorrows cannot forget the sense of weariness and pain that for four years has been unbroken. No elation of triumph lights the features . . . The States which lay 'out of their proper practical relation to the Union,' in his own phrase, must be brought back into a proper practical relation."[76]

It is fitting that Lincoln should set out to be photographed alone, with a *pencil,* on the very day that Lee surrenders to Grant with his *sword* at Appomattox. Lincoln's image remains to be drawn into the accumulating meaning of the event he authorized, but from which he was absent.[77]

It is also fitting that the (last) official portrait of the president would ultimately stand in for an official reproduction of the surrender scene itself. An official rendering of this scene of surrender would be explicitly rejected some years later, by Grant himself. The story of this rejection picks up the thread of the displaced person in the Thomas Nast print, Robert E. Lee, who goes on to find an authority in his very undoing. Vanquished, accused by some of treason, literally undone and fearing imprisonment, Lee stands alone in the scene. Nevertheless, the widely reproduced, necessarily speculative graphic representations of the surrender scene at Appomattox assisted Lee's resurgent popularity: "By showing the Confederate commander in the same scenes, more or less as Grant's equal—even if only to bring added luster to the Union victor—these graphics present Lee in surrender, but not humiliation, suggesting that reunion could be accomplished without subjugation."[78] But the problems of recognition at Appomattox show just how complicated these calibrations are. Ulysses S. Grant effectively erases the scene of the Confederate surrender from the collective memory because the familiarity of the enemy makes the scene impossible. This is a *civil war,* after all. And the family likeness problem causes Grant to reject a congressional committee's proposal to commission a painting of Lee's surrender at Appomattox for the rotunda of the United States Capitol: "He said he would never take part in producing a picture that commemorated a victory in which his own countrymen were the losers."[79]

Sovereignty at the Scene?

As if the paradoxes at work in representing the singular sovereign were not enough, we are getting a sense of all the subsidiary difficulties of representing the sovereign *in context,* especially in transformational contexts, like surrenders, that highlight the mechanical apparatus of power. President Grant's out-and-out refusal to allow a reproduction of his own military victory over his countrymen suggests another set of considerations. As I noted earlier, the victorious sovereign must consider what kind of image can sustain his own dignity and force as it reproduces the necessarily passive stance of *accepting* the surrender from the vanquished. He must consider what kind of imaging credit must be given to the sovereign proxies in the field (his generals). And here we need to add the further consideration of what *kind* of vanquished enemy is now in his hands and what this does to the sovereign's ability to appear at the scene of surrender. Is the vanquished a former countryman, as in the case of a civil war? Is the vanquished a former noble foe? Or is the vanquished a former despicable or unrecognizable foe?

It may indeed seem unbecoming to commission images of countrymen surrendering to oneself. In a certain sense these enemies never existed, in that they were not recognized. Scenes of their surrender might only add to the misrecognition problem. Of course, misrecognition scenes can cut both ways, and the vanquished can strategically misrecognize the victor. We recall here the much worked-on paintings of the confusion of the Persian princesses, unsure who is the real Alexander. We encounter more modern misrecognitions as well. General Grant's Lieutenant Horace Porter, present at the Appomattox surrender, reports that Lee replies to Grant's claim that they had met before in Mexico some years earlier with the casual statement, "Yes . . . I know I met you on that occasion and I have often thought of it and tried to recollect how you looked, *but I have never been able to recall a single feature.*"[80]

When the vanquished is a former noble foe, the chivalric magnanimity of the sovereign can achieve full flower. But even here there is often a relay of proxies that both bring the sovereign to the scene through his mediators (in a form of effigy that constitutes surrogacy) and manage to keep the sovereign self withheld. Philip IV is present in Breda in the figure of Spinola, in the flags and banners, and maybe in the mysterious piece of paper in the corner of Velázquez's painting (representing the paper-driven Habsburg bureaucracy), but he was not actually present at the scene and is not found in the painting of it (or in Maino's painting; only his woven image is on display in Brazil).

Absent sovereigns could always count on participants and witnesses to describe the scenes of surrender when such descriptions were of a piece with sovereign glory. As the English occupied and colonized India in the mid-1800s, British officials wrote frequently to Queen Victoria to describe the elaborately choreographed ritual surrenders of the last rulers of the Sikh empire. On one of these occasions Governor General Dalhousie, the director of the spectacle, wrote, "Your majesty may well imagine the pride with which the British Officers looked on such a scene, and witnessed this absolute subjection and humiliation of so powerful an enemy."[81]

When a vanquished foe is felt not to be powerful, but rather to be despicable or ignoble, the sovereign and his proxies may absent themselves both from the actual scenes and from their representations. When there are clear asymmetries of status between the two sides, genre problems result. Stephen Greenblatt describes a design study by Albrecht Dürer for a monument to celebrate a sixteenth-century victory of German nobility and princes over rebellious peasants. These peasants, one might guess, would not be given the option of surrender with terms (advantageous or not), and thus Dürer's drawing shows a peasant slumped atop a tall column of agricultural products, with a sword stuck in his back. Greenblatt writes, "The princes and nobles for whom such monuments were built could derive no dignity from the triumph, any more than they could derive dignity from killing a mad dog . . . Indeed in the economy of honor [the peasants] are not simply a cipher but a deficit, since even a defeat at the hands of a prince threatens to confer upon them some of the prince's store of honor, while what remains of the victorious prince's store can be tarnished by the unworthy encounter."[82] What cannot be recognized (the peasant) might suggest what cannot be represented. Yet it is the victor that becomes the impossible subject of the rendering of the victory here.

Peasants were ignoble foes, and the German generals at the end of World War II were perhaps despicable ones. General Dwight D. Eisenhower absented himself from the ceremony of signing the surrender documents when the German military officials came to his headquarters in Reims. He did, however, send his proxies—his subordinate officers and his pens: "Jodl, von Friedeburg and Oxenius bowed stiffly before taking their seats on the opposite side of the table. Four copies of the surrender documents, bound in plain gray paper covers, lay on the table. Eisenhower, refusing to treat directly with the German officers, was not present in the room but waited in his office down the corridor, pacing up and down impatiently . . . Two special fountain pens were produced, one solid gold and the other gold plated, both of them the personal property of General Eisenhower. The gold-plated one was handed to the blanched but impassive General Jodl who was the first to sign the surrender agreement."[83] There are no paintings of this scene.

The Uncopied

And if it is true that the psychology of the imagination neither can nor should work upon static figures—if it can only learn from images that are in the process of deformation . . .[84]

It is hard enough to represent the singularity that is the sovereign essence. It is harder still, it seems, to capture the vanishing sovereignty of the defeated. Before taking on the dilemmas associated with this strange task of representing the disappearance of the *unrepresentable,* we need to remember that some agent of the defeated, perhaps a proxy, must accomplish the necessary performative speech acts and demonstrative gestures in order for conflict to end. Whether it will be the individual sovereign or one or several of his proxies is a question with both political and semiotic resonance. As described in the preceding chapter, the site of surrender is inevitably both highly charged and emptied out. It is a place of metaphysical transformation of individual and collective identity. Proxies for supreme sovereigns who are defeated in battle may act as provisional buffers, preventing the public drama of a Richard II, who must "undo myself" with his own tongue, hands, and breath. Left to their own devices, proxies may themselves undergo a literal and figurative undoing in the stead of a vanished sovereign. The Florentine Giovanni Villani, a contemporary commentator writing about the fourteenth-century siege and surrender of Calais, made note of the details of the actions of capitulating town elders: "Those of Calais, seeing the departure of the king of France and his host, negotiated with the king of England to surrender their land, to save the people from the foreigners. Coming out of the town bare-chested with a noose around their necks, they asked him for mercy."[85]

Some defeated sovereigns do not simply withdraw, like Philip VI at Calais or the president of the Confederacy, Jefferson Davis. They might undo themselves through suicide, like Adolf Hitler, leaving their proxies to undergo the necessarily disjunctive formal surrender proceedings. Some, like Emperor Hirohito, surprise observers when they make the decision to surrender and then absent themselves from the ceremony. Such presentings and absentings are subject to hermeneutical interpretation that ultimately refer back to questions of sovereign identity. In the case of Hirohito's no-show, commentators made the following assessment: "The emperor did not participate in these proceedings, nor did any representative of the imperial family or the Imperial Household Ministry . . . And even after the Japanese learned that the emperor would be personally spared this ordeal, they still assumed that an intimate representative from the court, perhaps blood kin to the sovereign, would be required to sign the surrender documents on his behalf. The emperor's complete exclusion from the great morality play of September 2nd was a heartening signal to the Japanese side, for it intimated that the victors might be willing to disassociate the emperor from ultimate war responsibility."[86] Those who did attend the ceremony were well aware of their proxy duty, however. Toshikazu Kase, a Japanese diplomatic member of the party who boarded the ship, reveals the self-consciousness of an emulated presence: "I was the one who advocated wearing those swallow coats, not because we want to pay respect to American generals, but because we were representing our sovereign"[87] (plate 16).

Whether it is the supreme sovereign or his proxies who present themselves to do the work of surrender, the vanquished inevitably endure a kind of representational imperialism that comes along with their performative acts (the signing of the document, the oaths of loyalty, the declarations of surrender) and demonstrative gestures. They are drawn, painted, photographed, and filmed, their image captured often, though not exclusively, in the act of surrendering. These portraits and portrayals may include the inserted images of the victor as well, sometimes in unusual places and figures. The variations on a theme of portraying the victor and the vanquished as a couple (recall the characterization of MacArthur and Hirohito's photograph as a "wedding photo") call forth a theory of sovereignty in surrender that is both political and metaphysical and that relies on the plays of likeness in portraits and copies.

Recall the focus on the singularity of the sovereign in theories of sovereign power, the way the sovereign both brings law and stands outside it, the exceptionalism that generates the theological doctrine of the king's two bodies, the immortal, unrepresentable power that stands out and stands above. A necessary and ultimately unresolvable paradox of this concept is that outside the domestic domain of absolute mastery, the sovereign finds himself in a state of "independent vulnerability in the external zone of competing sovereignties."[88] Wars and other violent conflicts that arise between these competing sovereign entities (each of whom may claim the same territory, the same people) bring about a conceptual as well as a physical conundrum. A co-constituting system of sovereigns (states and individuals) seems logical on its face: sovereign nations, with clear boundaries, ruling their own subjects and ignoring or respecting the subjects of other nations. However, not only does this system not exist empirically, in spite of gestures in that direction in the form of international courts and legislative bodies, it cannot, according to the theory of sovereignty, be maintained conceptually.[89] Wars and other conflicts only highlight the reality of what one theorist calls "the anarchic realm" that appears in the place of such a system.[90]

The situation is best described by Elaine Scarry in her chapter on war in *The Body in Pain:*

> In consenting to enter into war, the participants enter into a structure that is a self-canceling duality. They enter into formal duality, but one understood by all to be temporary and intolerable, a formal duality that, by the very force of its relentless insistence on doubleness, provides the means for eliminating and replacing itself by the condition of singularity (since in the end it will have legitimized one side's right to determine the nature of certain issues). A first major attribute here is the transition, at the moment of the entry into war, from the condition of multiplicity to the condition of the binary; a second attribute is the transition, at the moment of ending the war, from the condition of the binary to the condition of the unitary.[91]

War initiates the time of the unidentified pretender. Yet both parties must act "as if" the enemy has the type of agency that derives from sovereignty. But this condition of *twinning* seems not to be indefinitely sustainable.[92] One sovereign will emerge as "true," one as "false." War is the state of the deferral of this identification. Surrender is a mechanism for its (provisional, recalling the return motif that is never ending) resolution.

Given the sheer impossibility of suspending the sovereign order that war nevertheless seems to demand, the repositionings and recompositions of power and fealty must be evident at conflict's end. The reregnant sovereign image must be fixed, particularly in relation to that of the now revealed pretender.

It is in this context that the many portraits and likenesses that are generated by surrenders begin to make sense. The victor claims not only the loyalty and submission of the vanquished but his image as well. Thus not only do we find portraits of the victors taken at the moments of their triumph—the last photo of Lincoln, the nested tapestry rendering of Philip IV by Maino, the engraving of the Archduchess Isabella by Rubens, the photos of Truman in the Oval Office reading the Japanese acceptance of the demand that they surrender unconditionally—but we also find portraits of the defeated commissioned by the victors.[93]

General Jonathan Wainwright, the American general forced to surrender to the Japanese in the Philippines in 1942, wrote a book about his long ordeal, plaintively titled *General Wainwright's Story: The Account of Four Years of Humiliating Defeat, Surrender, and Captivity.* After a long siege under excruciating conditions, Wainwright surrendered at Corregidor in May 1942. Wainwright and his fellow officers endured the formal surrender ceremony, and then, "After another period of waiting [for the arrival of General Masaharu Homma] we were suddenly ordered to move off the porch and line up on the lawn in front of the steps. This was for the benefit of Jap[anese] newsreel and still-camera men. They took our pictures over and over again for about thirty minutes."

Worse still, some time later on a ship taking him to a prison camp at Karenko, he again found himself the object of his captors' artistic attention: "I was led out on the ship's deck and, over my protests, made to pose for a Jap[anese] artist. He was doing a painting of my surrender to Homma. It was to go to the imperial palace in Tokyo when completed. It was an ambitious affair, for at Manila I had been forced to seat myself at a table—formerly the University Club's main dining table—and arrange Beebe, Pugh, Dooley, and Carroll about me, as we had been on the day we met Homma. Many photographs of us had been taken that day at Manila, to help the artist who was making sketches of my face. He was pretty overwhelmed by the fact that the painting, when finished, would be presented to Hirohito. I remember saying to myself, as I sat there posing on the little steamer going to Karenko, 'Douglas will get that painting one of these fine days.'"[94]

The formal pose of the defeated presents an unusual form of undoing. The subject of the rendering can attempt to imagine himself reappearing in a scene of reversal, as Wainwright does when he anticipates Douglas MacArthur's reclaiming the painting in an Allied victory. Alternatively, the vanquished can attempt to demand a realistic portrayal of captivity that withholds submission and identification with the new sovereign. The latter strategy shows up in the varied dreams of reconfigured portraits, from those voiced by Native Americans in the nineteenth-century United States to those of members of the so-called Sikh diaspora in England in the late twentieth century.

Both of these alternative imaginings revolve around the strange phenomenon of effigies worn around the neck of the defeated. European in origin, these "peace medals" consisted of large medallions bearing the image, or silhouette, of the victorious sovereign. So, for example, in Franz Winterhalter's 1854 portrait of Maharaja Dalip Singh, the last ruler of the Sikh empire, Dalip Singh is shown wearing a large medal on which Queen Victoria's image prominently appears. In the United States, at about the same time, Native Americans, some of whom were incarcerated by government officials, displayed the effigies of such presidents as James Monroe and Martin Van Buren. Many of these chiefs and other Native Americans were painted in native dress by such artists as George Catlin and Charles Bird King. Often the "peace medal" was highlighted in the renderings. These individuals, like the Native American leader Black Hawk, were then triply caught—by the United States officials who incarcerated them, by the medal and its sovereign image worn around the neck, and by the artist who rendered the portrait. In Catlin's *Letters and Notes on the Manners, Customs, and Conditions of North American Indians* (1833), he mentions that Black Hawk and other Sauks imprisoned at Jefferson Barracks challenged the painters to paint them wearing a ball and chain, a more realistic rendering of their condition. This was not done.[95]

On the other hand, history and its revisions do sometimes provide for a reversion of a representational unmaking. In 1993 a new Sikh version of Winterhalter's portrait of Dalip Singh replaced the effigy of Queen Victoria with that of Maharaja Ranjit Singh.

Like lovers wearing locks of hair entwined in a locket around their necks, the cross-referencing portraits of victors and vanquished enact and represent relationships. These are clearly relationships of power, announced at the conclusion of a contest to determine who wears whom around his neck.

CHAPTER 5

The Deep Structure of Surrender

The point to be stressed in this connection is that the terms "victory," "defeat," and "stalemate," when used to characterize the final outcome of wars rather than the outcome of military engagements, are not absolute, but relative concepts. If a war ends asymmetrically, this is because the loser regards as final the asymmetrical outcome achieved at a certain time.

—Paul Kecskemeti, *Strategic Surrender: The Politics of Victory and Defeat*

On the rotating wheel of fortune of victory and defeat, the positions of above and below are always being exchanged. The winner rises up in the world, while the loser falls. All Western languages use the verb *to fall* to distinguish a heroic warrior's death from ordinary dying. And the monuments erected to those who have fallen in battle are an attempt to lift them back up.

—Wolfgang Schivelbusch, *The Culture of Defeat*

Let us pray that peace be now restored to the world and that God will preserve it always. These proceedings are closed.

—Douglas MacArthur's declaration at the end of the signing of the Japanese surrender on the USS *Missouri*

A TRIP to the local notary public sounded innocuous enough. Notaries are paid witnesses, neither representatives of the state nor partisan advocates. They simply countersign official documents. Nevertheless, as this book has demonstrated, there is a gravity about all witnesses; countersigners are aware of being implicated as cosigners to a particular version of reality.

My seventeen-year-old son wanted his senior driver's license, the license that in Pennsylvania entitles the bearer to drive after 11 P.M. To receive it, he needed a parent or guardian to sign his application, verifying his abilities and credentials. But the signing needed to take place in the presence of a notary public. Swarthmore, Pennsylvania, is a small town, founded by Quakers. The local notary is an elderly woman who is serious about her job but neither commanding nor intimidating. The document to be signed could be understood as enhancing individual freedom and solidifying one's public identity, one of several official passports to adulthood. Yet I felt my anxiety grow as the notary took out her stamp pad and her crimping seal and I prepared to affix my signature. What was the nature of this anxiety? How did this straightforward, automatic transaction come to loom ominously before me as a very specific form of surrender?

The task was obvious and simple—sign my name. But unquestionably, much of my anxiety was about performing that act. I was asked for my own driver's license as the repository of a previous signature, and the inevitable comparison between my most contemporary version and this older one was imminent. Suddenly I wondered if I would be able to reproduce my "usual" signature or if something unrecognizable and alien would scrawl itself on the document and put my identity in doubt. Could I be accused of forging my own signature? Signature under scrutiny. But under the scrutiny of whom or what? Surely this pale and quietly businesslike woman could not be the source of the anxiety. Or could she? The notary public requires that bona fide identities be proved and committed in order that these identities might be performatively transformed. My own authority to name, demonstrate, and perform my identity was being tested and given over to another. The state and its surveillance and licensing privileges hovered like a specter in the room. Substantively, I was indeed surrendering a certain juridical control over my son; I was surrendering a part of his childhood, a childhood that was swiftly vanishing. Thus the signing of this document had become a strangely intimate act of identity transformation witnessed by an official stranger. The private becomes public as both the signature and the self (or the self through the signature) are claimed by the state. Hillel Schwartz writes of notaries, "They became the chief repositories of legal precedent . . . Notarizing transforms the private into the public, the transient into the timely, then into the timeless."[1]

And yet we do this all the time. We sign our names in front of witnesses at the supermarket, the bank, the school, the doctor's office, the town square (where petitions are solicited). We leave traces of our selves on all these documents, scattering our identity among myriad institutions and interested parties. And every time we do this, our identity is transformed in some manner—we become the identity created or represented on that document. Thus it should not seem strange that all of these issues and conditions are accentuated in signing a document that literally calls itself an "instrument of surrender." Such documents of self-undoing are the very exemplars of political transformation, recognition, authority, authenticity, exposure, and commitment.

Borderline Scrutinies

The panic and disorder of flight and retreat in battle might appear to be a kind of surrender. Leaving the field is one way to surrender it to one's opponent. Nevertheless, in the conventions of surrender that have evolved over centuries in the West, surrenders almost always require a return to the scene of battle, a kind of ceremonial reenactment of the enmity as identities and relations—indeed, the very field itself—are reconfigured. Yet it is also a sign of commitment (at least temporarily) to end the fighting. One must stay and sign. This study of surrender has reached into the manifold mechanisms of this complex and strained social interaction in order to analyze how it is accomplished.

I have examined three signal cases of military surrender—Breda, Appomattox, and Tokyo Bay—that have left a dense trail of documents and images. And I have noted many other historical instances of surrender occurring across different times and cultures. The approach used here, termed the political semiotic, analyzes both the interactional features of an archetypal event (surrender) and its social and cultural epistemological conditions and forms. Thus surrenders are necessarily demonstrated, performed, and represented. And they necessarily involve witnessing, exchanges, and sovereignty. The underlying model of social reality is one in which social relations are built up and decomposed through and with the available social and cultural forms of cognition and interaction. Catching this movement analytically is possible only using such an approach, one that provisionally separates the ceaseless flow of action and interaction from the congealing codifications (in documents, gestures, or images) that seek to reflect and reroute social identities and political relations. Only the cultural and political semiotic approach is capable of delineating the mechanisms of the deep structure of culture in action where values and ideas pulsate along the pathways and nodes of the various practices.[2] The three aspects or conditions of this cultural and political semiotic—the performative, the demonstrative, and the representational— are the elemental features of social transformations. Finally, this framework incorporates the insight, solidified after the linguistic turn and the practice turn, that culture refers not just to values and ideas, but to practices as well.

While military or political surrenders are explicit, event-focused transactions aimed at ending violent conflicts, issues of identity and subjecthood have come to loom large in this analysis. Surrenders do alter identities and relationships as they engage the mechanisms of the transfer of power. This goes beyond the former antagonists' taking on the paired identities of victor and vanquished. It goes beyond the fact that people(s) are attached to their possessions and are loath to surrender them, to give them over to another. It occurs because what must be handed over in surrenders has something of the very self attached. When it is a name, a territory, a weapon (the ability to defend oneself), or sovereignty, the transfers of surrender can eviscerate sovereign selfhood.

Undoing war, undoing conflict, undoing sovereignty—all of this is surrender's project. It is a project, as we have seen, that is necessarily liminal. Surrenders mark the limits of war, both the limits of its fighting and the limits of its contested terrains. These limits serve to reorient all combatants and thus create a field (of positions and relations) that is no longer a battlefield. Scrutinizing this threshold of war and peace, what do we find?

Ceremonies that bring antagonists together to mark and make a historical turn inevitably distill down into a binary structure. Victor and vanquished must orient toward each other in a manner that provisionally can be described as a mirror. Two sovereigns, or their proxies, similar in position, recognize each other as the exchanges commence. But a normal mirror simply reverses the direction of the identical reflection it hosts. This mirror of surrender is more akin to those found in a fun house or a circus. The reflections are distorted and exaggerated. The victorious sovereign can be up on a horse while the vanquished kneels below; the victorious general can sign a leather-bound instrument of surrender while the vanquished signs one bound in rough canvas[3] (plate 17).

Of course, in cases of expressive and diplomatic magnanimity of the victor toward the defeated, these asymmetries and distortions can be muted. Diffidence can generate more semiotic symmetry, or more semiotic nervousness. Such concerns may have lain behind the fact that there was no single surrender document that was signed by both Grant and Lee (where the obviously subordinated signature of Lee would have cohabited on the page with the superordinate signature of Grant). The editors of Grant's *Memoirs* insert a clarifying note about the Appomattox documents that indicates the mythological slippage around this sensitive point: "There is a popular error to the effect that Generals Grant and Lee each signed the articles of surrender. The document in the form of a letter was signed only by General Grant . . . and General Lee immediately wrote a letter accepting the terms and handed it to General Grant."[4] Whatever their eventual fates, Grant and Lee end this part of their conflict without a textual "handshake."

Magnanimous reticence might also have accounted for the initial inversion and eventual reversion of names on the surrender document signed by Union general William T. Sherman and Confederate general Joseph E. Johnston in the vexed negotiations on the western front of the Civil War. According to Jay Winik, when Johnston and Sherman met on April 26, 1865, to codify Johnston's decision to surrender rather than engage in an extended guerrilla war, "Sherman then graciously allowed Johnston's name to go first in the articles of surrender (Grant later reversed them so that Sherman's name would come first when they were published in the Northern press)."[5]

Even with such qualifications, the mirror-image framework of the antagonists presents an impossible dualism; one simply cannot have two sovereign claimants ruling over one territory or people. At the point of surrender the vanquished party *becomes* the reflection of the victorious other, and thus the other's subject (in whatever designated variation on that theme; e.g., slave, vassal). The vanquished is the double of the victorious sovereign only in the same way Felibien claims that Hephaestion *is* Alexander in the painting by Le Brun. The sovereign is reflected in all his subjects.

However, the direction of influence is not unilateral. As a consequence of the myriad exchanges and recognitions (and misrecognitions) of surrender encounters, the victor may also absorb something of the identity or image of the vanquished. This absorption tends to be implicit, as if its explicit recognition would put in doubt the newly codified hierarchy of power. Writing about the "Requirement" that sixteenth-century Spanish conquerors read to the natives of their newly possessed lands, requiring their submission to Spain and to Catholicism, Patricia Seed details all of this instrument's borrowed Islamic conventions and traditions: "Since enemies, even mirror-image ones, deny each other's legitimacy, traditional Islamic customs could not be acknowledged as a model for Spanish political authority."[6] Here the long history of Spanish-Muslim warfare actually works toward a kind of worldview incorporation, even as it is not officially recognized.

Uneasy Appearances

To fully appreciate the work of the mechanisms of the political semiotic, we need to recall the contradictions described in the previous chapter's discussion of the appearance of the sovereign at scenes of surrender. The sovereign must appear before his subjects, his image must circulate, his ubiquity must be sustained. At the same time, the sovereign must withhold appearance, must not be commonly visible, must be exceptional, powerful, invisible. Similarly, images and proxies of the sovereign must have something of the sovereign's true essence attached to them. At the same time, they must never be identical copies; the sovereign must exceed representation.[7]

In surrender, the vanquished sovereign undergoes an alchemical *reappearance*. He is revealed as base metal, that aspect of the "king's two bodies" that is mortal, imperfect. He is clearly subordinate to the victor, no longer exceptional or divine. He is "just" a person. That is the true disgrace of surrender, no matter how magnanimous the victor. The sovereign is simply human. This is most explicitly relevant to the defeated and undone sovereign, but it is implicitly relevant to the victor as well. As detailed in the previous chapter, the ceremony of surrender is dangerous for all attendant sovereigns because it reminds the *witnesses* of what can happen to a sovereign: that he is just human and can be stripped of power—that he can be displaced.

As always, these dangers play themselves out as variations on a theme of presentation and representation. At the scene of a surrender, the victorious sovereign might even be caught off guard not by a resumption of battle, but by an errant foe. In the surrender ceremony at Yorktown in 1781, during the American War of Independence, the British general Charles Cornwallis was to have rendered his sword directly to the victor, General George Washington. Barry Schwartz writes of this scene, "As the victorious commander [Washington] was entitled to receive the sword of surrender directly from Cornwallis, his vanquished counterpart. Cornwallis never showed up; instead, he delivered his sword to Washington through an aide. Refusing to accept the instrument himself, Washington instructed Cornwallis's aide to present it to his own aide, General Lincoln."[8] In these absences and deflections, away from the first-line representatives and drawing the seconds into the action, the exchanges of the surrender scene reposition the threshold even as they attempt to cross it.

In John Trumbull's painting of this surrender (plate 18), a painting that hangs in the Capitol rotunda, Washington appears as an éminence grise, hovering in the background of the scene of surrender on his horse while his second accepts Cornwallis's sword. He is present in a manner similar to the tapestry image of Philip IV in the painting by Maino, similar to General Dwight Eisenhower's sequestering himself down the hall from the actual signing of the surrender of the Germans in the schoolhouse in Reims: there but not really there, present in a way that maintains his zone of exceptionality in the midst of such a dangerous transaction.

These paradoxes are rich and patterned—within their constraints there is flexibility, hence the possibility that the inflection of the surrender ceremony can range from humiliation to magnanimity. A certain amount of stage managing is necessary to keep up "appearances," but the defeated may always attempt to improvise a way out of complete subjection.

The Political Semiotic at Conflict's End

When much is at stake, a pause in the action provides respite and a ground for reorientation. Surrender may be viewed as a pause in the face of the impositions of victory and defeat in war. The participants gather: sovereigns, proxies, foot soldiers, and witnesses. This book has sought to take them all seriously, to take seriously their positions vis-à-vis the transactions of exchange and transformation. We must have an image not just of Ulysses S. Grant, but of his staff member, the Native American colonel E. S. Parker, who wrote out the final copy of the surrender at Appomattox and who was portrayed paper in hand in Thomas Nast's *Palm Sunday* etching. We must trace the appearances and positions of the Dutch soldiers in Velázquez's *Surrender of Breda* and of the Spanish soldiers in Callot's *Map of the Siege of Breda* as much as we attend to the figures of Ambrogio Spinola and Justin of Nassau. As we analyze the work of MacArthur's many pens, we must note the enveloping mass of U.S. Navy sailors draping themselves over the ship that hosts the surrender of the Japanese. As we move through a final assessment of the demonstrative, the performative, and the representational aspects of surrender, we will fix our attention on the victors, on the vanquished, and on those who interpret the meaning of their actions.

Demonstration and Deictics

It was called the Battle of Antietam. The name derived from Antietam Creek, a beautiful winding stream with wooded banks. Because the Union named the battles after geographical features, and because the North won, the name stuck. But in the South, it was known as the Battle of Sharpsburg—the Confederacy named battles after nearby towns. By either name, when it was over, 12 hours after it began at sunrise on the morning of September 17, 1862, it was the greatest single day of blood sacrifice in American history.[9]

Whenever and wherever certain types of action are to commence or stop—whenever, in other words, the world changes—the attention of those involved must be focused. Gazes must be drawn, names must be announced, spaces must be mapped. A clearing, literal and figurative, emerges and acts as a gravitational field. Demonstrations are a necessary part of social transformations because they let relevant parties get their bearings, find the action, and take things in.

Demonstrations also work to identify the relevant parties. Contacts and communication along any number of mediated routes attempt to rivet the attention of those whom the ongoing situation has already designated as implicated. This is where demonstrations are revealed to be dependent on prior performative acts of authorization. Central actors, formal witnesses, and bystanders "who shall have been present" at an act of transformation demonstrate their involvement through posture, eye contact, physical involvement, and other gestures in the central acts of recognition and exchange. Those witnesses who then render these involvements, who copy them in a variety of media, seek to direct the attention of others who will view or hear or read these representations and so on as the network of cross-witnesses expands.[10]

As these mechanisms are tracked, it becomes clear that it is virtually impossible to disentangle the work of the demonstrations from that of the performatives and the representations. They all depend on each other to keep the situation moving and evolving and taking form. This is so even as each aspect seems to take a different temporal stance toward social situations: the demonstrative looks toward the future ("over there you will see the exchange of the key, the signing of the document"); the performative asserts its dominion over the present order of things ("I surrender!"); the representational looks toward events in the past in order to reproduce them and their effects. But we have seen how the looping symbolic interactions of emergent situations give the lie to this sort of temporal partitioning and claim staking. Most important, perhaps, inasmuch as surrenders appear to mark breaks, gaps, disappearances, and appearances of new powers and political entities, the political semiotic conditions of their evolution suggest the continuous influence of preconditions. By way of analogy, the necessary excretion of the past into the emergent present is captured well by Pierre Bourdieu's discussion of the attempts at innovation in the juridical field. The analogy is clear to all situations that claim for themselves a transformative agenda: "Nonetheless, the will to transform the world by transforming the words for naming it, by producing new categories of perception and judgment and by dictating a new vision of social divisions and distributions, can only succeed if the resulting prophecies or creative evocations are also, at least in part, wellfounded pre-visions, anticipatory descriptions. These visions only call forth what they proclaim—whether new practices, new mores or especially new social groupings—because they announce what is in the process of developing. They are not so much the midwives as the recording secretaries of history."[11]

Demonstrations insist that participants and "recording secretaries" (roles that can be concurrent and reversible, as we have seen) take notice. In directing vision, hearing, and action, however, they can meet with resistance. Parties to a situation can decide not to pay attention, not to follow the pointing finger or the directions of a map or a conversation. Inattention and distraction, literal and figurative looking away, can jam the mechanisms of a transformative event like a surrender. How far distraction can and ought to be interpreted as resistance is partly an empirical, partly a theoretical question. For example, William Craig writes about the project of persuading the Japanese to accept the Potsdam Declaration, which levied an ultimatum promising complete destruction unless they surrendered, and about the delay in gaining this acceptance: "Rather than make a decision on the Declaration, Japan preferred to wait for some progress in Moscow. When reporters asked Premier Suzuki for a reaction to the Allied message, *he meant to tell them* that the Government would 'withhold comment' on it for the time being. Unfortunately, he used the word *mokusatsu* to describe his attitude. In Japanese, *mokusatsu* means 'take no notice of, treat with silent contempt, ignore.'"[12] Was this difference in meaning, the former seeming to reflect ambivalence or delay, the latter appearing to signify purposive inattention, merely a matter of mistranslation? Or did it reflect differences over the nature and degree of resistance toward the demonstrations and performatives of the ultimatum?

Degrees of resistance are difficult to determine in any case. More important for this analysis is the ability to recognize the dynamic relationships between the subject positions of victor and vanquished and between the demonstrative stances of attention and distraction. When directions are given (in both senses of the word), they may be recognizably followed or they may be ignored. In any transfer of power, it is crucial that the transactions and exchanges that accomplish the transfer be recognized by the network of cross-witnesses. Thus, whatever their motivation, acts of inattention reveal an unquiet situation, one that has not yet settled down. They also indicate instances of nonrecognition.

Recognition is a key term for each of the analytic phases of the political semiotic. It is the term that signifies the effectiveness of all socially and culturally relevant actions in social life. Performatives operate only in conditions of their recognizability, and thus uptake. Demonstratives work only when the demonstrations are legible and their directionality can be followed. Representations must be recognized as mimetic in some measure. Thus, recognition is a crucial condition of the demonstrations that draw attention. Troubles or ambiguities over recognition can impede progress. For example, contradictory indications about when a besieged city or fortress may and must surrender (under the codified rules of siege warfare) often leaned on open interpretations about such things as exactly how many provisions were remaining and how wide the breach in the wall was. Contradictory ideas about how to characterize the nature of transactions between antagonists at the conclusion of the peace (negotiations, declarations, the presentation of terms) often hinged on how the entities involved in the transactions were, or were not, recognized. On the one hand, the victor's complete nonrecognition of the political integrity of the vanquished could, as we have seen in the case of the German surrender in World War II and the Confederate army surrender in the American Civil War, lead to a demonstration of that nonrecognition in the renaming of the act of surrender itself. On the other hand, acceptance (however distracted or inadvertent it might be) of a particular presentation of reality may be held to imply de facto recognition. For example, Patricia Seed notes, "Dutch writers recognized other states' claims to territory based upon map names . . . They insisted that when Englishmen and other Europeans used Dutch names, they were proving Dutch discovery and hence entitlement to New Netherlands."[13]

In all these variations, it is critical to chart how the conventions of demonstration do their work. They may be shared, but the situation may still be interpreted in divergent, unsettled ways. Or they may not be shared, in which case the parties work to impose their own. As always, the interest here is in the mechanics of this work. A particular feature of language, deictics, may be understood as a *micromechanics* of demonstration. Close attention to the indexical demonstrations of such deictic markers as pronouns and adverbs of time and place can illuminate the passages of the transformations of surrender. If we take the framing of surrenders as a pause or a gap, we would do well to rummage around within them to delineate their deferrals and distractions as much as their attentions and recognitions.

Deictic Deferrals

Each time a surrender is attempted, and each time one is achieved, the parties to it will have generated a living archive of documents, maps, diagrams, pictures, flags, and so forth. Within each of these cultural and political missives, deictical features perform the work of connecting the item to the larger social situation that it is both marking and making. We might recall the discussion of deictics in chapter 2, and Michael Silverstein's conceptualizing the way they make "explicit the structure of ongoing events." Here the emphasis is on the relation between deictic *deferral* and situational development.

Deictic deferral refers to contradictory or uncoordinated deictical features within any one text-image (it can also refer to contradictions among several text-images). Thus the meaning and location of the situational referent is deferred—waiting, as it were—to see the direction in which the indexical features will settle. Examples of deictic deferral include pronominal and adverbial oscillations and alternations, slides back and forth from active to passive voice, and doublings in representations.

We have encountered many examples of this deictical nervousness. General Lee surrendered at Appomattox and referred to "our army" of the Confederacy. This deictic persistence on the threshold of undoing took witnesses there by surprise. In fact, within a few weeks, Lee gave interviews to Northern newspapers in which the anticipated switch was effected. Writing about a *New York Herald* interview Lee gave, Jay Winik notes, "Where just weeks earlier . . . whenever Lee had said 'the country' he had meant the South, and whenever he said 'we' he had meant the Confederacy. But now, the reporter was struck by the degree to which Lee talked throughout, freely and noticeably, as 'a citizen of the United States.'"[14] This liminality of Lee's was also reflected in what might be considered a kind of spatial deictic ambiguity. Lee's position in Thomas Nast's *Harper's Weekly* lithograph appears to be both near Grant and far away from him at the same time. Is he, on May 20, 1865, near or far, here or there, one of us or one of them?

We also find instances when there are pronominal slides between first person and third person (a slide of responsibility), slides between formal and informal (a slide of recognition), and slides between first-person singular and first-person plural (a slide of responsibility or solidarity or both).

Another modality by which deictic deferral is accomplished is pictorial doubling—the repetition in one image of a figure or figures that signals different time points. They may be simultaneously portrayed as up close and in the present and as far away and in the past. Thus there are two Ambrogio Spinolas in the map of the siege and surrender of Breda by Callot and, however abstractly, in the painting by Velázquez.[15]

In cases of particularly charged surrenders, where the pronominal linguistic shifters are overdetermined and form the background of antagonist relations, such as those coming at the end of civil wars, a more explicit distraction may also claim the central protagonists. This was certainly the case at Appomattox. The North and the South were once merged ("us" and "them" were once all "us"; "here" and "there" were once all "here") and soon would be again. Meanwhile, the suturing work of the surrender agreement had to acknowledge the defeat of the South, the victory of the North, and the simultaneous recombining of the sundered parts. This complex and contradictory project seemed to particularly affect the victor, General Grant, and to deflect his central participation in signing the surrender as he kept getting distracted. His own memoirs reveal this rather tellingly as he recounts the meeting with General Lee:

> We soon fell into a conversation about old army times . . . Our conversation grew so pleasant *that I almost forgot the object of our meeting.* After the conversation had run on in this style for some time, General Lee called my attention to the object of our meeting, and said that he had asked for this interview for the purpose of getting from me the terms I proposed to give his army. I said that I meant merely that his army should lay down their arms, not to take them up again during the continuance of the war unless duly and properly exchanged. He said that he had so understood my letter. *Then we gradually fell off again into conversation* about matters foreign to the subject which had brought us

together . . . when Gen. Lee again interrupted the course of the conversation by suggesting that the terms I proposed to give his army ought to be written out.[16]

Even with his own citizenship and membership issues, Lee seemed to have been less subject to distraction, seeking to bring Grant's attention back to the business at hand.

Performatives and Transformations

When J. L. Austin first wrote about performative speech acts, he called attention to the way word and deed coincide in them.[17] Uttering certain words or phrases, in certain contexts, with certain specified authorizations, actually changes the world (that being a world composed of identities and relationships). "We find the defendant not guilty" makes the defendant legally not guilty and thus free to leave the courtroom. In this sense, performatives seem quintessentially presentist in their temporal location. They aim to grab the present as it passes and, before it knows what is happening, reroute it. When this present has anticipated itself to be in the very business of transformation and undoing, it is easy to see that it would be especially hard for its incumbents to find secure ground in the midst of its declarations, orders, promises, verdicts, and the like.

Disorientation in the face of the performatives of surrender thus incorporates more than whatever resistance one might reasonably expect to find.[18] For the vanquished, it is a disorientation that is permeated by a sense of existential loss. Reorientation requires the positioning of a new identity after the undoing of the old. The range of new identities runs the gamut from absolute humiliation (slavery, imprisonment, statelessness) to a kind of individual reconstitution as legitimate subjects (the Confederate soldiers transformed back into small farmers), with a variety of hybrid types in between.[19]

Of course, there are many modalities of performatives that stake claims to sovereignties, persons, armies, and territories. As Patricia Seed cataloged in her study of overseas conquests of European powers, the Spanish read the "Requirement"; the French planted crosses and standards; the English built houses and fences, enclosing (thus claiming) land; and the Dutch drew maps that, in essence, performed the discovery of the territories represented. We may view these acts as combinations of demonstrations, performatives, and representations. But for those who viewed them as changing the world, they were the actual mechanisms of conquest, not just evidence of conquest.

However, since performatives involve recognition and uptake by those whose world is being changed, the role of force and violence must be recalled, as it has throughout this book. Superior force, or its assumption, backs up the orders, ultimatums, and demands of the victor. This is so regardless of the willingness of the vanquished to proceed through the surrender as ordered. As we have seen in the case of the bilingual surrender treaty of al-Azraq and King James, it does not always determine the interpretation, or gloss, that will be given to the surrender. Nor does it preempt the projection of alternative identities and reversals of power into the future.[20]

Representations

> If an entire culture is regarded as a text then everything is at least potentially in play both at the level of representation and at the level of event. Indeed it becomes increasingly difficult to maintain a clear, unambiguous boundary between what is representation and what is event. At the very least, the drawing or maintaining of that boundary is itself an event.[21]

> Successful performances overcome the deferral of meaning that marks *différance:* The signifiers seem to become the signified, the mere action of performing to determine its effect. Successful performances do not eliminate social power, but they make it invisible.[22]

A certain wishful thinking affects the victors in most surrenders; they believe that this victory will definitively put the matter, or matters, to rest. Even as the return cycle is invigorated by the surrender, it is clear that the victor aims to stop it by permanently achieving peace. Franklin Delano Roosevelt went so far as to articulate this desire in a policy. At the press conference held after the meeting with Allied leaders at Casablanca in 1943, Roosevelt referred to "the utter necessity of our standing together after the war to secure a peace based on principles of permanence."[23] It is the work of representations of surrenders to reflect these themes of permanence, timelessness, and transcendent power. Representation aims at reiteration, pressing home the configurations and compositions that have been performatively accomplished. Representations of surrender (at least those rendered by the victorious parties) seek to capture and extend the outcomes of conflict in space and in time. They have a normative component: the way things appear at a particular moment is the way they will always be and should be. In this way, they are monumentalizing.

But the representations of surrender scenes themselves seem to have a special burden. They may try to capture the very moment of its acts of undoing and reversion, but such moments are in the business of disappearing and reappearing. We have already taken note of the existential disorientation of such intervals in the deictic alternations, the referential slidings, and the dialectic between absorption and distraction. But how do you represent this transitional moment in genres (like history paintings) that aim to monumentalize? This problem is especially salient in what Wendy Steiner claims is the antinarrativist program of art from the Renaissance and after that aims to capture a single moment. She writes, "By prohibiting repeated subjects, painting could depict identity as either a single frozen moment or an eternal essence, but not as a continuity constantly modified by time."[24]

What are the consequences of freezing a particular moment when one party is saying to another, "I surrender"? Does it have the effect of extending that performative in an endless, or timeless, repetition?[25] Is the represented vanquished thus caught in this repeating temporal loop of surrendering, over and over again, like Prometheus with the long-winged eagle daily eating his regenerating liver? Justin of Nassau's key is forever suspended, Darius's family is forever in supplication, the two princesses in Rubens's painting are forever precariously balanced on that pontoon midway between France and Spain.

Of course, different representational media will accomplish this monumentalizing of the transition differently. Recalling the discussion of "genre displacement" in chapter 2, it is important to stress that events like surrenders live only with and through genres and media of representation, communication, and interaction. An analysis of the deep structure of such events must have the capacity to articulate the opportunities and constraints for taking power and making meaning that each genre holds. Language signifies differently from gesture, which signifies differently from figural images. The power to make one's chosen meaning stick through time and across space depends on both the choice and the use of specific genres. In the case of events that can transform identity and sovereignty, a given genre's power to successfully compel subjects and witnesses depends as much on what Hayden White calls the power to "represent the moral under the aspect of the aesthetic" as it does on its dissemination.[26]

Technological innovation in media of representation obviously has consequences for making meanings overt and convincing. But even with the differing capacities of medieval iconography, cartographic maps, and film, the artist who renders surrender is nevertheless attempting to capture something of an ineffable moment of transformation and make it timeless. There are practical problems associated with these efforts as well, primarily a temporal lag. In the ten years, 1625–35, that it took Velázquez to paint *The Surrender of Breda,* the town was on the verge of reverting to Dutch control. And it was not long after General Wainwright's portrait was painted by the Japanese artist for the imperial palace in Tokyo that Wainwright's stubborn thought that "Douglas will get that painting one of these fine days" turned out to be true. Even when it is not a question of a reversion to a prior state, renderings of and encomiums to conquests and surrenders can quickly become out of date. Roger Chartier quotes from a sonnet Molière wrote celebrating Louis XIV's conquest of Franche-Comté: "Mais nos chansons, Grand Roi, ne sont pas si tôt prêtes, / Et tu mets moins de temps à faire tes conquêtes / Qu'il ne faut pour les bien louer."[27] The conqueror marches on as the rendering lags behind.

The condition of representation thus raises the basic question regarding all transformations: Is this temporary, or is this permanent? The mythos of return in surrender would claim a cyclical temporality that is simply returning things to their original and natural state. The phases of surrender play with the cyclical and linear conceptions of time. The surrender brings a return. But the surrender marks a break. *Copies* of surrender may, among other things, be a mechanism by which these alternating visions of the temporality of surrender are adjudicated. On the one hand, the copy clearly announces its differentiation from the original act; thus the surrender is positioned as a singular event in time. On the other hand, the copy suggests a ritual repetition; thus the surrender is a repeatable, reiterable state, out of time itself.

Copies and Their Inversions

If surrenders are fundamentally about undoings, and if they precipitate, in their own turn, motifs and motives of revenge and retaking, then it should not surprise us that the "return" surrender, if and when it occurs, may be framed as a kind of anticopy of the first. In these cases where history repeats itself in its forms but reverses itself in its content, much attention may be paid to the details of the ceremony. Perhaps the most famous case of the anticopy is the surrender of the German generals on November 11, 1918, to the French officer Marshal Ferdinand Foch at Compiègne in Foch's railroad car office (a converted dining car), in which the kaiser's officers accepted the humiliating terms of the armistice that ended World War I, and the "return" surrender of the French to Hitler in the very same railroad car on June 21, 1940. This symmetry was quite purposeful. German army engineers demolished the walls of the museum where Foch's railroad car was displayed and dragged it to the very same spot where it had housed the original German surrender. In the years between 1918 and 1940 the original site had been made into a memorial complex commemorating the German surrender. The Germans destroyed the plaques and statues, undoing the representations of their own surrender. Of course, since the end of World War II, this site has been restored.

The example above demonstrates once again how adept visual images of surrender are in metaphorically sustaining the repetitive performative mantra "I surrender," even when the victor and the vanquished switch positions. Comparisons and juxtapositions of images from the past and the present are often used to make points about the reiteration or reversal of historical trajectories. W. J. T. Mitchell quotes the first President Bush as having said, "The specter of Vietnam has been buried forever in the desert sands of the Arabian Peninsula." He goes on to make the representational dimension of such undoings of undoings explicit when he writes, "Or perhaps the moral was put more pointedly by Dan Rather, as he juxtaposed file footage of the last U.S. helicopter rising from the American embassy in Saigon and live footage of a helicopter landing at our embassy in Kuwait City. 'Of course,' Rather said, 'an image doesn't tell us everything.'"[28] The two counterimages (retreat from an embassy versus claiming of an embassy) are thus linked across a sea of differences in time, space, and political context.

Finally, presidential candidate Albert Gore employed a number of strategies of repetition in his concession speech (a speech already touched on in chapter 1). He begins the speech by noting that he has just telephoned George W. Bush to definitively concede the election. Then, in a reference to his original *revoked* concession phone call immediately after the contested election in November 2000, he says, "And I promised him that I wouldn't call him back this time." In other words, he assures Bush that the surrender will stand as a singular act that breaks the cycle. A few lines later, Gore employs another repetitive rhetorical device when he brings historic concessions to bear on his current act: "Almost a century and a half ago, Senator Stephen Douglas told Abraham Lincoln, who had just defeated him for the presidency, 'Partisan feeling must yield to patriotism. I'm with you, Mr. President, and God bless you.' Well, in that same spirit, I say to President-elect Bush that what remains of partisan rancor must now be put aside, and may God bless his stewardship of this country."[29]

These examples illuminate several relevant functions of repetition in social action generally. One of these functions is to demonstrate that some event or action is not just a random episode; rather, it is a part of a system that will have a temporal extension (whether it will stand permanently or will be revoked). This thinking, I claim, was actually behind the decision to drop not just one but two bombs on Japan in order to induce the Japanese to surrender unconditionally at the end of World War II. One bomb is an incident; two bombs imply a system of production.[30] Finally, repetitions can solidify relationships and augment power. Thus does Admiral Perry's flag return for a second visit to Tokyo Harbor—repetition in the service of repossession.

Plate 1. Diego Velázquez, *The Surrender of Breda* (courtesy Erich Lessing/Art Resource, NY)

Plate 2. Jacques Callot, *The Siege of Breda* (Rosenwald Collection, photograph ©2002 Board of Trustees, National Gallery of Art, Washington)

Plate 3. Jusepe Leonardo, *The Surrender of Julich* (reproduced by permission, rights reserved © Museo Nacional del Prado–Madrid)

Plate 4. German civilians view corpses at Buchenwald, April 16, 1945 (U.S. Army Signal Corps photograph, U.S. National Archives and Records Administration)

Plate 5. Spectators and photographers on the USS *Missouri*, September 2, 1945 (U.S. National Archives and Records Administration)

Plate 6. John Trumbull, *The Resignation of General Washington*

Plate 7. Raphael, *The Marriage of the Virgin*, Pinacoteca di Brera, Milan (courtesy Scala/Art Resource, NY)

EMBLEMA XXXIX.

IN bellum ciuile duces cùm Roma pararet,
    Viribus & caderet Martia terra suis:
Mos fuit in partes turmis coëuntibus easdem,
    Coniunctas dextras mutua dona dare.
Fœderis hæc species: id habet concordia signum,

Plate 8. Andrea Alciati, *Concordia* (courtesy of Swarthmore College Rare Books Collection)

EMBLEMA CLXVII.

BELLORVM cepiſſe ferunt monumenta viciſſim
Scutiferum Aiacen, Hectoráque Iliacum.
Baltea Priamides, rigidum Telamonius enſem,
Instrumenta ſua cepit vterque necis.
Enſis enim Aiacem confecit; at Hectora functum

Plate 9. Andrea Alciati, *In dona hostium* (courtesy of Swarthmore College Rare Books Collection)

Plate 10. Simone Martini, *Guidoriccio da Fogliano* (courtesy Erich Lessing/Art Resource, NY)

Plate 11. Thomas Nast, *Palm Sunday, Harper's Weekly,* 1865

Plate 12. Charles Le Brun, *The Queens of Persia at the Feet of Alexander* (courtesy Réunion des Musées Nationaux/Art Resource, NY)

Plate 13. Peter Paul Rubens, *The Exchange of Princesses at Hendaye* (courtesy Erich Lessing/Art Resource, NY)

Plate 14. Juan Bautista Maino, *The Recapture of Bahia* (courtesy Scala/Art Resource, NY)

Plate 15. Alexander Gardner, "The Last Sitting," portrait photograph of Abraham Lincoln

Plate 16. Japanese surrender signatories aboard the USS *Missouri*, September 2, 1945 (U.S. National Archives and Records Administration)

Plate 17. General Douglas MacArthur signing the surrender document on the USS *Missouri*, September 2, 1945 (U.S. National Archives and Records Administration)

Plate 18. John Trumbull, *The Surrender of Cornwallis at Yorktown*

Underrepresentation and the Civil War

In the midst of so many copies, we are struck by occasions of their absence. As I noted earlier, Grant rejected the idea of a congressionally commissioned painting of the surrender at Appomattox. In addition, as an early twentieth-century historian put it, "No photographer was present at Appomattox, that supreme moment in our national history, when Americans met for the last time as foes on the field. Nothing but fanciful sketches exist of the scene inside the McLean home."[31] In this remarkably photographed war, it is indeed noteworthy that no photograph exists of Lee surrendering to Grant. Perhaps the absence of representation, or the presence of representations that are known to be the products of imagination and not of authorized witnesses, indicates something about the unrepresentability of surrenders after civil wars. Civil wars are demonstrably unnatural in ways noted earlier. Surrenders that bring about the reabsorption of errant brethren are perhaps better left in an uncommemorated past. This accords with a general theoretical aporia around civil wars described by Arno Mayer: "Tellingly, there is no treatise on civil war to equal Clausewitz's *On War*. To date, civil war has been essentially blind and wild, in part for being impregnated with vengeance and re-vengeance."[32] Civil war surrenders may remain a kind of blind spot, surrenders whose representation would reveal an impossible return.

On the Threshold of Assumptions and Divestments

> The gaze of the painter arrests the flux of phenomena, contemplates the visual field from a vantage-point outside the mobility of duration, in an eternal moment of disclosed presence; while in the moment of viewing, the viewing subject unites his gaze with the Founding Perception, in a moment of perfect recreation of that first epiphany.[33]

Chapter 1 promised a theoretical agenda that might link surrender, understood as a transfer of power and a reconfiguration of identity at conflict's end, to analogous social transformations. These events and situations include inaugurations, foundings, annunciations, coronations, resignations, marriages and divorces, sacrifices, and tributes. While varying in their focus on, and consequences for, individuals or collectivities, all these different types of events position their participants at the limits of their old worlds (on the "limen") and propel them into new ones. Identities change, names change, orientations in time and space change, loyalties change, commitments change, and rights change. The complex nature of these transformations of identity, fealty, sovereignty, and relationships must obviously be explored by examining specific empirical cases and the relevant media and actions of ratification and representation that carry these transitions forward in time.[34] But I may suggest a few things here at the end of this study of surrender.

Norman Bryson's insight about the connection between the viewing subject, gazing perhaps at a history painting, and the founding perception that crystallized the scene instantiates what I have been calling the network of cross-witnessing. It is in the context of such a network that founding perceptions anticipate literal foundings of societies, those occasions that are specifically in the business of arresting the flux of phenomena to declare the emergence of something new. In marking the gaps between the end of one regime and the beginning of another, surrenders are in this sense siblings to acts of founding as well as acts of resignation. We have already seen one famous national American image, John Trumbull's mural of George Washington resigning his commission (plate 6; one of eight such historical paintings lining the circumference of the rotunda of the United States Capitol).[35] This painting draws an important connection between surrenders and other signal events that make and mark social and political boundaries.

One of four scenes Trumbull painted for the rotunda, it marks a critical move by Washington to, in essence, surrender to Congress at the Annapolis Statehouse in 1783. Scholars have noted the importance of this voluntary resignation (as well as *President* Washington's later resignation) in allaying the anxiety about dictatorial, imperial interventions in the life of the new republic. I would go a step further. The positioning of this painting in the Capitol rotunda alongside that of the signing of the Declaration of Independence strikes me as key. The ability to incorporate a modality of surrender into the very fabric of a chartered founding gives legitimacy to the foundational act. There must be an end before there can be a beginning. And since the ends of surrender are always also restitutions, permanence and legitimacy are ensured through transition.

But foundings also and emphatically make the claim that they bring something new to the world. Thus they must look outside the extant, constituted system of legitimate social relations and borrow their authority from some other epistemological realm. Political theorist Bonnie Honig explicates the Derridean reading of this borrowing and writes, "No act of foundation . . . possesses resources adequate to guarantee itself . . . each and every one necessarily needs some external, systematically illegitimate guarantee to work."[36]

These systematically illegitimate guarantees can include the mythos of return, the divine right of kings, the idea of the king's two bodies, or simply the signatures of countersigners whose own authority is not imminently in need of further confirmation.

Enacting and representing such leaping social occasions becomes all the more complicated with this realization. As I noted earlier, Thomas Dumm has written of the several procedural and symbolic quandaries of enacting resignations, quandaries that bear precisely on the visible *site* of the resignation. Dumm understands resignations as "attempts to mark the site of a trauma, to contain it, and to remove its effects."[37] But what does the site look like? What form does it take—where trauma has once been and now is no longer, even as it still casts its shadow? It can be simply a white piece of paper, blank and expectant. Or it can be a piece of paper with a monogram or a letterhead. In assessing something as simple as the paper on which to write a letter of resignation, Dumm considers the complexity of using institutional letterhead. The person resigning is both still of the place and, immediately on writing the letter and signing it, not of the place. The paper and the signature are sites of transformation—sites that host, authorize, and perform these transformations. Linking the acts of resignation directly to the acts of original signing, we understand that resignings are made possible and conditioned by prior acts of signing, or signing *on to,* something. The twin acts of signing and re-signing are existentially linked.[38] Both the beginning and the end of tenure are marked by the signature, a signature that ironically undoes itself through this mirror-image repetition. Repetition functions in this context, as in others we have seen, as erasure. This suggests something important about the relation between beginnings and endings—that they are made of the same "stuff," and that it is the stuff of existence and identity.

Which finally brings me to my final question, a question I have had to pose to myself. Why, of the many sites and ceremonies of surrender historically documented, have I primarily chosen to investigate scenes of surrender that expresses decorum and magnanimity above all else? The surrenders at Breda and at Appomattox have been assessed as magnanimous in their terms and in their treatment of the vanquished generals. The surrender on the USS *Missouri* is framed in a more stringent manner—after all, it was "unconditional." Nevertheless, the Japanese emperor was allowed to remain sovereign. As Toshikazu Kase, a Japanese diplomat and member of the party boarding the ship to sign the surrender documents, recounts, "Here is the victor [MacArthur] announcing the verdict to the prostrate enemy. He can impose a humiliating penalty if he so desires. And yet he pleads for freedom, tolerance and justice. For me, who expected the worst humiliation, this was a complete surprise."[39] As noted earlier, art scholars have indicated that conventional artistic representations of surrender show triumph of the victor and humiliation and supplication of the vanquished.[40] Perhaps the alternative emphasis here reflects my own diffidence in the face of humiliation, my own inclination to turn away from scenes of shame. Or is it perhaps simply that episodes of magnanimity generate the most lavish representational trail?

Magnanimous ceremonies of surrender can be viewed as acts of partial salvaging (of reputations, identity, honor). Even where the cause of one's enemy is reviled, the bravery or honor of the warrior can be recognized. In his memoirs, General Grant wrote that on seeing and shaking hands with General Lee, "I felt anything rather than rejoicing at the downfall of a foe who had fought so long and valiantly, and had suffered so much for a cause, though that cause was, I believe, one of the worst for which a people ever fought, and one for which there was the least excuse."[41]

Salvaging missions are knives that can cut both ways, as anyone knows who has read about the development of formulas for surrender after World War I and then after World War II. Nevertheless, they may reveal something about our deepest human longings. Writing about the *Iliad,* Jorge Luis Borges noted, "Men have sought kinship with the defeated Trojans, and not with the victorious Greeks. This is perhaps because there is a dignity in defeat that hardly belongs to victory."[42] While the vanquished is the direct beneficiary of magnanimity, such gestures are always performed for the third party: the observer, the witness, the sovereign authority, other sovereign authorities in a world system, History with a capital *H*. They are the gestures of a power that is attempting, for whatever motive and for however brief a moment, to suture the timeline where power, myth, and history intersect.

Notes

CHAPTER ONE

1. This section was probably politically censored and left out of the First Quarto text of the play (1597) but reinstated in the First Folio of 1623.
2. J. L. Austin, *How to Do Things with Words,* 2nd ed. (Cambridge, MA: Harvard University Press, 1975); italics mine.
3. Giorgio Agamben, *Remnants of Auschwitz: The Witness and the Archive,* trans. Daniel Heller-Roazen (New York: Zone Books, 1999), 106–7.
4. William Shakespeare, *Richard II,* 4.1.202–22. The linguist Émile Benveniste asserts a fundamental difference between the first-person and second-person pronouns "I" and "you" and those of the third person. Of the "I," Benveniste writes that it "signifies the person uttering the present instance of discourse containing I." On the contrary, third-person pronouns "only serve as abbreviated substitutes" and have the property of "never being reflective of the instance of discourse." Émile Benveniste, "The Nature of Pronouns," in *Problems in General Linguistics,* ed. Émile Benveniste, trans. Mary Elizabeth Meek (Coral Gables, FL: University of Miami Press, 1971), 218. Thus Richard's switch from I to "Richard" indicates a radical rupture in the self and the concomitant loss of agency as Richard becomes the substitute for an "I" no longer agentic in the present discursive situation.
5. It is a fact of the brutality of war that slaughters often occur when soldiers or civilians are literally not allowed to surrender. Writing about the bloody campaign of the Confederate guerrilla fighter Nathan Bedford Forrest to take the Union garrison Fort Pillow during the Civil War, Jay Winik notes that "many of the blacks, estimated at 100—and a number of whites as well—were not allowed to surrender and were butchered in cold blood instead, even as they fell to their knees and with uplifted hands screamed for mercy." Jay Winik, *April 1865: The Month That Saved America* (New York: HarperCollins, 2001), 281.
6. See the discussion of changing shapes of genres in Wendy Griswold, "A Methodological Framework for the Sociology of Culture," in *Sociological Methodology,* vol. 17, ed. Clifford Clogg (Washington, DC: American Sociological Association,

1987), 1–35. Also see the discussion of discourse genres and their necessary evolution by William Hanks: "Practice as inscribed in time is always de-totalized, in that it remains unfinished and emergent. Hence, the unitary wholeness of genre, which is axiomatic in formalist approaches, becomes a problematic achievement in a practice-based framework . . . Hence neither the genre nor the individual work can be viewed as a finished product unto itself, but remains partial and transitional." William Hanks, "Discourse Genres in a Theory of Practice," *American Ethnologist* 14, no. 4 (1987): 681.

7. See Barbara Donagan, "Codes and Conduct in the English Civil War," *Past and Present,* no. 118 (1988): 65–95. Writing about the surrender of the Parliamentary Foot at Lostwithiel in 1644, Donagan describes an instance of the latter form of betrayal when the Cornish people attacked the retreating Parliamentarians after they had surrendered. In spite of the treachery of the Royalist populace, however, Donagan points to the generally progressive development of codified agreements such as this one: "Articles of surrender provided a restraining framework rather than a guarantee of performance. The attempts of authorities to enforce them rather than to collaborate in their breach was in itself a brake on the legitimation of revenge" (91).

8. Patricia Seed's discussion of the development of the Spanish "Requirement" (declaration of war) in *Ceremonies of Possession in Europe's Conquest of the New World, 1492–1640* (Cambridge: Cambridge University Press, 1995), which was read as a central part of the Spanish sixteenth-century possession ceremonies in New World colonies, demonstrates the Islamic roots of this official document: "The Requirement most closely resembles the unique ritual demand for submission characteristic of the military version of an Islamic jihad" (72). Nevertheless, these incorporated Islamic conventions and ideas could not, according to Seed, be overtly acknowledged by the Spanish, for whom Islam remained the enemy: "Since enemies, even mirror-image ones, deny each other's legitimacy, traditional Islamic customs could not be acknowledged as a model for Spanish political authority" (93).

9. For an interesting analysis of the contested meanings of sixteenth-century Tudor martyrs, in which those ritualistically burned at the stake were suspected of suicide rather than martyrdom, see Seymour Byman, "Ritualistic Acts and Compulsive Behavior: The Pattern of Tudor Martyrdom," *American Historical Review* 83, no. 3 (1978): 625–43. The key to such diacritical moves turns out to have been the martyrs' participation in highly formalized behavior up to and including their burning at the stake.

10. Yael Zerubavel, *Recovered Roots: Collective Memory and the Making of Israeli National Tradition* (Chicago: University of Chicago Press, 1995).

11. Frontline, "Waco: The Inside Story," page 5 of transcript. ABC television documentary, October 17, 1995.

12. James Tabor, "Religious Discourse," in *Armageddon in Waco,* ed. Stuart Wright (Chicago: University of Chicago Press, 1995), 266.

13. Peter Burke, *Eyewitnessing: The Uses of Images as Historical Evidence* (Ithaca, NY: Cornell University Press, 2001), 149.

14. Chandra Mukerji, "The Political Mobilization of Nature in 17th Century French Formal Gardens," *Theory and Society* 23 (1994): 651–77.

15. Discussing the evolution of knighthood and its relation to the economic and political autonomy and dependency of cities and towns, Michael Harney notes, "Both epic and chivalric romance are preoccupied with sieges. However, while in the former genre the protagonist is the besieger, in the romance the hero sides with the besieged." Michael Harney, "Siege Warfare in Medieval Hispanic Epic and Romance," in *The Medieval City under Siege,* ed. Ivy A. Corfis and Michael Wolfe (Woodbridge, UK: Boydell, 1995), 179.

16. Jorge Arditi, *A Genealogy of Manners: Transformations of Social Relations in France and England from the Fourteenth to the Eighteenth Century* (Chicago: University of Chicago Press, 1998), 77. In a similar manner, art historian Hubert Damisch discusses the opportunism of social forms that utilize rather than promote emergent aesthetic genres. Describing the illusionistic perspectivalism of the Renaissance theatrical stage, he notes, "One can maintain that this form of theater corresponded in allegorical terms to the ideal of an aristocratic society, centered on the figure of the prince, and that it implied a radical transformation of the scenic conception of the Middle Ages: while the medieval theater addressed a popular or 'democratic' public, its scenic elements consisting of facing 'houses' so disposed that spectators could move to keep track of the unfolding action, the Italian theater conformed to another conception. But does this mean that the perspective scene was able to prevail only in the age of absolutism, when architects were charged with the task of conceiving theaters for the few and primarily for the pleasure of the prince, who was to be placed in a privileged position? . . . On the contrary, absolutist discourse discovered the advantages deriving from such a configuration only belatedly." Hubert Damisch, *The Origin of Perspective,* trans. John Goodman (Cambridge, MA: MIT Press, 1995), 396–97.

17. Paul Kecskemeti, *Strategic Surrender* (Stanford, CA: Stanford University Press, 1958), 5.

18. Arditi notes, "The emergence of practices leading to an assuagement of dispersed forms of violence, both through the establishment of a formal apparatus of law and through transformations in behavior, therefore involves a complete reconfiguration of the body politic and generates the conditions for the concentration of the means of violence conducive to the development of the modern nation-state." Arditi, *Genealogy of Manners,* 63.

19. Bombardment alternated with starvation as the primary method used by the besieger, this alternation being a function of the ability of the walls of a city or bastion to withstand the enemy's attack. Strong medieval walls could defend against catapults and rams, but not against the gunpowder-fueled cannon called the bombard. In its turn, the architecture of the bastion walls developed the innovation of the *trace italienne,* a new type of fortification with low walls made of a thick, sloping earth layer and external ditches. The key to the *trace italienne* lay in the external geometry of these walls and in the fact that cannonballs fired against them would bury themselves in the soil. Bert Hall writes about the changing face of siege warfare, "It soon became clear that a town protected by

the *trace italienne* could not be captured by the traditional methods of battery and assault. It had to be encircled and starved into surrender. This meant that warfare lost much of its earlier mobility and fluidity, becoming instead a 'struggle for strongholds, a series of protracted sieges.'" Bert S. Hall, "The Changing Face of Siege Warfare: Technology and Tactics in Transition," in *The Medieval City under Siege,* ed. Ivy A. Corfis and Michael Wolfe (Woodbridge, UK: Boydell, 1995), 260.

20. John W. Wright, "Sieges and Customs of War at the Opening of the Eighteenth Century," *American Historical Review* 39, no. 4 (1934): 629.

21. Referring to General McClellan's dismissal and the appointment of such "new men" as Grant, Sherman, and Sheridan, Wolfgang Schivelbusch notes how these new men "readily adapted modern industrial methods to the conduct of war, an innovation that produced—among other things—the scorched earth policy." Wolfgang Schivelbusch, *The Culture of Defeat,* trans. Jefferson Chase (New York: Henry Holt, 2003), 57.

22. Barbie Zelizer, *Remembering to Forget: Holocaust Memory through the Camera's Eye* (Chicago: University of Chicago Press, 1998), 11.

23. Colonel Bertram Kalisch, of the United States Army, was chosen to direct all the pictorial coverage of the signing of the surrender documents, being assigned one deputy from each of the three United States services. In his recounting of the logistics and decisions about this coverage, he notes that the USS *Missouri*'s main deck "offered daylight for the photographic units, as well as more space for all concerned." Bertram Kalisch, "Photographing the Surrender Aboard the USS *Missouri,*" *Proceedings of the United States Naval Institute* 81, no. 8 (1955): 867.

24. Bernard Weinraub, "Threats and Responses: Articles of Capitulation. Iraqis Told 'Sign Here' to Surrender—as Lee Did," *New York Times,* May 20, 2003, A14, col. 6. But of course surrender is a tricky business, and several of these Iraqi troops feigned surrender with white flags as a way of drawing the United States forces into an ambush.

25. Albert Gore's concession speech, printed in the *New York Times,* December 14, 2000, A26.

26. Quincy Wright, "How Hostilities Have Ended: Peace Treaties and Alternatives," *Annals of the American Academy of Political and Social Science* 392 (1970): 59. Virginia Page Fortna, a political scientist studying the durability of peace, finds some benefit to conclusions of conflict that end more definitively: "Wars that end in a tie are much (twenty-seven times) more likely to be repeated than those that end with a decisive victory for one side." Virginia Page Fortna, "Scraps of Paper? Agreements and the Durability of Peace," *International Organization,* 57, no. 2 (2003): 351.

27. Randall Collins, "Forward Panic," chap. 3 in *Violent Conflict* (forthcoming, 2006), 7.

28. Niall Ferguson, "Prisoner Taking and Prisoner Killing in the Age of Total War," *War in History* 11, no. 2 (2004): 151. Ferguson notes that most surrenders do indeed involve collectivities—units or whole armies as opposed to individual soldiers (153).

29. On the state of field theory generally in sociology, see John Levi Martin, "What Is Field Theory?" *American Journal of Sociology* 109 (2003): 1–49.

30. This advance draws from the work of such linguistic anthropologists as Michael Silverstein, whose analysis of deictics, or "shifters," incorporates both the pragmatic work of context-dependent switches of pronouns and adverbs of time and space and the subtending referential meanings as well. As Silverstein writes, "Deictics, as we saw, presuppose the referent from previous discourse, for example, as well as the speaker or hearer location, and refer to the locus of the presupposed referent relative to that of speaker or hearer." Michael Silverstein, "Shifters, Linguistic Categories, and Cultural Description," in *Language, Culture, and Society,* 2nd ed., ed. Benjamin Blount (Prospect Heights, IL: Waveland Press, 1995), 212.

31. On this dialectic see Jeffrey C. Alexander's article "Cultural Pragmatics: Social Performance between Ritual and Strategy," *Sociological Theory* 22, no. 4 (2004), and Bonnie Honig, "Declarations of Independence: Arendt and Derrida on the Problem of Founding a Republic," in *Rhetorical Republic: Governing Representation in American Politics,* ed. Frederick M. Dolan and Thomas L. Dumm (Amherst: University of Massachusetts Press, 1993), 202–15.

32. Pierre Bourdieu, "The Force of Law: Toward a Sociology of the Juridical Field," *Hastings Law Journal* 38 (July 1987): page 1 of downloaded article.

33. Algirdas J. Greimas, *On Meaning: Selected Writings in Semiotic Theory,* trans. Paul J. Perron and Frank H. Collins (Minneapolis: University of Minnesota Press, 1997), 23.

34. For an analysis of the temporal, spatial, and action parameters of another archetypal social situation, the standoff, see Robin Wagner-Pacifici, *Theorizing the Standoff: Contingency in Action* (Cambridge: Cambridge University Press, 2000). The current study of surrender represents an attempt to work with and expand beyond the analytical program articulated in that book.

35. William Ian Miller, "Weak Legs: Misbehavior Before the Enemy," *Representations* 70 (Spring 2000): 36.

36. Art historian Rudolf Arnheim develops an alternative semiotic schema with the analogous terms "centricity" and "eccentricity." Unlike Greimas, Arnheim idealizes a certain concept of balance (both psychological and figural) in which "neither total self-centeredness nor total surrender to outer powers can make for an acceptable image of human motivation." Rudolf Arnheim, *The Power of the Center* (Berkeley: University of California Press, 1988), 2.

37. In his book *Lee at Appomattox and Other Papers,* Charles Francis Adams recounts the following scene between General Robert E. Lee and Henry Wise, a former governor of Virginia. Wise, having grown impatient with General Lee's refusal to see that he was in an endgame with General Grant during the waning days of his campaign in the United States Civil War, responds tellingly to a question posed by Lee: "Growing more serious, General Lee inquired what he thought of the situation. 'Situation?' said the bold old man. 'There is no situation! Nothing remains General Lee but to put your poor men on your poor mules and send them home in time for spring ploughing.'" Charles Francis Adams, *Lee at Appomattox and Other Papers* (New York: Houghton, Mifflin, 1902), 7.

38. *Oxford English Dictionary—Online Edition* (Oxford: Oxford University Press, 1989).
39. *OED* definition 1b of "surrender" as a verb states, "To give up (letters patent, tithes) into the hands of the sovereign." *Oxford English Dictionary—Online Edition* (Oxford: Oxford University Press, 1989).
40. Ibid. *OED* definition 2 states, "To give up (something) out of one's own possession or power into that of another who has or asserts a claim to it . . . to give up the possession of (a fortress, town, territory) to an enemy or assailant."
41. The earliest examples provided for both of these meanings come from the fifteenth century.
42. The absence of such an authority at conflict's end militates against surrender as an option for termination. Referring to the imminent end of the European phase of World War II, Reiner Hansen writes: "Towards the end of March 1945, the British government became convinced that once Germany had been completely overpowered, there would in all probability no longer be any military or civil authority capable of signing such an instrument of surrender. As a consequence, the victors would have to resort to a different procedure and unilaterally proclaim total German defeat and their assumption of supreme authority in Germany. Accordingly, the surrender document was redrafted by the European Advisory Commission into the form of a declaration." Reiner Hansen, "Germany's Unconditional Surrender," *History Today* 45, no. 5 (1995): 34. A more contemporary example comes from the second Gulf War of 2003. Referring to a photograph of American military commanders sitting behind a table and surveying the scene at one of Saddam Hussein's palaces, Wolfgang Schivelbusch noted that, unlike at previous surrender ceremonies, "there were no vanquished on the other side of the table . . . The absence of the vanquished from their place at the table of surrender resonated as a sinister silence, like a tragedy ending without a dying hero's last words." Wolfgang Schivelbusch, "The Loneliest Victors," *New York Times,* April 22, 2003, A25. These absences at the ultimate scenes of surrender raise the important issue of the variable relation between small surrenders of individual soldiers or military units and large surrenders of armies and political leaders, an issue I will address at length in chapter 4.
43. Jacques Derrida, *Given Time: I. Counterfeit Money,* trans. Peggy Kamuf (Chicago: University of Chicago Press, 1992).
44. Maurice Godelier, *The Enigma of the Gift,* trans. Nora Scott (Chicago: University of Chicago Press, 1999), 12.
45. Stephen Greenblatt develops an analysis of this weaving together of the religious and secular imperatives of what he calls "Christian imperialism" in his discussion of Columbus's acts of taking possession of the New World for the Spanish Crown in *Marvelous Possessions: The Wonder of the New World* (Chicago: University of Chicago Press, 1991), 68–72.
46. It is interesting that contemporary theorists and practitioners of "conflict resolution" never use the term "surrender." According to political scientist Marc Howard Ross, it is not in their vocabulary—partly for its imperialist loading and

partly because surrender is, despite its apparent clarity, understood never to really resolve things.

47. In our radically postmodern world, a world in which events are decontextualized and only loosely connected, it is fascinating to find this cyclical notion of retaking retooled by the mass media representations of historical events. At the end of the first Gulf War, CBS news anchor Dan Rather consciously juxtaposed images from the Vietnam War and the Gulf War to make visually clear the notion of historical return, articulated publicly by then President George H. W. Bush. W. J. T. Mitchell writes about this occurrence, "As George Bush so aptly put it: 'The specter of Vietnam has been buried forever in the desert sands of the Arabian Peninsula.' Or perhaps the moral was put more pointedly by Dan Rather, as he juxtaposed file footage of the last U.S. helicopter rising from the American embassy in Saigon with live footage of a helicopter landing at our embassy in Kuwait City." W. J. T. Mitchell, *Picture Theory* (Chicago: University of Chicago Press, 1994), 16.

48. Kyoko Inoue, *MacArthur's Japanese Constitution: A Linguistic and Cultural Study of Its Making* (Chicago: University of Chicago Press, 1991), 7. Inoue provides an explanation for this nuance in the configuration of subordination: "It appears that the Foreign Ministry 'inaccurately' translated two key phrases to prevent further opposition by the extremist military commanders and then defended its translations by insisting that it had the prerogative of providing the official interpretation of all diplomatic documents" (7).

49. Ferguson, "Prisoner Taking and Prisoner Killing," 174.

50. Many thanks to both Kennosuke and Aya Ezawa for these sociolinguistic clarifications.

51. Wright, "Sieges and Customs of War," 639.

52. Quoted in Adams, *Lee at Appomattox and Other Papers*, 6.

53. Hannah Arendt, *The Human Condition* (Chicago: University of Chicago Press, 1958), 244, 246.

54. Thanks to Jonathan LeBreton for recalling that Grant sent food to the starving soldiers in Lee's army during the settling of the surrender agreement.

55. Pierre Bourdieu, "Structures, Habitus, Power: Basis for a Theory of Symbolic Power," in *Culture/Power/History: A Reader in Contemporary Social Theory*, ed. Nicholas B. Dirks, Geoff Eley, and Sherry Ortner (Princeton, NJ: Princeton University Press, 1994), 196.

56. Jonathan Crary, *Techniques of the Observer: On Vision and Modernity in the Nineteenth Century* (Cambridge, MA: MIT Press, 1991), 98.

57. In another context, I have put forward a model of the relation between what I call ur-texts and texts-in-action. Certain historically sedimented and paradigmatic texts are typically referenced and quoted in the contingent, action-oriented texts of ongoing social situations. For a discussion of this model, see Wagner-Pacifici, *Theorizing the Standoff*.

58. Roger Chartier, *On the Edge of the Cliff: History, Language, and Practices*, trans. Lydia G. Cochrane (Baltimore: Johns Hopkins University Press, 1997), 99.

59. On this gap see Jacques Derrida, *Margins of Philosophy,* trans. Alan Bass (Chicago: University of Chicago Press, 1982), and Alexander, "Cultural Pragmatics."

60. Louis Marin, "Towards a Theory of Reading in the Visual Arts: Poussin's 'The Arcadian Shepherds,'" in *Calligram: Essays in New Art History from France,* ed. Norman Bryson (Cambridge: Cambridge University Press, 1988), 72.

61. Luc Boltanski adumbrates Adam Smith's formulation of the ideal spectator in this way: "Smith defines a model or a structure that is a system of places comprising positions whose occupants are not specified. Each anticipates how he will be imagined by the other and the composition of these anticipations generates an equilibrium." Luc Boltanski, *Distant Suffering: Morality, Media, and Politics* (Cambridge: Cambridge University Press, 1999), 39.

62. Crary, *Techniques of the Observer;* Wendy Steiner, *Pictures of Romance: Form against Context in Painting and Literature* (Chicago: University of Chicago Press, 1988); Marin, "Towards a Theory of Reading in the Visual Arts"; Michel Foucault, *The Order of Things: An Archeology of the Human Sciences* (New York: Pantheon, 1971); and Svetlana Alpers, *The Art of Describing: Dutch Art in the Seventeenth Century* (Chicago: University of Chicago Press, 1983).

63. Crary, *Techniques of the Observer,* 34.

64. See Gridley McKim-Smith and Marcia L. Welles, "Topographical Tropes: The Mapping of Breda in Calderón, Callot, and Velázquez," *Indiana Journal of Hispanic Literatures* 10, no. 1 (1992): 185–212: "As though subjected to a process of distillation, the myriad events of the historical narrative occurring as a process over time are purified of extraneous materials and reduced to one essential timeless event in the painting" (188).

65. Marin, "Towards a Theory of Reading in the Visual Arts," 67.

66. As I noted earlier, Chandra Mukerji makes the case that landscape and landscape design must also be read as a representational medium that constitutes the power of the copy: "The conquests of the French army were not just written about in celebratory languages, but dug into hillsides and dredged along waterways." Mukerji, "Political Mobilization of Nature," 652.

67. Ernst Kantorowicz discusses the progress of the problem of continuity of kings and the thirteenth-century innovation regarding ceremonies of coronation: "Both France and England thus succeeded in abolishing the 'little interregnum' arising between the king's accession and his coronation . . . The new king's government was legalized by God and the people alone, opulo faciente et Deo inspirante. The Church, as Marsiglio of Padua said, had merely to 'signify.'" Ernst Kantorowicz, *The King's Two Bodies: A Study in Mediaeval Political Theology* (Princeton, NJ: Princeton University Press, 1957), 329.

CHAPTER TWO

1. The difference between cosigners and countersigners is important for mapping the role of the witness. Cosigners share in the collective action of bringing something into being or of undoing something that exists. Countersigners guarantee

the first-line signatures. In spite of these structural differences, witnesses can be either cosigners (in which case all signers may witness each others' signing) or countersigners (ratifying the authenticity and authority of the first-line signers). In her careful consideration of Hannah Arendt's and Jacques Derrida's readings of the problem of founding a republic, Bonnie Honig notes that cosigners figure in Arendt's analysis of the "we" in "We hold . . . ," while countersigners are called forth by Derrida's recognition of the need for "another subjectivity . . . to sign, in order to guarantee it, this production of signature." Bonnie Honig, "Declarations of Independence: Arendt and Derrida on the Problem of Founding a Republic," in *Rhetorical Republic: Governing Representations in American Politics,* ed. Frederick M. Dolan and Thomas L. Dumm (Amherst: University of Massachusetts Press, 1993), 212.

2. Jonathan Brown and J. H. Elliott, *A Palace for a King: The Buen Retiro and the Court of Philip IV* (New Haven, CT: Yale University Press, 1980), 178.

3. Ibid., 179.

4. Chandra Mukerji, "Unspoken Assumptions: Voice and Absolutism at the Court of Louis XIV," *Journal of Historical Sociology* 11, no. 3 (1998): 286. For the development of the military drill and its importance in increasing efficiency and obedience of the soldiers in sixteenth- and seventeenth-century Western Europe, see William H. McNeill, *The Pursuit of Power: Technology, Armed Force, and Society since A.D. 1000* (Chicago: University of Chicago Press, 1982).

5. Jonathan I. Israel, *The Dutch Republic and the Hispanic World: 1606–1661* (Oxford: Clarendon Press, 1982), 107.

6. McNeill, *Pursuit of Power,* 128.

7. Gerrat Barry quoted in Brown and Elliott, *Palace for a King,* 179.

8. Ibid., 181.

9. Christine Smith writes, "Spinola's leniency in the treaty of Breda did not wholly meet with Spanish approval. We know that later, in 1630, when he had successfully besieged Casale and was about to negotiate peace, Count Olivares deprived him of this power and fixed the terms himself. To this Spinola could only say: 'They have taken my honour.' He is said to have been so broken by this that it was the cause of his death a few weeks later." Christine Smith, "Sources for 'The Surrender of Breda' by Diego Velázquez," *Vassar Journal of Undergraduate Studies* 20 (1966): 6.

10. Geoffrey Parker dates this Dutch retaking of Breda to 1637 (though there is some disagreement on this date). See Geoffrey Parker, ed., *The Thirty Years' War,* 2nd ed. (New York: Routledge, 1997).

11. "The enemy left in good order in files of four . . . Our troops lined up in two parallel rows forming an avenue between which they passed until they had all marched away. Then the keys of the fortress were turned over [to Spinola]." Translated and quoted in John F. Moffitt, "Diego Velázquez, Andrea Alciati and the Surrender of Breda," *Artibus et Historiae* 3, no. 5 (1982): 86.

12. Quoted in Smith, "Sources for 'The Surrender of Breda,'" 6.

13. Shirley B. Whitaker, "The First Performance of Calderón's *El Sitio de Breda,*" *Renaissance Quarterly* 31, no. 4 (1978): 526.

14. Svetlana Alpers, *The Art of Describing: Dutch Art in the Seventeenth Century* (Chicago: University of Chicago Press, 1983), 139.

15. Gridley McKim-Smith and Marcia L. Welles, "Topographical Tropes: The Mapping of Breda in Calderón, Callot, and Velázquez," *Indiana Journal of Hispanic Literatures* 10, no. 1 (1992): 194.

16. Patricia Seed, *Ceremonies of Possession in Europe's Conquest of the New World, 1492–1640* (Cambridge: Cambridge University Press, 1995), 160.

17. In terms of the kind of map-inspired self-recognition of dynastic subjects transformed into nationalists, Richard Helgerson notes that "nowhere was this impact greater than in the Netherlands . . . Through eighty years of intermittent war, from the 1560s to the 1640s, the Dutch fought to free themselves from their monarchic overlord, the king of Spain. In those circumstances, maps had an extraordinarily potent effect. They stood almost alone for the nation and for whatever national identity the Dutch managed to forge . . . In the Netherlands maps—most particularly the survey ordered by the Habsburg emperor Charles V, when in the 1540s he decided to unite the seventeen provinces as a single administrative unit—made the nation." Richard Helgerson, "The Folly of Maps and Modernity," in *Literature, Mapping, and the Politics of Space in Early Modern Britain,* ed. Andrew Gordon and Bernhard Klein (Cambridge: Cambridge University Press, 2001), 253.

18. Seed, *Ceremonies of Possession,* 168.

19. Martin Jay, "Scopic Regimes of Modernity," in *Vision and Visuality,* ed. Hal Foster (Seattle, WA: Bay Press, 1988), 12.

20. McKim-Smith and Welles, "Topographical Tropes," 194.

21. "If the commander [of a fortress] surrendered prematurely, he was brought to trial before a military tribunal; and in such cases the penalties were mandatory." John W. Wright, "Sieges and Customs of War at the Opening of the Eighteenth Century," *American Historical Review* 39, no. 4 (1934): 630. Note also that a commander could be accused of an "overripe" surrender.

22. Svetlana Alpers writes that "despite the mapped background (Velázquez's art contained much of what I am considering as the northern mode), Velázquez presents a human relationship steeped in artistic tradition, which he further stages on the basis of the account of Breda given in a contemporary play . . . To record history in maps and their related illustrations is to emphasize certain aspects rather than others: history is pictured by putting before our eyes an enriched description of the place rather than the drama of human events." Alpers, *The Art of Describing,* 161.

23. I thank T. Kaori Kitao for this apt and poignant phrase.

24. Brown and Elliott, *Palace for a King,* 180.

25. Giorgio Agamben, *Remnants of Auschwitz: The Witness and the Archive,* ed. and trans. Daniel Heller-Roazen (New York: Zone Books, 1999), 26.

26. Ibid., 17.

27. Here it is important to note the distinction, remarked on by Jacques Derrida, between testimony understood as an essentially moral act of "sworn faith" and testimony as evidence in a legal proof: "Bearing witness is heterogeneous to the

administration of a legal proof or the display of an object produced in evidence. Witnessing appeals to the act of faith with regard to a speech given under oath." Jacques Derrida, "'A Self-Unsealing Poetic Text': Poetics and Politics of Witnessing," trans. Rachel Bowlby, in *Revenge of the Aesthetic: The Place of Literature in Theory Today,* ed. Michael P. Clark (Berkeley: University of California Press, 2000), 188. Consideration of the hybrid nature of witnessing as performative, demonstrative, and representational provides a way of analytically teasing apart these often copresent understandings of the act of testimony.

28. Hillel Schwartz, *The Culture of the Copy: Striking Likenesses, Unreasonable Facsimiles* (New York: Zone Books, 1996), 214.

29. Ibid.

30. Donald Black, *The Social Structure of Right and Wrong* (San Diego, CA: Academic Press, 1998), 97.

31. H. E. Goemans, *War and Punishment: The Causes of War Termination and the First World War* (Princeton, NJ: Princeton University Press, 2000), 33.

32. Agamben, *Remnants of Auschwitz,* 35.

33. Philippe-Joseph Salazar, "Rhetoric and Reconciliation in South Africa: Arguing for Democracy in the New Millennium," paper presented at Swarthmore College, 1999.

34. Erving Goffman, *Forms of Talk* (Philadelphia: University of Pennsylvania Press, 1981), 128.

35. Barbie Zelizer, *Remembering to Forget: Holocaust Memory through the Camera's Eye* (Chicago: University of Chicago Press, 1998), 73.

36. Zelizer, *Remembering to Forget,* 102.

37. Salazar, "Rhetoric and Reconciliation," 9.

38. The transformation of soldiers into witnesses is a common aspect of surrender ceremonies. Brigadier General Joshua Lawrence Chamberlain was the Union officer in charge of the surrender ceremony at Appomattox in the ending days of the American Civil War. In the journal he kept of that ceremony, he wrote about the demeanor and experience of the Union soldiers, now dispatched as witnesses to the formal surrender of Confederate arms: "On our part not a sound of trumpet more, nor roll of drum; not a cheer, nor word, nor whisper or vaingorying . . . but an awed stillness rather, and breath-holding, as if it were the passing of the dead . . . How could we help falling on our knees, all of us together, and praying God to pity and forgive us all!" Quoted in Jay Winik, *April 1865: The Month That Saved America* (New York: HarperCollins, 2001), 197–98.

39. Brown and Elliott, *Palace for a King,* 181.

40. Brown and Elliott are undisturbed by the distraction. They note the disaligned witnesses and conclude: "For the onlookers, the ceremony seems to be one of those important but fleeting moments of history that come and go before you can take it in. A few of the soldiers turn toward the two main figures, but most of them seem to be caught by inner or outer distractions" (ibid., 184).

41. Onlookers and eavesdroppers can become witnesses, but only if their observations of the scene are drawn up into its sedimenting meaning. Barbie Zelizer writes about the varieties of witnesses witnessing the liberation of the concen-

tration camps and the mechanisms of their inclusion: "The most common way of representing the act of witnessing was in layers: liberated inmates watched German civilians, reporters watched officials, and everyone watched the corpses. One reporter watched a US soldier who in turn watched a group of German civilians. The horror of it caused many women to faint. Others sobbed and put their hands to their eyes . . . An American MP ordered them to take their hands down. He told them to have a good look and never forget what they had seen." Zelizer, *Remembering to Forget,* 72.

42. Jonathan Crary, *Techniques of the Observer: On Vision and Modernity in the Nineteenth Century* (Cambridge, MA: MIT Press, 1991), 52.

43. Martin Meisel, *Realizations: Narrative, Pictorial, and Theatrical Arts in Nineteenth-Century England* (Princeton, NJ: Princeton University Press, 1983), 45.

44. Crary writes, "But the movement and temporality so evident in the camera obscura were always prior to the act of representation; movement and time could be seen and experienced, but never represented." Crary, *Techniques of the Observer,* 34.

45. Alpers, *Art of Describing;* Norman Bryson, "The Gaze in the Expanded Field," in *Vision and Visuality,* ed. Hal Foster (Seattle, WA: Bay Press, 1988); Jay, "Scopic Regimes of Modernity"; Louis Marin, "Towards a Theory of Reading in the Visual Arts: Poussin's 'The Arcadian Shepherds,'" in *The Art of Art History: A Critical Anthology,* ed. Donald Preziosi (Oxford: Oxford University Press, 1998); and Meisel, *Realizations.*

46. Wendy Steiner, *Pictures of Romance: Form against Context in Painting and Literature* (Chicago: University of Chicago Press, 1988).

47. Michael Fried, *Absorption and Theatricality: Painting and Beholder in the Age of Diderot* (Berkeley: University of California Press, 1980). Children often reveal themselves to be the purest and thus most recalcitrant of witnesses. They look where they want to and avert their gaze aggressively. Barbie Zelizer notes that "German children were portrayed in a refusal to bear witness: one shot showed a small boy looking straight at the camera and away from the bodies that took up the majority of photographic space, his glance communicating an act of witnessing that was in essence not-witnessing." Zelizer, *Remembering to Forget,* 104.

48. In his analysis of the deictic, or indexical, network of Poussin's *Arcadian Shepherds,* Louis Marin considers the apparent absence of a source of enunciation for the painting. He writes, "Now, if the characteristic of the 'historical' enunciative modality is that events narrate themselves in the story as if nobody were speaking, this means that the whole deictic network has to be erased in the narrative message." Marin, "Towards a Theory of Reading," 263. But this merely raises the question, in the context of historical painting, Who gets to be Nobody? Assuming that Nobody is the victor is probabilistically reasonable. Yet Velázquez's painting seems, improbably, to incorporate both victor and vanquished in the Nobody of the enunciative modality.

49. Thanks to Professor James Maraniss for assistance with the translation and interpretation of *El sitio de Breda.*

50. Benedict Anderson's discussion of the importance of the daily newspaper is directly relevant here. Overcoming spatial and temporal distance is precisely the

task of newspapers. By dint of this overcoming, they make possible a solidary politics of the nation. See Benedict Anderson, *Imagined Communities: Reflections on the Origin and Spread of Nationalism* (London: Verso Press, 1991).

51. Meisel, *Realizations,* 22. John Durham Peters finds philosophical resonance for this in John Locke's *Essay concerning Human Understanding.* Peters says of Locke that "among the various standards he offers [for believing the reports of others], key is a hierarchy of testimony determined by the witness's proximity to the event: 'any Testimony, the farther off it is from the original Truth, the less force and proof it has.'" John Durham Peters, "Witnessing," *Media, Culture and Society* 23 (2001): 723.

52. In chapter 3 I examine Hugo's rendering of the path to and terms of the surrender of Breda.

53. Peters, "Witnessing," 726.

54. In his analysis of referential practices of native speakers of Yucatec Maya, anthropologist William Hanks refers to these various modalities of knowing and referencing as "Ostensive Evidential adverbs," the evidential basis of which "is reflected in the clear focus of the forms on the sensory access that participants have to referents—tactual, visual, auditory—olfactory, or known for certain without current evidence." William Hanks, "Metalanguage and Pragmatics of Deixis," in *Intertexts: Writings on Language, Utterance, and Context* (New York: Rowman and Littlefield, 2000), 85–86.

55. W. J. T. Mitchell, *Picture Theory* (Chicago: University of Chicago Press, 1994), 5. Mitchell is himself attempting to move across the channels, to actually picture theory (as opposed to theorizing in language about pictures).

56. Of course, presence is ratified only ex post facto, through the traces it leaves. Derrida writes about the impossibility of contemporaneous revelation of presence and does so by insisting on a grammatical future perfect past: "The witness is the one who will have been present. He or she will have attended, in the present, the thing of which he is witness." Derrida, "Self-Unsealing Poetic Text," 187.

57. Hannah Arendt, *On Revolution* (New York: Viking Press, 1963), 81.

58. Luc Boltanski, *Distant Suffering: Morality, Media and Politics* (Cambridge: Cambridge University Press, 1999), 7.

59. Conversely, distanced observation may take steps to meet the criteria of proximal witnessing. One might read Boltanski's adumbration of the spectator's meeting the moral demands of spectatorship as a description of a spectator *becoming* a witness. In this case he "must not only observe on his own but also put himself in the position of reporting to a third party both what he has seen and the emotion the spectacle aroused in him, how he was affected by it." Ibid., 49.

60. Peters, "Witnessing," 728.

61. Boltanski writes, "It is because the spectator is without ties and prior commitments that his report, his testimony, can be put forward as credible." Boltanski, *Distant Suffering,* 29.

62. For example: "Such categories as tense unite in a single segmentable sign vehicle a referential or quasi-semantic meaning and an indexical or pragmatic one. The

referential value of a shifter, moreover, depends on the presupposition of its prag-matic value." Michael Silverstein, "Shifters, Linguistic Categories, and Cultural Description," in *Language, Culture, and Society,* 2nd ed., ed. Benjamin Blount (Prospect Heights, IL: Waveland Press, 1995), 197.

63. Ibid., 204.

64. Thanks to Randy Collins for this insight.

65. Ann Uhry Abrams, "National Paintings and American Character: Historical Murals in the Capitol Rotunda," in *Picturing History: American Painting, 1770–1930,* ed. William Ayres (New York: Rizzoli in association with Fraunces Tavern Museum, 1993), 67.

66. Of the resignation ceremony, carefully devised by Congress, Barry Schwartz writes, "Although it was Washington who first raised the question of how he should resign his commission, 'whether in writing or at an Audience,' it was Congress that decided on the latter. And it was Congress, too, that designed the framework for that self-abnegation commonly ascribed solely to Washington's character." Barry Schwartz, *George Washington: The Making of an American Symbol* (Ithaca, NY: Cornell University Press, 1987), 139.

67. "Where there is not, in the verbal formula of the utterance, a reference to the person doing the uttering, and so the acting by means of the pronoun 'I' . . . then in fact he will be 'referred to' in one of two ways . . . [one being] in written utterances (or 'inscriptions'), by his appending his signature (this has to be done because, of course, written utterances are not tethered to their origin in the way spoken ones are)." J. L. Austin, *How to Do Things with Words* (Cambridge, MA: Harvard University Press, 1975), 60.

68. Bonnie Honig quotes Derrida as pushing on this paradox in his consideration of signatures on the Declaration of Independence: "The signature invents the signer. This signer can only authorize him- or herself to sign once he or she has come to the end, if one can say this, of his or her own signature, in a sort of fabulous retroactivity." Bonnie Honig, "Declarations of Independence," 212.

69. "In order to guarantee that power and secure their innovation, they had to combine their performative with a constative utterance. They needed another 'subjectivity' . . . to sign, in order to guarantee it, this production of signature," for "in this process," Derrida argues, "there are only countersignatures." Honig, "Declarations of Independence," 214.

70. Derrida, "Signature, Event, Context," in *Margins of Philosophy,* trans. Alan Bass (Chicago: University of Chicago Press, 1982), 328.

71. Witness signatures mark commitments in the legal sphere, since they aid in the production of evidence. A recent front-page article in the *New York Times* discusses changes in strategies of witness identification of suspects in criminal cases: "Photographs of suspects are showed to the witness in sequence. Once the witness identifies the suspect, the photographs must be signed. The rejected photos are merely initialed. The signed and initialed photos become evidence." "New Jersey Trying a New Way for Witnesses to Pick Suspects," *New York Times,* July 21, 2001, A1.

72. See Robert I. Burns and Paul E. Chevedden, "A Unique Bilingual Surrender Treaty from Muslim-Crusader Spain," *Historian* 62, no. 3 (2000): 521.

73. Horace C. Porter, "The Surrender at Appomattox," *Civil War Times,* May 2000, 70.

74. Jonathan M. Wainwright, *General Wainwright's Story: The Account of Four Years of Humiliating Defeat, Surrender, and Captivity,* ed. Robert Considine (New York: Doubleday, 1946), 280.

75. Translation of August 12, 1945, response of Americans to Japanese acceptance. Quoted in William Craig, *The Fall of Japan* (New York: Dial Press, 1967), 145.

76. Translation of Foreign Minister Mamoru Shigemitsu's credentials. National Archives of the United States, *The End of the War in the Pacific: Surrender Documents in Facsimile* (Washington, DC: Government Printing Office, 1945), 9.

77. An original draft of the surrender proclamation to be read by the emperor used common, undignified pronominal forms: "To the Kawabe group, the document was an insult to the Throne and the personage of Hirohito." Craig, *Fall of Japan,* 246. Ultimately a more appropriate draft was prepared with imperial indexical terms.

78. Wainwright, *General Wainwright's Story,* 135; italics mine.

79. Bryson, "Gaze in the Expanded Field," 103.

80. In characterizing the vanishing point of Cartesian perspectivalism, Martin Jay writes that "the basic device was the idea of symmetrical visual pyramids or cones with one of their apexes the receding vanishing or centric point in the painting, the other the eye of the painter or the beholder." Jay, "Scopic Regimes of Modernity," 6. Further writings on the vanishing point include Bryson, "Gaze in the Expanded Field"; Brian Rotman, *Signifying Nothing: The Semiotics of Zero* (New York: St. Martin's Press, 1987); and Marin, "Towards a Theory of Reading."

81. Rotman, *Signifying Nothing,* 19.

82. Bryson, "Gaze in the Expanded Field," 89–90.

83. Michael Baxandall discusses the meaning of Fra Roberto's discussion of this Angelic Colloquy for fifteenth-century representations of the Annunciation in *Painting and Experience in Fifteenth Century Italy: A Primer in the Social History of Pictorial Style* (Oxford: Oxford University Press, 1988), 51.

84. Personal communication from Patricia Reilly regarding the political controversy surrounding the ring.

85. Now, some of this distraction is simply a function of the Albertian convention regarding historical paintings. In Leon Battista Alberti's Renaissance treatise *Della pittura,* he indicates that historical paintings can be more effective if a character is introduced who actually looks out at the viewer, capturing the viewer's attention and indicating the important part of the story. Velázquez multiplies this Albertian character by at least four—an intriguing gesture of overdoing in such an understated painting. Surely more is going on here than the accidental multiplication of the viewer-attracting character of the *istoria.*

86. "The Contract of Marriage between Lewis XIII, King of France, and the most Serene Lady Anne of Austria, Infanta of Spain. Concluded at Madrid the 22d of

August, 1612," in *A General Collection of Treatys, Declarations of War, Manifestos, and Other Publick Papers* (London: Printed by J. Darby for A. Bell in Cornhill, and E. Sanger, 1710), 180. This marriage was one of a matched pair of marriages organized largely by Marie de Médicis for her son, Louis XIII, and her daughter, Elizabeth (betrothed to Philip IV of Spain, Anne's brother). This marriage exchange was programmed to fundamentally transform the relationship between France and Spain, which had been consistently hostile.

87. Thanks to both Thomas De Gloma and Randy Collins for comments on these questions on the compositions of interactions. Donald Black, in writing about those third parties who act as settlement agents, also comments on the compositional aspects of these relations: "Generally, the intimacy between the agent and each of the principles is about equal, so that the three parties together form an isosceles triangle of relational distance." Black, *Social Structure of Right and Wrong,* 123.

88. In fact it was only in the fifteenth century that signatures on paintings and etchings migrated from their previous position outside the actual work (often on the sculptural frames) and were incorporated within the work itself: "À la même époque, la localisation de la phrase entière se modifie et le registre de la signature abandonne se cadre sculpte pour se situer dans l'espace interne de l'oeuvre, celui du champ iconique." Charles Sala, "La signature à la lettre et au figure," *Poétique* 18 (1987): 121.

CHAPTER THREE

1. Carl von Clausewitz, *On War,* quoted in Niall Ferguson, "Prisoner Taking and Prisoner Killing in the Age of Total War," *War in History* 11, no. 2 (2004): 151. The full quotation is: "[Captured] artillery and prisoners are therefore at all times regarded as the true trophies of victory, as well as its measure, because through these things its extent is declared beyond a doubt."

2. This moment of recognition and misrecognition refers most particularly to the victor's receiving from the vanquished the recognition of rightful sovereignty. I will take up this issue at length in chapter 4.

3. Charles Francis Adams, *Lee at Appomattox and Other Papers* (New York: Houghton, Mifflin, 1902), 25.

4. Rudolf Arnheim, *The Power of the Center* (Berkeley: University of California Press, 1988), 2.

5. Lewis A. Coser, "The Termination of Conflict," *Journal of Conflict Resolution* 5, no. 4 (1961): 348.

6. Randall Collins, "Violent Conflict and Social Organization: Some Theoretical Implications of the Sociology of War," *Amsterdams Sociologisch Tijdschrift* 16, no. 4 (1990): 72.

7. Lorraine White, "Spain's Early Modern Soldiers: Origins, Motivation and Loyalty," *War and Society* 19, no. 2 (2001): 40.

8. Miller writes, "Panic usually involves large numbers in headlong flight and however harmful its consequences it hardly makes sense to hand over the entire army to the firing squad . . . In battle the soldier may not succumb to fear unless substantial numbers of his fellows give in at the same time." William Ian Miller, "Weak Legs: Misbehavior Before the Enemy," *Representations* 70 (Spring 2000): 30–31.

9. Marc Ross, personal communication.

10. Moffitt dates the painting later than other Velázquez scholars do; that is, only shortly before 1640 (as opposed to 1635). See John F. Moffitt, "Diego Velázquez, Andrea Alciati, and the Surrender of Breda," *Artibus et Historiae* 3, no. 5 (1982): 75–90.

11. William H. McNeill, *The Pursuit of Power: Technology, Armed Force, and Society since A.D. 1000* (Chicago: University of Chicago Press, 1982).

12. See Chandra Mukerji, "Unspoken Assumptions: Voice and Absolutism at the Court of Louis XIV," *Journal of Historical Sociology* 11, no. 3 (1998): 286.

13. John W. Wright, "Sieges and Customs of War at the Opening of the Eighteenth Century," *American Historical Review* 39, no. 4 (1934): 631.

14. Anne Armstrong, *Unconditional Surrender* (New Brunswick, NJ: Rutgers University Press, 1961), 14. See also Quincy Wright, "How Hostilities Have Ended: Peace Treaties and Alternatives," *Annals of the American Academy of Political and Social Science* 392 (1970): 55.

15. Thanks to Barry Schwartz of the University of Georgia for providing me with this polling instrument. The poll goes on to ask subjects their opinions about requiring unconditional surrender of "our enemies" and about making public the fact that the United States was requiring unconditional surrender.

16. Concerning the war between the Athenians and the Melians in 416 BCE, which followed the Melians' refusal to surrender sovereignty, Heinz Waelchli and Dhavan Shah write, "After a siege that lasted from the summer of 416 BC to that winter, the Melians surrendered to the Athenians, who killed all men of military age and sold the women and children for slaves. Subsequently, the Athenians sent out five hundred colonists and inhabited the island themselves." Heinz Waelchli and Dhavan Shah, "Crisis Negotiation between Unequals: Lessons from a Classic Dialogue," *Negotiation Journal* 10, no. 2 (April 1994): 138.

17. Roosevelt quoted in John L. Chase, "Unconditional Surrender Reconsidered," *Political Science Quarterly* 70, no. 2 (1955): 260.

18. "Indeed the demand for political capitulation was unprecedented in international law. In contrast to armistice treaties, international law regarded, and continues to view, surrender as a purely military agreement concluded between the armed forces of the warring parties." Reiner Hansen, "Germany's Unconditional Surrender," *History Today* 45, no. 5 (1995): 34.

19. Wright, "How Hostilities Have Ended," 57.

20. Hansen, "Germany's Unconditional Surrender," 35.

21. Quoted in Jay Winik, *April 1865: The Month That Saved America* (New York: HarperCollins, 2001), 215.

22. Edwin Cole Bears, "'We Have to Save the People': Efforts to End the War after Lee's Surrender Collide Head-on with Politics—and the Murder of a Peacemaker," *Civil War Times,* May 2000, 41.

23. Raymond G. O'Connor, *Diplomacy for Victory: FDR and Unconditional Surrender* (New York: W. W. Norton, 1971), 60.

24. Chase, "Unconditional Surrender Reconsidered," 263.

25. See Eviatar Zerubavel, "Lumping and Splitting: Notes on Social Classification," *Sociological Forum* 11, no. 3 (1996): 421–33.

26. Quoted in William Craig, *The Fall of Japan* (New York: Dial Press, 1967), 66–67.

27. Ibid., 125.

28. Ibid., 145.

29. For the debate within the Truman administration about the consequences and advisability of retaining the emperor, see Kyoko Inoue, *MacArthur's Japanese Constitution: A Linguistic and Cultural Study of Its Making* (Chicago: University of Chicago Press, 1991), 6–7, n. 1; and Craig, *Fall of Japan,* 59. In chapter 4 I will address the question of sovereignty in surrenders most directly, and I will take up this decision again in that chapter.

30. Ruti Teitel, *Transitional Justice* (Oxford: Oxford University Press, 2000), 124.

31. It is not always clear who will be paying reparations to whom. As late as February 1865, President Abraham Lincoln had returned from an unsuccessful peace conference with representatives of the Confederacy off Hampton Roads and "suggested to his cabinet that the United States pay the insurgent Southern states $400 million as compensation for their lost slaves—if they surrendered by April 1. The Union cabinet was unanimous in its rejection." Winik, *April 1865,* 34.

32. These *nontransfers* also participate in and constitute a kind of compositional field of exchange. If a defeated soldier is allowed to retain his sword, for example, such permission references both an object and a specific paradigm of exchange. The victor *gives* a strange kind of "gift" to the vanquished. In a paradoxical way, he gives him "back" his own, now theoretically alienated sword.

33. Of course, the network of cross-witnesses has various degrees of freedom to confirm or negate the interpretation of these tendencies in their performative, demonstrative, and representational actions.

34. Georg Simmel, "Exchange," in *Georg Simmel: Individuality and Social Forms,* ed. and intro. Donald Levine (Chicago: University of Chicago Press, 1971), 67.

35. Perhaps implicitly suggesting a link between the arts of war and the giving of gifts, Chandra Mukerji writes about humanity's sustained engagement with armaments and their deployment: "These acts of material assault are just as much material means of organizing relations as gift-giving." Chandra Mukerji, "The Political Mobilization of Nature in 17th Century French Formal Gardens," *Theory and Society* 23 (1994): 655.

36. Pierre Bourdieu, "Structures, Habitus, Power: Basis for a Theory of Symbolic Power," in *Culture/Power/History: A Reader in Contemporary Social Theory,* ed. Nicholas B. Dirks, Geoff Ely, and Sherry Ortner (Princeton, NJ: Princeton University Press, 1994), 166.

37. Jacques Derrida, *Given Time: I. Counterfeit Money,* trans. Peggy Kamuf (Chicago: University of Chicago Press, 1992), 41.

38. Bourdieu, "Structures, Habitus, Power," 186.

39. Coser, "Termination of Conflict," 348.

40. Christine Smith, "Sources for 'The Surrender of Breda,' by Diego Velázquez," *Vassar Journal of Undergraduate Studies* 20 (1966): 10.

41. Writing about forced resignations—surrenders of a sort—Thomas Dumm describes a similar dynamic: "The receipt of the letter is crucial to the resignation because it is the moment of communication, the act of transmission of the sign of resignation . . . The letter of resignation becomes a collaborative act." Thomas Dumm, *A Politics of the Ordinary* (New York: New York University Press, 1999), 55.

42. Robert I. Burns, S.J., and Paul E. Chevedden, "A Unique Bilingual Surrender Treaty from Muslim-Crusader Spain," *Historian* 62, no. 3 (2000): 524–25.

43. Douglas Botting, *From the Ruins of the Reich: Germany 1945–1949* (New York: Meridian Books, 1985), 90.

44. Letter from U.S. Grant to R. E. Lee, April 7, 1865, reproduced in Ulysses S. Grant, *Personal Memoirs of U.S. Grant* (New York: Charles Webster, 1886), 478.

45. Giorgio Agamben, *Homo Sacer: Sovereign Power and Bare Life,* trans. Daniel Heller-Roazen (Stanford, CA: Stanford University Press, 1998), 85.

46. Coser, "Termination of Conflict," 349.

47. Maurice Godelier, *The Enigma of the Gift,* trans. Nora Scott (Chicago: University of Chicago Press, 1999), 19.

48. Coser notes that for some nations "the capital symbolizes the very existence of the nation, then its fall will be perceived as defeat and will lead to the acceptance of the terms of the victor." This he claims was true for Paris in 1871 and 1940. Coser, "Termination of Conflict," 350.

49. Kim Lane Scheppele writes abut the surrender of the Hungarian army at the end of World War II and the capture of the holy crown of Saint Stephen. The crown guard "only agreed to turn the crown over to the Americans if they got not just a property receipt, but also a statement saying that the crown had been given 'asylum' in America." Kim Lane Scheppele, "Counter-constitutions," unpublished manuscript, 2002.

50. Wright, "How Hostilities Have Ended," 52.

51. H. E. Goemans, *War and Punishment: The Causes of War Termination and the First World War* (Princeton, NJ: Princeton University Press, 2000), 33.

52. "After three sieges of Jativa in 1239, 1240, and 1244, [King] James settled for a qualified surrender that gave the semblance of political subjugation while leaving the city with its ruling house, its population, its defenses, and its army all intact." Burns and Chevedden, "Unique Bilingual Surrender Treaty," 529.

53. Roger Chartier, *On the Edge of the Cliff: History, Language, and Practices,* trans. Lydia G. Cochrane (Baltimore: Johns Hopkins University Press, 1997), 87.

54. Burns and Chevedden, "Unique Bilingual Surrender Treaty," 523; italics mine.

55. Quoted in Roger Chartier, *Forms and Meanings: Texts, Performances, and Audiences from Codex to Computer* (Philadelphia: University of Pennsylvania Press, 1995), 44.

56. Nevertheless, historian Michael Biggs, while tracing the origins of cartography and European state formation, notes that "to my knowledge there has been no systematic research on the role of maps in treaty documents, let alone the negotiation process." Michael Biggs, "Putting the State on the Map: Cartography, Territory, and European State Formation," *Comparative Study of Society and History* 41 (1999): 388.

57. Ibid., 380.

58. Chandra Mukerji, *Territorial Ambitions and the Gardens of Versailles* (Cambridge: Cambridge University Press, 1997), 3.

59. Indeed, concern over accuracy in actual maps was rudimentary. In this period of the long Thirty Years' War, the ability, as well as the desire, to stay current with the political territorial alignments and realignments was beyond the capability of the mapmakers: "In the initial stages of the Dutch revolt, to be sure, the situation was in flux and the outcome uncertain. By the armistice of 1607, however, the United Provinces were clearly separate from the remaining Habsburg possessions . . . Yet Blaeu, like other cartographers, did not record it on the map. And when his son Joan prepared the multivolume Atlas Major, he used the same plate again." Biggs, "Putting the State on the Map," 393.

60. Simone Zurawski, "New Sources for Jacques Callot's Map of the Siege of Breda," *Art Bulletin* 70, no. 4 (1988): 623. I will take up Callot's map again in chapter 5 when I discuss the role of maps in framing sovereignty.

61. President Washington's Farewell Address, September 17, 1796, in James D. Richardson, ed., *A Compilation of the Messages and Papers of the Presidents, 1789–1897,* vol. 1 (Washington, DC: United States Congress, 1899).

62. Horace C. Porter, "The Surrender at Appomattox," *Century Magazine,* 1887, republished in *Civil War Times,* May 2000, 70.

63. Winik, *April 1865,* 217.

64. White, "Spain's Early Modern Soldiers," 43. These soldiers included Italian, English, German, and Burgundian troops along with Spanish and Flemish ones.

65. "Covered wagons which would not be examined were to permit the garrison to bring with them unseen deserters from the enemy. Were these deserters to march with the troops they would be instantly recognized and the victorious general would be under the necessity of having them shot or hanged which he wished to avoid." Wright, "Sieges and Customs of War," 642.

66. Barbara Donagan, "Codes and Conduct in the English Civil War," *Past and Present,* no. 118 (February 1988): 88.

67. Zurawski, "New Sources," 633.

68. Hermannus Hugo, *The Siege of Breda: By the Armes of Phillip the Fourth,* trans. Captaine Barry (1627; Ilkley, UK: Scolar Press, 1975), 142.

69. Collins, "Violent Conflict and Social Organization," 69.

70. See Michael Mallory and Gordon Moran, "Precisazioni e aggiornamenti sul 'Caso' Guido Riccio," *Bollettino Senese di Storia Patria* 92 (1985): 334–43, for a discussion of a recent discovery of another fresco on the same wall as Guidoriccio and the emergent doubts about attribution of the Guidoriccio fresco.

71. Michael Mallory and Gordon Moran recount the story of the Guidoriccio investigation and the placement of the fresco on the wall with the other paintings in "The Guido Riccio Controversy in Art History," in *Confronting the Experts,* ed. Brian Martin (Albany, NY: SUNY Press, 1996), 131–54.

72. Brian Keith Axel, *The Nation's Tortured Body: Violence, Representation, and the Formation of the Sikh "Diaspora"* (Durham, NC: Duke University Press, 2001), 51–52.

73. Hugo, *Siege of Breda,* 129.

74. Winik, *April 1865,* 68.

75. Grant, *Personal Memoirs,* 485.

76. Winik, *April 1865,* 294.

77. National Archives of the United States, *The End of the War in the Pacific: Surrender Documents in Facsimile* (Washington, DC: U.S. Government Printing Office, 1945), 9.

78. Quoted in Winik, *April 1865,* 194.

79. Transcript of concession speech of Albert Gore, *New York Times,* December 14, 2000, A26.

80. Article 1, Surrender Agreement between Magistrates and Burgers of Breda and Ambrogio Spinola, transcribed in Hugo, *Siege of Breda,* 138.

81. Thomas Nast, *Harper's Weekly,* May 20, 1865, 312–13.

82. Cf. Hansen, "Germany's Unconditional Surrender," 34.

83. "Of the several thousand Confederate soldiers taken prisoner by the Federals after the battle of Five Forks on April 1 [about a week before Appomattox] not even a full 100 would swear the oath of allegiance to the Union." Winik, *April 1865,* 131.

84. "The outward civility of the Appomattox surrender hid a terrible secret: a shared animosity that would not heal for generations." Gary W. Gallagher, "There Is Rancor in Our Hearts . . . Which You Little Dream Of," *Civil War Times,* May 2000, 54.

85. Teitel, *Transitional Justice,* 154.

86. Paul Kecskemeti, *Strategic Surrender: The Politics of Victory and Defeat* (Stanford, CA: Stanford University Press, 1958), v, 10.

87. General Jonathan Wainwright of the U.S. Army in the Philippines during World War II wrote about his actions immediately after his decision to surrender to the Japanese: "Then I order the men of Corregidor and the other fortified islands in the bay to destroy all remaining weapons of greater than .45 caliber before noon, as well as all other military and naval stores, equipment and ships." Jonathan M. Wainwright, *General Wainwright's Story: The Account of Four Years of Humiliating Defeat, Surrender, and Captivity,* ed. Robert Considine (New York: Doubleday, 1946), 120.

88. Armstrong, *Unconditional Surrender,* 18.

89. Michael Balfour, "The Origin of the Formula: 'Unconditional Surrender' in World War II," *Armed Forces and Society* 5, no. 2 (1979): 291.

90. Quoted in Herbert P. Bix, "Japan's Delayed Surrender: A Reinterpretation," *Diplomatic History* 19, no. 2 (1995): 219.

91. Grant quoted in Porter, "Surrender at Appomattox," 70. Note the way Ambrogio Spinola's chaplain, Hermannus Hugo, sought to deride the gathering, largely English, army of the German general Ernst Graf von Mansfield, viewed as a potential savior by the besieged city of Breda: "Isabella, having often tried the honesty of that well known man, thought it best to signify by silence how little credit he had with her, and how little she feared his sudden gathered and unexpert army, *fitter for the plough than for the war*" (italics mine). Here the soldiers are revealed as truly farmers, never having undergone the transmutation into soldiers. Hugo, *Siege of Breda,* 96.

92. Grant, *Personal Memoirs,* 490.

93. Porter, "Surrender at Appomattox," 74.

94. Grant, *Personal Memoirs,* 494.

95. John Wright writes of a defeated garrison found guilty of sedition, "Then the infantry marched out without muskets, carrying only their swords; but these could not be worn by their side and were carried drawn and under their arms, pointing to the rear." Wright, "Sieges and Customs of War," 639.

96. Ibid., 641.

97. Henry W. Elson, *The Civil War through the Camera* (Springfield MA: Patriot, 1912), pt. 16.

98. Jonathan Brown and J. H. Elliott, *A Palace for a King: The Buen Retiro and the Court of Philip IV* (New Haven, CT: Yale University Press, 1980), 180.

99. William Hanks, "Metalanguage and Pragmatics of Deixis," in *Intertexts: Writings on Language, Utterance, and Context* (New York: Rowman and Littlefield, 2000), 69.

100. Arnheim, *Power of the Center,* 76.

101. Algirdas J. Greimas, *On Meaning: Selected Writings in Semiotic Theory,* trans. Paul J. Perron and Frank H. Collins (Minneapolis: University of Minnesota Press, 1997), 31.

102. Although this key exchange is not mentioned in Hermannus Hugo's *Obsidio Bredana,* it is mentioned in an anonymous account of the siege and surrender titled *Carta tercera que vino a un cavallero:* "The enemy left in good order in files of fours . . . Our troops lined up in two parallel rows forming an avenue between which they passed until they had all marched away. Then the keys of the fortress were turned over [to Spinola]." Quoted in Moffitt, "Diego Velázquez, Andrea Alciati, and the Surrender of Breda," 86.

103. Brown and Elliott refer to another famous surrender in the history of Spain, the surrender of Granada to Ferdinand and Isabella in 1492: "On that occasion the Moorish king Boabdil, in the words of a contemporary, 'came out on horseback accompanied by many caballeros, with the keys in his hands and he wanted to dismount to kiss the king's hand, and the king would not let him get off his horse . . . And the Moorish king kissed his arms and gave him the keys, and said: "Take, sir, the keys of your city. I and all of us within it, are yours." '" Brown and Elliott, *Palace for a King,* 182.

104. Craig, *Fall of Japan,* 241.

105. Brian Axel reproduces a historian's account about the work with turbans: "In the eighteenth and nineteenth centuries, an Indian would place his turban at the feet of the conqueror as a sign of complete surrender. This was also used in a metaphoric sense to ask a great favor of someone, indicating a willingness to become their slave." Axel, *Nation's Tortured Body,* 59.

106. Bonnie Honig, "Declarations of Independence: Arendt and Derrida on the Problem of Founding a Republic," in *Rhetorical Republic: Governing Representations in American Politics,* ed. Frederick M. Dolan and Thomas L. Dumm (Amherst: University of Massachusetts Press, 1993), 210, 213.

107. Recall here the discussion of the complex nature of the "vanishing point" in pictorial representations of surrender developed in chapter 2.

108. Dumm, *Politics of the Ordinary,* 54.

109. "When a monopoly of force is formed, pacified social spaces are created which are normally free from acts of violence." Norbert Elias, *Civilizing Process,* vol. 2, *Power and Civility,* trans. Edmund Jephcott (New York: Pantheon Press, 1982), 235.

110. Jorge Arditi, *A Genealogy of Manners: Transformations of Social Relations in France and England from the Fourteenth to the Eighteenth Century* (Chicago: University of Chicago Press, 1998), 79.

111. Roland Barthes, quoted in Rudolf Arnheim, *Power of the Center,* 114.

112. The general director of all pictorial coverage of the surrender, Colonel Bertram Kalisch of the U.S. Army, notes how the photographers reordered the space for their own, representational, imperatives: "The surrender table was centered with Navy exactness right in the middle of the deck . . . we relocated the table by pushing it up within eight feet of our platform, an ideal spot for our lenses." Bertram Kalisch, "Photographing the Surrender Aboard the USS *Missouri,*" *Proceedings of the United States Naval Institute* 81, no. 8 (1955): 868.

113. Craig, *Fall of Japan,* 300.

114. Hugo, *Siege of Breda,* 129.

115. Quoted in Winik, *April 1865,* 182.

116. Randall Collins makes a similar point about perception on the battlefield itself: "The individual overcomes fear by displacing his attention to symbolic tokens which structure the perceptual field among the chaos of the battlefield." Randall Collins, "Violent Conflict and Social Organization: Some Theoretical Implications of the Sociology of War," *Amsterdams Sociologisch Tijdschrift* 16, no. 4 (1990): 69.

117. Hanks, "Metalanguage and Pragmatics of Deixis," 90.

118. For example, in the formulation of the unconditional surrender policy of World War II, "Secretary Hull objected to the policy [of unconditional surrender] not only on tactical grounds but also because he felt that it 'logically required the victor nations to be ready to take over every phase of the national and local governments of the conquered countries, and to operate all governmental activities and properties.' We and our Allies were in no way prepared to undertake this vast obligation." Chase, "Unconditional Surrender Reconsidered," 278.

119. Louis Marin, "Towards a Theory of Reading in the Visual Arts: Poussin's 'The Arcadian Shepherds,'" in *The Art of Art History: A Critical Anthology,* ed. Donald Preziosi (Oxford: Oxford University Press, 1998), 268.

CHAPTER FOUR

1. André Felibien, *Recueil de Descriptions de Peintures* (Geneva: Minkoff Reprint, 1973), 32. Several other painters chose to paint this scene, with similar figural placements, including Tiepolo and Veronese.

2. "This migration of the 'Soul,' that is, of the immortal part of kingship, from one incarnation to another as expressed by the concept of the king's demise is certainly one of the essentials of the whole theory of the King's Two Bodies." Ernst H. Kantorowicz, *The King's Two Bodies: A Study in Medieval Political Theology* (Princeton, NJ: Princeton University Press, 1957), 13. Of course, this apparently anachronistic analogy must take into account that the theory of the king's two bodies, developed in the medieval period, postdated the historical Alexander. However, Veronese and others painted this scene of doubled identity in the centuries that followed the development of the concept.

3. Kantorowicz addresses this temporally oriented plurality in his reference to Shakespeare's Macbeth, who "conjures up that uncanny ghostly procession of Macbeth's predecessor kings whose last one bears the 'glass' showing the long file of successors. By this fiction, at any rate, the plurality of persons necessary to make up the corporation was achieved—a plurality that is which did not expand within a given Space but was determined exclusively by Time. This was doubtless the prevailing theory until early modern times." Kantorowicz, *King's Two Bodies,* 387.

4. Georg Simmel, "Superiority and Subordination as Subject Matter of Sociology," in *German Sociology,* ed. Uta Gerhardt (New York: Continuum Press, 1998), 2.

5. Felibien, *Recueil de Descriptions,* 31.

6. Thanks to William Turpin for this information.

7. *Oxford English Dictionary—Online Edition* (Oxford: Oxford University Press, 1989).

8. Jens Bartelson, *A Genealogy of Sovereignty* (Cambridge: Cambridge University Press, 1995). 25.

9. Giorgio Agamben, *Homo Sacer: Sovereign Power and Bare Life,* trans. Daniel Heller-Roazen (Stanford, CA: Stanford University Press, 1998), 41.

10. Jean Bethke Elshtain traces the concept of sovereignty to the ancient Roman *dominus:* "Absolute domination over a 'domestic' arena is the mark of the sovereign dominus." Jean Bethke Elshtain, "Rethinking Sovereignty," in *Post-realism: The Rhetorical Turn in International Relations,* ed. Francis A. Beer and Robert Hariman (East Lansing: Michigan State University Press, 1996), 173.

11. Kantorowicz notes regarding Baldus de Ubaldus's theory of the phoenix, "Evidently, Baldus [ca. 1327–1400] had a clear analogy in mind. To him, the

Phoenix represented one of the rare cases in which the individual was at once the whole existing species so that indeed species and individual coincided. The species of course was immortal, the individual mortal. The imaginary bird, therefore, disclosed a duality: it was at once Phoenix and Phoenix-kind, mortal as an individual, though immortal too, because it was the whole kind." Kantorowicz, *King's Two Bodies,* 387.

12. Ibid., 316.

13. Certainly there have mostly been hybrid forms found in history. For example, writing of the emergence of "England" during the Elizabethan period, Richard Helgerson notes that "a kingdom whose boundaries are determined by the language of its inhabitants is no longer a kingdom in the purely dynastic sense, but neither, so long as it goes on identifying itself with the person of a hereditary monarch, is it quite a nation." Richard Helgerson, *Forms of Nationhood: The Elizabethan Writing of England* (Chicago: University of Chicago Press, 1992), 2.

14. Benedict Anderson, *Imagined Communities: Reflections on the Origin and Spread of Nationalism* (London: Verso Press, 1991).

15. Kantorowicz, *King's Two Bodies,* 299, quoting Baldus de Ubaldus.

16. President Washington's Farewell Address, September 17, 1796, in James D. Richardson, ed., *A Compilation of the Messages and Papers of the Presidents, 1789–1897,* vol. 1 (Washington, DC: United States Congress, 1899), 214.

17. Quincy Wright, "How Hostilities Have Ended: Peace Treaties and Alternatives," *Annals of the American Academy of Political and Social Science* 392 (1970): 54.

18. Paul Kecskemeti, *Strategic Surrender: The Politics of Victory and Defeat* (Stanford, CA: Stanford University Press, 1958), 144.

19. Deeply philosophical issues regarding human agency and self-understanding are necessarily suggested here but can only be touched on. For example, scholars have noted the way language and its grammar call coherent individuals into being and sustain them through time. Linguists such as Émile Benveniste elaborated on the way the act of enunciation, relying on the insertion of the self-presenting deictical feature of the "I," brings both the present and the subject into being. Philosopher Ferdinand Gonseth developed an analysis of the syntactic basis of the individual: "In order that a real person should not have the feeling to be somebody else from one day to the next it is necessary that something should persist in him which is profoundly characteristic for this person; the syntactic person is a theoretical form of this 'something.'" Ferdinand Gonseth, *Time and Method: An Essay on the Methodology of Research,* trans. Eva Guggenheimer (Springfield, IL: Charles C. Thomas, 1972), 162. Intertwined with this linguistic base of personhood is the experience of the body and its generation of something Maurice Merleau-Ponty called the *schéma corporel:* "The concrete, always changing self-awareness that actors have of their own bodily position in space is . . . dynamic, as is the body in motion." William Hanks, *Intertexts: Writings on Language, Utterance, and Context* (New York: Rowman and Littlefield, 2000), 20.

20. Ronald Forsyth Millen and Robert Erich Wolf, in their book on the Medici cycle, argue that Marie is, in fact, present in the painting in a symbolic, or more precisely, emblematic manner: "But the presence of the caduceus tells us that

Maria herself is present, and that this, though it has been thought so, is not a picture from which Maria is absent . . . Rubens . . . by recourse to her essential emblem, ensured her presence as presiding genius in a painting which 'concerns other persons more than the Queen Mother herself.'" Ronald Forsyth Millen and Robert Erich Wolf, *Heroic Deeds and Mystic Figures* (Princeton, NJ: Princeton University Press, 1989), 163. This seems more likely than the musing of Louis Hourticq, in his "Memoranda," in which he notes Marie's absence and speculates on its meaning: "C'est la seule fois qu'elle n'apparait pas; sa maturité a-t-elle donc craint la comparaison avec la jeunesse irrésistable des deux princesses?" Louis Hourticq, *La galerie Médicis de Rubens au Louvre* (Paris: Henri Laurens, 1921), 44.

21. Margaret Carroll, "The Erotics of Absolutism: Rubens and the Mystification of Sexual Violence," *Representations* 25 (Winter 1989): 3–29. Complicating these scenes even more is the ambiguous question of the gender of the allegorical figures of Spain and France in the *Exchange* painting. Art historians generally code them as female, and yet in the real ceremony of exchange it was two men, the Duc de Guise and the Duque de Uceda, who escorted the princesses to the floating pontoon exactly midway between the two banks of the Bidassoa River (and thus equidistant from both countries), and these men were, of course, proxies for Louis XIII and Philip IV, a topic to be taken up below. Art historian Sarah R. Cohen makes the case for an androgynous personification of France in this and other paintings in Rubens's cycle, a personification that portrays the nation as a cavalier, performing a virtuoso role. Interestingly, given my analysis of the appearance of swords in other scenes of surrender, Cohen also notes that both France and Spain conspicuously show off their swords in this painting: "Both personifications carry long swords in the manner of the male nobility, that of France protruding conspicuously as it rides suspended from a baldric on the figure's left side." Sarah R. Cohen, "Rubens's France: Gender and Personification in the Marie de Médicis Cycle," *Art Bulletin* 85, no. 3 (2003): 507.

22. See Chandra Mukerji, *Territorial Ambitions and the Gardens of Versailles* (Cambridge: Cambridge University Press, 1997), 3.

23. Of course, the reestablished equilibrium is one that now, theoretically, has a supplement (also on both sides) of possible offspring. The taboo against incest made this impossible in the former pairings.

24. Yoshikuni Igarashi, "The Bomb, Hirohito, and History: The Foundational Narrative of the United States–Japan Postwar Relations," *Positions* 6, no. 2 (1998): 276.

25. Quoted in ibid., 273.

26. Hannah Arendt, *The Human Condition* (Chicago: University of Chicago Press, 1958), 245.

27. "Hobbes treated [sovereignty] as the power to coerce, by law and in accordance with laws, or without law and in disregard of it." Scott Gordon, *Controlling the State: Constitutionalism from Ancient Athens to Today* (Cambridge, MA: Harvard University Press, 1999), 28.

28. The work of Max Weber, Robert Cover, Giorgio Agamben, Pierre Bourdieu, and Lewis Coser, among others, analyzes this complicated interdependency of violence, power, and law. All struggle to track the basic asymmetry of the force/law dialectic. This asymmetry is well captured in the following statement by the British foreign minister during the parliamentary debate over the impending war against Iraq in September 2002: "Law without force is no *law;* force without law is no *law.*" But of course, force without law is still *force.*

29. J. L. Austin, *How to Do Things with Words,* 2nd ed. (Cambridge, MA: Harvard University Press, 1975), 163.

30. Ruti Teitel, *Transitional Justice* (Oxford: Oxford University Press, 2000), 59.

31. Hermannus Hugo, *The Siege of Breda: By the Armes of Phillip the Fourth,* trans. Captaine Barry (1627; Ilkley, UK: Scolar Press, 1975), 146.

32. William Craig, *The Fall of Japan* (New York: Dial Press, 1967), 232.

33. Here the pronouns "I" and "you" are special in that they actualize the situation and the speakers at hand. Third-person pronouns refer to other situations or present nonparticipants. As Émile Benveniste noted, "Pronouns do not constitute a unitary class but are of different types depending on the mode of language of which they are the signs. Some belong to the syntax of a language, others are characteristics of what we shall call 'instances of discourse,' that is, the discrete and always unique acts by which the language is actualized in speech by a speaker." Émile Benveniste, *Problems in General Linguistics,* trans. Mary Elizabeth Meek (Coral Gables, FL: University of Miami Press, 1971), 217.

34. Douglas Botting, *From the Ruins of the Reich: Germany, 1945–1949* (New York: Median Books, 1985), 89.

35. Edwin Cole Bears, "'We Have to Save the People': Efforts to End the War after Lee's Surrender Collide Head-on with Politics—and the Murder of a Peacemaker," *Civil War Times,* May 2000, 41.

36. Rudolf Arnheim, *The Power of the Center* (Berkeley: University of California Press, 1988), 14.

37. Clifford Geertz, "Centers, Kings, and Charisma: Reflections on the Symbolics of Power," in *Local Knowledge* (New York: Basic Books, 1983), 134–35.

38. See the work of Norbert Elias in this regard, in particular *The Civilizing Process,* vol. 2, *Power and Civility,* trans. Edmund Jephcott (New York: Pantheon, 1982).

39. Michael Biggs, "Putting the State on the Map: Cartography, Territory, and European State Formation," *Comparative Study of Society and History* 41 (1999): 375.

40. Lorraine White, "Spain's Early Modern Soldiers: Origins, Motivation, and Loyalty," *War and Society* 19, no. 2 (2001): 42.

41. Leon Battista Alberti, *Della pittura,* quoted in Hubert Damisch, *A Theory of /Cloud/: Toward a History of Painting,* trans. Janet Lloyd (Stanford, CA: Stanford University Press, 2002), 112.

42. I thank Roger Friedland for clarifying this point.

43. Roger Chartier, *Forms and Meanings: Texts, Performances, and Audiences from Codex to Computer* (Philadelphia: University of Pennsylvania Press, 1995), 44.

44. Craig, *Fall of Japan,* 209.

45. Robert L. Burns, S.J., and Paul E. Chevedden, *Negotiating Cultures: Bilingual Surrender Treaties in Muslim-Crusader Spain under James the Conqueror* (Leiden: Brill Books, 1999), 37.
46. Ibid., 49.
47. "As a result of the social field in which official Maya was produced, and to which it was addressed, the texts themselves contain a mixture of native Maya modes of representation along with Spanish bureaucratic and Franciscan doctrinal discourse. They include prominently the letters to the crown, chronicles, and land surveys . . . boundary works . . . yielding two or more contradictory interpretations." William Hanks, "Discourse Genres in a Theory of Practice," *American Ethnologist* 14, no. 4 (1987): 669.
48. Elias, *Civilizing Process,* 60. Writing about the "Requirement," a sixteenth-century imperial Spanish document demanding that conquered peoples in the New World submit, or surrender, to Spain and accept both Spanish authority and Catholicism, historian Patricia Seed makes a compelling case that it had its roots in Islamic customs and ritual forms of conquest: "The Requirement most closely resembles the unique ritual demand for submission characteristic of the military version of an Islamic jihad . . . According to Islamic tradition, the Prophet Muhammad would write to those against whom he was starting a jihad, 'Now then I invite you to Islam [surrender to Allah].'" Patricia Seed, *Ceremonies of Possession in Europe's Conquest of the New World, 1492–1640* (Cambridge: Cambridge University Press, 1995), 76. Of course, Seed argues, the Spanish could not themselves recognize the traces of their own former conquerors in their own instruments of conquest.
49. See Kyoko Inoue, *MacArthur's Japanese Constitution: A Linguistic and Cultural Study of Its Making* (Chicago: University of Chicago Press, 1991), 7. See also Craig, *Fall of Japan,* 246, for discussion of the formal versus the vernacular presentation of the emperor's proclamation.
50. Chandra Mukerji, "Unspoken Assumptions: Voice and Absolutism at the Court of Louis XIV," *Journal of Historical Sociology* 11, no. 3 (1998): 284–85.
51. Jonathan Brown and J. H. Elliott, *A Palace for a King: The Buen Retiro and the Court of Philip IV* (New Haven, CT: Yale University Press, 1980), 180.
52. Hugo, *Siege of Breda,* 115.
53. Ulysses S. Grant, *Personal Memoirs of U.S. Grant* (New York: Charles Webster, 1886), 490.
54. Jay Winik, *April 1865: The Month That Saved America* (New York: HarperCollins, 2001), 169.
55. Biggs, "Putting the State on the Map," 386.
56. Of course, such relations could break down and loyalties could be split, with consequences for sovereign power: "When selecting recruits for the royal armies and garrisons, it seems certain that towns and villages showed far less concern than they did when recruiting soldiers for their own militia companies." White, "Spain's Early Modern Soldiers," 30.
57. Mukerji, "Unspoken Assumptions," 285.

58. Biggs, "Putting the State on the Map," 385. Writing about the Elizabethan map-maker Christopher Saxton and his attempt to signal the sovereign in the mapped realm, Richard Helgerson notes, "The harder the mapmaker tries, the larger and more elaborate he makes the signs of sovereignty, the more out of place they seem. Reduced in size and importance, they pass easily enough as mere labels, identifying marks like the place-names written elsewhere on the sheet. But expanded . . . they construct around themselves a representational space separate from and foreign to the space supposed by the map itself." Helgerson, *Forms of Nationhood,* 112.

59. "Towards the end of March 1945, the British government became convinced that once Germany had been completely overpowered, there would in all probability no longer be any military or civil authority capable of signing such an instrument of surrender. As a consequence, the victors would have to resort to a different procedure and unilaterally proclaim total German defeat and their assumption of supreme authority in Germany. Accordingly, the surrender document was redrafted by the EAC into the form of a declaration." Reiner Hansen, "Germany's Unconditional Surrender," *History Today* 45, no. 5 (1995): 35.

60. Bears, "'We Have to Save the People,'" 40.

61. Roger Chartier, *On the Edge of the Cliff: History, Language, and Practices,* trans. Lydia G. Cochrane (Baltimore: Johns Hopkins University Press, 1997), 87.

62. Sovereign images also appear before other sovereigns, as marriage advertisements or diplomatic gestures of amity or challenge. The network of sovereigns regarding each other's images suggests the visual rudiments of a transcendent apparatus of power that is, in structure and authority, never quite realized. I will take up this question at the end of this chapter.

63. In fact, an alternative reading of the relation between artist and sovereign in this painting is presented by Craig Owens: "For the painting represents not the painter's but the King's vision: Velázquez appears to have abdicated his own role as 'author' of the image to that superior authority that sustains him and his art." Craig Owens, "Representation, Appropriation, and Power," *Art in America* 70 (May 1982): 9–21.

64. Wolfgang Kemp, "The Theater of Revolution: A New Interpretation of Jacques-Louis David's *Tennis Court Oath,*" in *Visual Culture: Images and Interpretations,* ed. Norman Bryson, Michael Ann Holly, and Keith Moxey (Hanover, NH: University Press of New England for Wesleyan University Press, 1994), 223.

65. "A double meaning and a double function are thus assigned to representations: to make an absence present, but also to exhibit its own presence as image, hence to constitute the person who looks at it as the looking subject." Chartier, *On the Edge of the Cliff,* 91. "For the problem of the observer is the field on which vision in history can be said to materialize, to become itself visible. Vision and its effects are always inseparable from the possibilities of an observing subject who is both the historical product and the site of certain practices, techniques, institutions, and procedures of subjectification." Jonathan Crary, *Techniques of the*

Observer: On Vision and Modernity in the Nineteenth Century (Cambridge, MA: MIT Press, 1991), 5.

66. Quoted in Norman Bryson, *Word and Image: French Painting of the Ancien Régime* (Cambridge: Cambridge University Press, 1981), 54.

67. Edmund Plowden, "Commentaries or Reports," in Ernst H. Kantorowicz, *The King's Two Bodies: A Study in Medieval Political Theology* (Princeton, NJ: Princeton University Press, 1957), 7.

68. Jean Bodin quoted in Elshtain, "Rethinking Sovereignty," 176.

69. See Owens, "Representation, Appropriation, and Power," 17.

70. Gordon, *Controlling the State,* 49. This boundlessness may be one reason Michel Foucault was so reluctant to address power as a bounded concept.

71. Agamben, *Homo Sacer,* 24.

72. Our modern American popular culture version of this is the scene in the film *The Wizard of Oz* when Dorothy and her companions catch a glimpse of the "wizard" in the curtained booth and realize he is just a man pulling levers.

73. Jonathan Brown and J. H. Elliott develop a rich and detailed analysis of the painting and its sources. My own analysis is indebted to their discussion. Brown and Elliott, *Palace for a King,* 184–90.

74. Jay Winik gives historical context to this visual liminality: "Lee was, to put it bluntly, stateless, a man in limbo, without a country, a paroled prisoner of war living in occupied territory that was no longer the Confederate capital but not yet a Union state, and whose fate had yet to be decided by Northern authorities." Winik, *April 1865,* 313.

75. "Greater love hath no man than this, that a man lay down his life for his friends. ABRAHAM LINCOLN has done that. He has sealed his service to his country by the last sacrifice." *Harper's Weekly,* April 29, 1865, 258.

76. Henry W. Elson, *The Civil War through the Camera,* pt. 16 (Springfield, MA: Patriot, 1912).

77. See Barry Schwartz's magisterial study of the evolving reputation of Abraham Lincoln from the end of the Civil War to World War I, *Abraham Lincoln and the Forge of National Memory* (Chicago: University of Chicago Press, 2000).

78. Mark E. Neely Jr., Harold Holzer, and Gabor Boritt, "The Confederate Image: Prints of the Lost Cause," *Imprint: Journal of the American Historical Print Collectors Society* 12, no. 1 (1987): 5.

79. Ibid., 6. Artists of the level of renown of Thomas Eakins were known to have attempted to paint Lee's surrender to Grant. After some initial sketches in oil, however, Eakins gave up on the project. Art historian Carol Troyen explores why Eakins never carried this project forward, speculating about the difficulties of design or simple lack of personal interest. She does not, however, consider the existential problems associated with this surrender scene. Carol Troyen, "The Surrender of General Lee to General Grant: Thomas Eakins and History Painting," *Apollo* 495 (May 2003): 30–31. One further possibility is that Grant's action was all of a piece with a late nineteenth- and early twentieth-century construal of the Civil War and its aftermath as exclusively a conflict between and about whites, and avoiding its real subject, the black slave. Thus attention must be given to

scenes of reconciliation, with scenes of former conflict elided. See Kirk Savage, "The Politics of Memory: Black Emancipation and the Civil War Monument," in *Commemorations: The Politics of National Identity,* ed. John R. Gillis (Princeton, NJ: Princeton University Press, 1994).

80. Horace C. Porter, "The Surrender at Appomattox," *Civil War Times,* May 2000, 68; italics mine.

81. Brian Keith Axel, *The Nation's Tortured Body: Violence, Representation, and the Formation of a Sikh "Diaspora"* (Durham, NC: Duke University Press, 2001), 40.

82. Stephen Greenblatt, "Murdering Peasants, Status, and the Representation of Rebellion," *Representations* 1, no. 1 (1983): 10.

83. Botting, *From the Ruins of the Reich,* 90.

84. Damisch, *Theory of /Cloud/,* 19.

85. Kelly R. DeVries, "Hunger, Flemish Participation, and the Flight of Philip VI: Contemporary Accounts of the Siege of Calais, 1346–47," *Studies in Medieval and Renaissance History,* n.s., 12 (1990): 137.

86. John Dower, *Embracing Defeat: Japan in the Aftermath of World War II* (London: Penguin Books, 2000), 41. Political theorist Thomas Dumm gets at these decisions and their resonance by looking at the analogous case of letters of (forced) resignation. Writing about a professor who has been denied tenure, he asks, "In this situation why, after all she has already been through, must she perform such a task . . . she ponders what the resignation letter must contain. She faces representational issues, such as letterhead: Does she use the stationary of the place from which she is departing? To whom does she address her resignation? What does she say in the letter itself? . . . Would her silence be a monkey wrench thrown into the machine of rejection, fouling its works?" Thomas Dumm, *A Politics of the Ordinary* (New York: New York University Press, 1999), 53.

87. Quoted in James Brooke, "A Japanese Witness to History Adroitly Survived It," *New York Times,* November 8, 2003, A4.

88. Elshtain, "Rethinking Sovereignty," 175.

89. For a recent analysis of the complex and contradictory mandates of organizations like the United Nations, see Michael Hardt and Antonio Negri, *Empire* (Cambridge, MA: Harvard University Press, 2000).

90. "How can two states reach an agreement in an anarchic realm with no central authority to enforce its terms? This problem should be particularly severe in agreements to end a war because the settlement of a war almost always entails some shift in relative power between the belligerents." H. E. Goemans, *War and Punishment: The Causes of War Termination and the First World War* (Princeton, NJ: Princeton University Press, 2000), 10.

91. Elaine Scarry, *The Body in Pain: The Making and Unmaking of the World* (Oxford: Oxford University Press, 1985), 87.

92. See the fascinating article by Robert Paine on the foundational violence of biblical twins: "What twins alert us to, then, is how the issue of identity and the issue of rights are themselves 'twinned'; thus any apparent *sameness* raises a need for *distinction* (i.e., difference); and in resolving the issue, a resort to violence may be taken—certainly there is that suggestion in Genesis." Robert Paine, "'Am I

My Brother's Keeper?' (Genesis IV:9): Violence and the Making of Society," *Qualitative Sociology* 24, no. 2 (2001): 174.

93. Hermannus Hugo reports that "Isabella, whilst she remained at Antwerp, was drawn with the pencil of Rubens that excellent painter, and being graven with an instrument of brass, she saw herself crowned with a garland of oake, in an imperial table." Hugo, *Siege of Breda,* 153. William Craig reports that "the office was bedlam as photographers snapped pictures of the group centered around Truman's desk. Generals, admirals, statesmen, all listened as the Chief Executive, cool-looking in a summer suit, read from a paper: 'I have just received a note from the Japanese Government in reply to the message forwarded to that Government by the Secretary of State on August 11. I deem this reply a full acceptance of the Potsdam Declaration which specifies the unconditional surrender of Japan.'" Craig, *Fall of Japan,* 201.

94. Jonathan M. Wainwright, *General Wainwright's Story: The Account of Four Years of Humiliating Defeat, Surrender, and Captivity,* ed. Robert Considine (New York: Doubleday, 1946), 129, 174. Note the breezy way Wainwright uses the derogatory term "Jap" in his book, published right after the war in 1946.

95. Thanks to my colleague Kendall Johnson for this information, based on his own research. For more on the relation of peace medals to the politics of peace treaties between European colonizers and Native Americans, see Johnson's essay "Peace, Friendship, and financial Panic: Reading the Mark of Black Hawk in *Life of Ma-Ka-Tai-She-Kia-Kiak,"* paper presented at Tri-College Americanist Reading Group, February 13, 2003.

CHAPTER FIVE

1. Hillel Schwartz, *The Culture of the Copy: Striking Likenesses, Unreasonable Facsimiles* (New York: Zone Books, 1996), 214.

2. This approach shares many of the preoccupations and perspectives of the "strategies of action" approach to culture developed by sociologist Ann Swidler. While not explicitly focused on power, Swidler's great advance, following the pragmatist tradition, is to draw attention to the means and strategies of action rather than to give pride of analytical place to the ends. For a fully developed statement of Swidler's approach, see her *Talk of Love: How Culture Matters* (Chicago: University of Chicago Press, 2002).

3. "I stood out on the deck beneath one of the huge forward turrets and never had I seen so many generals and admirals in one spot in my life. Our Army and Navy officers were lined up on one side of a cleared deck space. At right angles to them was a line of foreign officers. Facing the American officers was a platform for cameramen. The fourth side of the square was left open for the Jap[anese] delegates. *A table in the center of the square, covered with an ornate cloth, held the surrender documents. The copy which was to be given the Jap[anese] was bound in canvas. The other, to be delivered to the US, was bound in leather."* Jonathan Wainwright, *General Wain-*

wright's Story: The Account of Four Years of Humiliating Defeat, Surrender, and Captivity, ed. Robert Considine (New York: Doubleday, 1946), 279; italics mine.

4. Ulysses S. Grant, *Personal Memoirs of U.S. Grant* (New York: Charles Webster, 1886), 494.

5. Jay Winik, *April 1865: The Month That Saved America* (New York: HarperCollins, 2001), 319.

6. Patricia Seed, *Ceremonies of Possession in Europe's Conquest of the New World, 1492–1640* (Cambridge: Cambridge University Press, 1995), 94.

7. Cf. the discussion of how divine, "real" essences exceed representation in Catherine Gallagher and Stephen Greenblatt, *Practicing New Historicism* (Chicago: University of Chicago Press, 2000), 107.

8. Barry Schwartz, *George Washington: The Making of an American Symbol* (Ithaca, NY: Cornell University Press, 1987), 140–41. Recall as well the absence of the Japanese emperor and any of the members of his family from the surrender signing on the USS *Missouri.*

9. Stephan A. Schwartz, "A Sacred Space," *Attaché,* September 2003, 52.

10. Recall here John Durham Peters's classification of different witness positions, outlined in chapter 2.

11. Pierre Bourdieu, "The Force of Law: Toward a Sociology of the Juridical Field," *Hastings Law Journal* 38 (July 1987): page 7 of downloaded article.

12. William Craig, *Fall of Japan* (New York: Dial Press, 1967), 67–68; italics mine.

13. Seed, *Ceremonies of Possession,* 163.

14. Winik, *April 1865,* 316.

15. As I noted earlier, this doubling up in one picture was a convention of medieval Western art, an art that could not or would not insist on an image's rendering of a single moment in time. However, its use is somewhat anachronistic in the renderings of Callot and Velázquez and necessarily spoke to different propositions about history and its progress.

16. Grant, *Personal Memoirs,* 490.

17. J. L. Austin, *How to Do Things with Words,* 2nd ed. (Cambridge, MA: Harvard University Press, 1975), 14–15.

18. For a very interesting discussion of resistance to imperatives in cultural narratives of modernity, see Greg Urban, *Metaculture: How Culture Moves through the World* (Minneapolis: University of Minnesota Press, 2001).

19. Brian Axel describes the condition of absolute humiliation of Sikhs surrendering to the British in the nineteenth century as being "at once transformed into prisoners and liberated as new colonial subjects." Brian Keith Axel, *The Nation's Tortured Body: Violence, Representation, and the Formation of a Sikh "Diaspora"* (Durham, NC: Duke University Press, 2001), 41.

20. In her study of the origin of private property, Carol Rose links possession claims to communication and to the necessity for unremitting communication. One might even say that she identifies a kind of perpetual machinery of performatives of the declarative type in the maintaining of property claimed: "Possession now begins to look even more like something that requires a kind of communication,

and the original claim to the property looks like a kind of speech, with the audience composed of all others who might be interested in claiming the object in question. Moreover, some venerable statutory law obligates the acquiring party to *keep on* speaking, lest he lose his title by 'adverse possession.'" Carol Rose, "Possession as the Origin of Property," *University of Chicago Law Review* 52 (1985): 79.

21. Gallagher and Greenblatt, *Practicing New Historicism,* 15.

22. Jeffrey C. Alexander, "Cultural Pragmatics: Social Performance between Ritual and Strategy," *Sociological Theory* 22, no. 4 (2004).

23. John L. Chase, "Unconditional Surrender Reconsidered," *Political Science Quarterly* 70, no. 2 (1955): 273.

24. Wendy Steiner, *Pictures of Romance: Form against Context in Painting and Literature* (Chicago: University of Chicago Press, 1988), 2–3.

25. Here I am following an approach that art historian Craig Owens claims is the one Foucault and Marin adopt in their analyses of works of art: "They are interested less in what works of art say, and more in what they do; theirs is a performative view of cultural production." Craig Owens, "Representation, Appropriation, and Power," *Art in America* 70 (May 1982): 10.

26. Hayden White, *The Content of the Form: Narrative Discourse and Historical Representation* (Baltimore: Johns Hopkins University Press, 1987), 25.

27. [But our songs, Great King, are not ready so soon / and you take less time to make your conquests / than [we] need to praise them properly.] Roger Chartier, *Forms and Meanings: Texts, Performances, and Audiences from Codex to Computer* (Philadelphia: University of Pennsylvania Press, 1995), 44.

28. W. J. T. Mitchell, *Picture Theory* (Chicago: University of Chicago Press, 1994), 16.

29. Albert Gore's concession speech, printed in the *New York Times,* December 14, 2000, A26.

30. "Admiral Purnell and General Groves had often discussed the importance of putting a second bomb on target as quickly as possible after the first in order to impress the Japanese with the fact that the United States was actually in production of the weapon, that the future held only the prospect of more and more atomic warfare. It was Purnell who had initially proposed that it would take two bombs to end the war." Craig, *Fall of Japan,* 75–76.

31. Henry W. Elson, *The Civil War through the Camera,* pt. 16 (Springfield, MA: Patriot, 1912), 19.

32. Arno Mayer, "Untimely Reflections," *Theory and Event* 5 (2003): 4.

33. Norman Bryson quoted in Martin Jay, "Scopic Regimes of Modernity," in *Vision and Visuality,* ed. Hal Foster (Seattle, WA: Bay Press, 1988), 7.

34. This is a project I expect to develop.

35. These eight paintings included two scenes of military surrender (surrender of Cornwallis at Yorktown and surrender of General Burgoyne at Saratoga), one scene of resignation, one scene of founding (Declaration of Independence), three scenes of discovery (landing of Columbus, embarkation of the Pilgrims, and discovery of the Mississippi by De Soto in 1541), and one scene of religious con-

version and colonial absorption (baptism of Pocahontas). See Anne Uhry Abrams, "National Paintings and American Character: Historical Murals in the Capitol Rotunda," in *Picturing History: American Painting, 1770–1930,* ed. William Ayres (New York: Rizzoli in association with Fraunces Tavern Museum, 1993); on commemorative imagery in the U.S. Capitol more generally, see Barry Schwartz, "The Social Context of Commemoration: A Study in Collective Memory," *Social Forces* 61, no. 2 (1982): 374–402.

36. Bonnie Honig, "Declarations of Independence: Arendt and Derrida on the Problem of Founding a Republic," in *Rhetorical Republic: Governing Representation in American Politics,* ed. Frederick M. Dolan and Thomas L. Dumm (Amherst: University of Massachusetts Press, 1993), 214.

37. Thomas Dumm, *A Politics of the Ordinary* (New York: New York University Press, 1999), 54.

38. Cf. Schwartz, *George Washington,* on the importance of Washington's several resignations for soldering and ensuring the founding of the United States. Thus, at its beginning the United States needed to play out both the performatives of founding: "We hold" (with the fifty-six signatures on the Declaration of Independence) and of resignation—needed to complete the cycle at least once at the beginning to see if the pattern of structured alternation of leadership would hold.

39. Quoted in James Brooke, "A Japanese Witness to History Adroitly Survived It," *New York Times,* November 8, 2003, A4.

40. Jonathan Brown and J. H. Elliott, *A Palace for a King: The Buen Retiro and the Court of Philip IV* (New Haven, CT: Yale University Press, 1980), 180.

41. Grant, *Personal Memoirs,* 489.

42. Jorge Luis Borges, "The Telling of the Tale," *Atlantic Monthly* 286 (September 2000): 63.

Bibliography

Abrams, Ann Uhry. "National Paintings and American Character: Historical Murals in the Capitol Rotunda." In *Picturing History: American Painting, 1770–1930*, edited by William Ayres, 65–80. New York: Rizzoli, 1993.

Adams, Charles Francis. *Lee at Appomattox and Other Papers*. New York: Houghton, Mifflin, 1902.

Agamben, Giorgio. *Homo Sacer: Sovereign Power and Bare Life*. Translated by Daniel Heller-Roazen. Stanford, CA: Stanford University Press, 1998.

———. *Potentialities*. Edited and translated by Daniel Heller-Roazen. Stanford: Stanford University Press, 1999.

———. *Remnants of Auschwitz: The Witness and the Archive*. Translated by Daniel Heller-Roazen. New York: Zone Books, 1999.

Alciati, Andrea. *Emblemata*. Leiden: Christophorum Raphelengium, 1599.

Alexander, Jeffrey C. "Cultural Pragmatics: Social Performance between Ritual and Strategy." *Sociological Theory* 22, no. 4 (2004): 527–73.

Alpers, Svetlana. *The Art of Describing: Dutch Art in the Seventeenth Century*. Chicago: University of Chicago Press, 1983.

———. "Describe or Narrate? A Problem in Realistic Representation." *New Literary History* 8 (Autumn 1976): 15–41.

Anderson, Benedict. *Imagined Communities: Reflections on the Origin and Spread of Nationalism*. London: Verso Press, 1991.

Arditi, Jorge. *A Genealogy of Manners: Transformations of Social Relations in France and England from the Fourteenth to the Eighteenth Century*. Chicago: University of Chicago Press, 1998.

Arendt, Hannah. *The Human Condition*. Chicago: University of Chicago Press, 1958.

———. *On Revolution*. New York: Viking Press, 1963.

Aristotle. *Nicomachean Ethics.* Translated by Terence Irwin. Indianapolis, IN: Hackett, 1985.

Armas, Frederick A. de. "At War with Primavera: Botticelli and Calderón's *El Sitio de Breda.*" *Hispania* 82 (1999): 436–45.

Armstrong, Anne. *Unconditional Surrender.* New Brunswick, NJ: Rutgers University Press, 1961.

Arnheim, Rudolf. *The Power of the Center.* Berkeley: University of California Press, 1988.

Austin, J. L. *How to Do Things with Words.* 2nd ed. Cambridge, MA: Harvard University Press, 1975.

Axel, Brian Keith. *The Nation's Tortured Body: Violence, Representation, and the Formation of a Sikh "Diaspora."* Durham, NC: Duke University Press, 2001.

Balfour, Michael. "The Origin of the Formula: 'Unconditional Surrender' in World War II." *Armed Forces and Society* 5, no. 2 (1979): 281–301.

Bartelson, Jens. *A Genealogy of Sovereignty.* Cambridge: Cambridge University Press, 1995.

Baxandall, Michael. *Painting and Experience in Fifteenth Century Italy: A Primer in the Social History of Pictorial Style.* Oxford: Oxford University Press, 1988.

———. *Patterns of Intention: On the Historical Explanation of Pictures.* New Haven, CT: Yale University Press, 1985.

Bears, Edwin Cole. "'We Have to Save the People': Efforts to End the War after Lee's Surrender Collide Head-on with Politics—and the Murder of a Peacemaker." *Civil War Times,* May 2000, 38–41, 76.

Bennett, Drew A. "Heads I Win, Tails You Lose: Forcing Unconditional Surrender on Germany." *Marine Corps Gazette* 86, no. 12 (2002): 42–44.

Benveniste, Émile. *Problems in General Linguistics.* Translated by Mary Elizabeth Meek. Coral Gables, FL: University of Miami Press, 1971.

Bernstein, Richard. *Philosophical Profiles: Essays in a Pragmatic Mode.* Philadelphia: University of Pennsylvania Press, 1986.

Biggs, Michael. "Putting the State on the Map: Cartography, Territory, and European State Formation." *Comparative Study of Society and History* 41 (1999): 374–405.

Bix, Herbert P. "Japan's Delayed Surrender: A Reinterpretation." *Diplomatic History* 19, no. 2 (1995): 197–225.

Black, Donald. *The Social Structure of Right and Wrong.* San Diego, CA: Academic Press, 1993.

Blau, Peter M. *On the Nature of Organizations.* New York: John Wiley, 1974.

Boltanski, Luc. *Distant Suffering: Morality, Media, and Politics.* Cambridge: Cambridge University Press, 1999.

Borges, Jorge Luis. "The Telling of the Tale." *Atlantic Monthly* 286 (May 2000): 63–65.

Botting, Douglas. *From the Ruins of the Reich: Germany, 1945–1949.* New York: Meridian Books, 1985.

Bouissac, Paul. *Circus and Culture: A Semiotic Approach.* Bloomington: Indiana University Press, 1976.

Bourdieu, Pierre. "The Force of Law: Toward a Sociology of the Juridical Field." *Hastings Law Journal* 38 (July 1987): 805–53.

———. "Structures, Habitus, Power: Basis for a Theory of Symbolic Power." In *Culture/Power/History: A Reader in Contemporary Social Theory,* edited by Nicholas B. Dirks, Geoff Eley, and Sherry Ortner, 155–99. Princeton, NJ: Princeton University Press, 1994.

Brooke, James. "A Japanese Witness to History Adroitly Survived It." *New York Times,* November 8, 2003.

Brooks, William E. *Grant of Appomattox.* New York: Bobbs-Merrill, 1942.

Brown, Jonathan, and J. H. Elliott. *A Palace for a King: The Buen Retiro and the Court of Philip IV.* New Haven, CT: Yale University Press, 1980.

Bryson, Norman. *Word and Image: French Painting of the Ancien Régime.* Cambridge: Cambridge University Press, 1981.

Burke, Peter. *Eyewitnessing: The Uses of Images as Historical Evidence.* Ithaca, NY: Cornell University Press, 2001.

Burns, Robert I., S.J., and Paul E. Chevedden. *Negotiating Cultures: Bilingual Surrender Treaties in Muslim-Crusader Spain under James the Conqueror.* Leiden: Brill Books, 1999.

———. "A Unique Bilingual Surrender Treaty from Muslim-Crusader Spain." *Historian* 62, no. 3 (2000): 510–34.

Byman, Seymour. "Ritualistic Acts and Compulsive Behavior: The Pattern of Tudor Martyrdom." *American Historical Review* 83, no. 3 (1978): 625–43.

Calderón de la Barca, Pedro. *Obras completas.* Edited and with an introduction by Angel Valbuena Briones. Madrid: Aguilar, 1952.

Carroll, Margaret. "The Erotics of Absolutism: Rubens and the Mystification of Sexual Violence." *Representations* 25 (Winter 1989): 3–29.

Chartier, Roger. *Forms and Meanings: Texts, Performances, and Audiences from Codex to Computer.* Philadelphia: University of Pennsylvania Press, 1995.

———. *On the Edge of the Cliff: History, Language, and Practices.* Translated by Lydia G. Cochrane. Baltimore: Johns Hopkins University Press, 1997.

Chase, John L. "Unconditional Surrender Reconsidered." *Political Science Quarterly* 70, no. 2 (1955): 258–79.

Cohen, Sarah R. "Rubens's France: Gender and Personification in the Marie de Médicis cycle." *Art Bulletin* 85, no. 3 (2003): 490–522.

Collins, Randall. *Violent Conflict: A Micro-sociological Theory.* Forthcoming, 2006.

———. "Violent Conflict and Social Organization: Some Theoretical Implications of the Sociology of War." *Amsterdams Sociologisch Tijdschrift* 16, no. 4 (1990): 65–82.

Coser, Lewis A. "The Termination of Conflict." *Journal of Conflict Resolution* 5, no. 4 (1961): 347–53.

Cover, Robert. *Narrative, Violence and the Law: The Essays of Robert Cover.* Edited by Martha Minow, Michael Minow, and Austin Sarat. Ann Arbor: University of Michigan Press, 1995.

Craig, William. *The Fall of Japan.* New York: Dial Press, 1967.

Crary, Jonathan. *Techniques of the Observer: On Vision and Modernity in the Nineteenth Century.* Cambridge, MA: MIT Press, 1991.

Damisch, Hubert. *The Origin of Perspective.* Translated by John Goodman. Cambridge, MA: MIT Press, 1995.

———. *A Theory of /Cloud/: Toward a History of Painting.* Translated by Janet Lloyd. Stanford, CA: Stanford University Press, 2002.

Derrida, Jacques. *Given Time: I. Counterfeit Money.* Translated by Peggy Kamuf. Chicago: University of Chicago Press, 1992.

———. *Margins of Philosophy.* Translated by Alan Bass. Chicago: University of Chicago Press, 1982.

———. "'A Self-Unsealing Poetic Text': Poetics and the Politics of Witnessing." Translated by Rachel Bowlby. In *Revenge of the Aesthetic: The Place of Literature in Theory Today,* edited by Michael P. Clark, 180–207. Berkeley: University of California Press, 2000.

DeVries, Kelly R. "Hunger, Flemish Participation, and the Flight of Philip VI: Contemporary Accounts of the Siege of Calais, 1346–47." *Studies in Medieval and Renaissance History,* n.s., 12 (1990): 131–81.

Donagan, Barbara. "Codes and Conduct in the English Civil War." *Past and Present,* no. 118 (February 1988): 65–95.

Dower, John. *Embracing Defeat: Japan in the Aftermath of World War II.* London: Penguin Books, 2000.

Dumm, Thomas. *A Politics of the Ordinary.* New York: New York University Press, 1999.

Duve, Thierry de. "How Manet's 'A Bar at the Folies Bergère' Is Constructed." *Critical Inquiry* 26 (Autumn 1998): 136–68.

Elias, Norbert. *The Civilizing Process.* Vol. 2. *Power and Civility.* Translated by Edmund Jephcott. New York: Pantheon, 1982.

Elshtain, Jean Bethke. "Rethinking Sovereignty." In *Post-realism: The Rhetorical Turn in International Relations,* edited by Francis A. Beer and Robert Hariman, 171–91. East Lansing: Michigan State University Press, 1996.

Elson, Henry H. *The Civil War through the Camera.* Springfield, MA: Patriot, 1912.

Felibien, André. *Recueil de Descriptions de Peintures et d'autre ouvrages fait pour le Roy.* Geneva: Minkoff Reprint, 1973.

Ferguson, Niall. "Prisoner Taking and Prisoner Killing in the Age of Total War." *War in History* 11, no. 2 (2004): 148–92.

Fortna, Virginia Page. "Scraps of Paper? Agreements and the Durability of Peace." *International Organization* 57, no. 2 (2003): 337–72.

Foster, Hal, ed. *Vision and Visuality.* Seattle, WA: Bay Press, 1988.

Foucault, Michel. "Afterward: The Subject and Power." In *Michel Foucault: Beyond Structuralism and Hermeneutics,* 2nd ed., edited by Hubert Dreyfus and Paul Rabinow, 212–21. Chicago: University of Chicago Press, 1983.

———. *The Order of Things: An Archeology of the Human Sciences.* New York: Pantheon, 1971.

Fried, Michael. *Absorption and Theatricality: Painting and Beholder in the Age of Diderot.* Berkeley: University of California Press, 1980.

———. *Realism, Writing, Disfiguration: On Thomas Eakins and Stephen Crane.* Chicago: University of Chicago Press, 1987.

Gallagher, Catherine, and Stephen Greenblatt. *Practicing New Historicism.* Chicago: University of Chicago Press, 2000.

Gallagher, Gary W. "There Is Rancor in Our Hearts . . . Which You Little Dream Of." *Civil War Times,* May 2000, 52–55.

Geertz, Clifford. *Local Knowledge.* New York: Basic Books, 1983.

Gillis, John, ed. *Commemorations: The Politics of National Identity.* Princeton, NJ: Princeton University Press, 1994.

Godelier, Maurice. *The Enigma of the Gift.* Translated by Nora Scott. Chicago: University of Chicago Press, 1999.

Goemans, H. E. *War and Punishment: The Causes of War Termination and the First World War.* Princeton, NJ: Princeton University Press, 2000.

Goffman, Erving. *Forms of Talk.* Philadelphia: University of Pennsylvania Press, 1981.

Gonseth, Ferdinand. *Time and Method: An Essay on the Methodology of Research.* Translated by Eva Guggenheimer. Springfield, IL: Charles C. Thomas, 1972.

Gordon, Scott. *Controlling the State: Constitutionalism from Ancient Athens to Today.* Cambridge, MA: Harvard University Press, 1999.

Grant, Ulysses S. *Personal Memoirs of U.S. Grant.* New York: Charles Webster, 1886.

Greenblatt, Stephen. *Marvelous Possessions: The Wonder of the New World.* Chicago: University of Chicago Press, 1991.

———. "Murdering Peasants, Status, and the Representation of Rebellion." *Representations* 1, no. 1 (1983): 1–29.

Griswold, Wendy. "A Methodological Framework for the Sociology of Culture." In *Sociological Methodology,* vol. 17, edited by Clifford Clogg, 1–35. Washington, DC: American Sociological Association, 1987.

Hall, Bert S. "The Changing Face of Siege Warfare: Technology and Tactics in Transition." In *The Medieval City under Siege,* edited by Ivy A. Corfis and Michael Wolfe, 257–75. Woodbridge, UK: Boydell, 1995.

Hanks, William. "Discourse Genres in a Theory of Practice." *American Ethnologist* 14, no. 4 (1987): 668–92.

———. *Intertexts: Writings on Language, Utterance, and Context.* New York: Rowman and Littlefield, 2000.

Hansen, Reiner. "Germany's Unconditional Surrender." *History Today* 45, no. 5 (1995): 34–40.

Hardt, Michael, and Antonio Negri. *Empire.* Cambridge, MA: Harvard University Press, 2000.

Harney, Michael. "Siege Warfare in Medieval Hispanic Epic and Romance." In *The Medieval City under Siege,* edited by Ivy A. Corfis and Michael Wolfe, 179–87. Woodbridge, UK: Boydell, 1995.

Helgerson, Richard. "The Folly of Maps and Modernity." In *Literature, Mapping and the Politics of Space in Early Modern Britain,* edited by Andrew Gordon and Bernhard Klein, 241–62. Cambridge: Cambridge University Press, 2001.

————. *Forms of Nationhood: The Elizabethan Writing of England.* Chicago: University of Chicago Press, 1992.

Hesse, Everett W. "Calderon and Velazquez." *Hispania* 35, no. 1 (1952): 74–82.

Honig, Bonnie. "Declarations of Independence: Arendt and Derrida on the Problem of Founding a Republic." In *Rhetorical Republic: Governing Representations in American Politics,* edited by Frederick M. Dolan and Thomas L. Dumm, 202–15. Amherst: University of Massachusetts Press, 1993.

Hourticq, Louis. *La galerie Medicis de Rubens au Louvre.* Paris: Henri Laurens, 1921.

Hugo, Hermannus. *The Siege of Breda: By the Armes of Phillip the Fourth.* 1627. Translated by Captaine Barry. Ilkley, UK: Scolar Press, 1975.

Igarashi, Yoshikuni. "The Bomb, Hirohito, and History: The Foundational Narrative of the United States–Japan Postwar Relations." *Positions* 6, no. 2 (1998): 261–302.

Inoue, Kyoko. *MacArthur's Japanese Constitution: A Linguistic and Cultural Study of Its Making.* Chicago: University of Chicago Press, 1991.

Israel, Jonathan I. *The Dutch Republic and the Hispanic World, 1606–1661.* Oxford: Clarendon Press, 1982.

Johnson, Dorothy. "Corporality and Communication: The Gestural Revolution of Diderot, David, and the Oath of the Horatii." *Art Bulletin* 71, no. 1 (1989): 92–113.

Kalisch, Bertram. "Photographing the Surrender Aboard the USS *Missouri.*" *Proceedings of the United States Naval Institute* 81, no. 8 (1955): 866–73.

Kantorowicz, Ernst H. *The King's Two Bodies: A Study in Medieval Political Theology.* Princeton, NJ: Princeton University Press, 1957.

Kecskemeti, Paul. *Strategic Surrender: The Politics of Victory and Defeat.* Stanford, CA: Stanford University Press, 1958.

Keegan, John. *A History of Warfare.* New York: Alfred A. Knopf, 1993.

Kemp, Wolfgang. "The Theater of Revolution: A New Interpretation of Jacques-Louis David's *Tennis Court Oath.*" In *Visual Culture: Images and Interpretations,* edited by Norman Bryson, Michael Ann Holly, and Keith Moxey, 202–24. Hanover, NH: University Press of New England for Wesleyan University Press, 1994.

Lee, Benjamin. *Talking Heads: Language, Metalanguage, and the Semiotics of Subjectivity.* Durham, NC: Duke University Press, 1997.

Luhmann, Niklas. "Communication about Law in Interaction Systems." In *Advances in Social Theory and Methodology: Toward an Integration of Micro- and Macro-Sociologies,* edited by Karin Knorr-Cetina and Aaron V. Cicourel, 235–52. Boston: Routledge and Kegan Paul, 1981.

MacCormack, Sabine. "History, Memory and Time in Golden Age Spain." *History and Memory* 4, no. 2 (1992): 38–68.

Mallory, Michael, and Gordon Moran. "Precisazioni e aggiornamenti sul 'Caso' Guido Riccio." *Bollettino Senese di Storia Patria* 92 (1985): 334–43.

Marin, Louis. "Towards a Theory of Reading in the Visual Arts: Poussin's 'The Arcadian Shepherds.'" In *The Art of Art History: A Critical Anthology,* edited by Donald Preziosi, 263–74. Oxford: Oxford University Press, 1998.

Martin, Brian, ed. *Confronting the Experts.* Albany: SUNY Press, 1996.

Martin, John Levi. "What Is Field Theory?" *American Journal of Sociology* 109 (2003): 1–49.

Mayer, Arno. "Untimely Reflections." *Theory and Event* 5 (2002): 4.

McKim-Smith, Gridley, and Marcia L. Welles. "Topographical Tropes: The Mapping of Breda in Calderón, Callot, and Velázquez." *Indiana Journal of Hispanic Literatures* 10, no. 1 (1992): 185–212.

McNeill, William. *The Pursuit of Power: Technology, Armed Force, and Society since A.D. 1000.* Chicago: University of Chicago Press, 1982.

Meisel, Martin. *Realizations: Narrative, Pictorial, and Theatrical Arts in Nineteenth-Century England.* Princeton, NJ: Princeton University Press, 1983.

Millen, Ronald Forsyth, and Robert Erich Wolf. *Heroic Deeds and Mystic Figures.* Princeton, NJ: Princeton University Press, 1989.

Miller, William Ian. "Weak Legs: Misbehavior Before the Enemy." *Representations* 70 (Spring 2000): 27–48.

Mitchell, W. J. T. *Picture Theory.* Chicago: University of Chicago Press, 1994.

Moffitt, John F. "Diego Velázquez, Andrea Alciati, and the Surrender of Breda." *Artibus et Historiae* 3, no. 5 (1982): 75–90.

Mohan, Uday, and Sanho Tree. "Hiroshima, the American Media, and the Construction of Conventional Wisdom." *Journal of American–East Asian Relations* 4, no. 2 (1995): 141–60.

Morgenthau, Hans. *In Defense of the National Interest: A Critical Examination of American Foreign Policy.* New York: Alfred A. Knopf, 1951.

Mukerji, Chandra. "The Political Mobilization of Nature in 17th Century French Formal Gardens." *Theory and Society* 23 (1994): 651–77.

———. *Territorial Ambitions and the Gardens of Versailles.* Cambridge: Cambridge University Press, 1997.

———. "Unspoken Assumptions: Voice and Absolutism at the Court of Louis XIV." *Journal of Historical Sociology* 11, no. 3 (1998): 283–315.

Neely, Mark E., Jr., Harold Holzer, and Gabor Boritt. "The Confederate Image: Prints of the Lost Cause." *Imprint: Journal of the American Historical Print Collectors Society* 12, no. 1 (1987): 2–12.

O'Connor, Raymond G. *Diplomacy for Victory: FDR and Unconditional Surrender.* New York: W. W. Norton, 1971.

Orr, Linda. "The Blind Spot of History: Logography." *Yale French Studies,* no. 73 (1987): 190–214.

Owens, Craig. "Representation, Appropriation, and Power." *Art in America* 70 (May 1982): 9–21.

Padron, Ricardo. "Mapping Plus Ultra: Cartography, Space, and Hispanic Modernity." *Representations* 79 (2002): 28–60.

Paine, Robert. "'Am I My Brother's Keeper?' (Genesis IV:9): Violence and the Making of Society." *Qualitative Sociology* 24, no. 2 (2001): 169–90.

Parker, Geoffrey. "Maps and Ministers: The Spanish Habsburgs." In *Monarchs, Ministers, and Maps,* edited by David Buisseret, 124–52. Chicago: University of Chicago Press, 1992.

————, ed. *Cambridge Illustrated History of Warfare*. Cambridge: Cambridge University Press, 1995.

————, ed. *The Thirty Years' War*. 2nd ed. New York: Routledge, 1997.

Peters, John Durham. "Witnessing." *Media, Culture and Society* 23 (2001): 715–31.

Petrucci, Armando. *Writing the Dead: Death and Writing Strategies in the Western Tradition*. Translated by Michael Sullivan. Stanford, CA: Stanford University Press, 1998.

Porter, Horace C. "The Surrender at Appomattox." *Civil War Times*, May 2000, 26–28, 62–75.

Reynolds, Joshua. *Discourses on Art*. Edited by Robert R. Wark. San Marino, CA: Huntington Library, 1959.

Richardson, James D., ed. *A Compilation of the Messages and Papers of the Presidents, 1789–1897*. Vol. 1. Washington, DC: United States Congress, 1899.

Rose, Carol. "Possession as the Origin of Property." *University of Chicago Law Review* 52 (1985): 73–88.

Rotman, Brian. *Signifying Nothing: The Semiotics of Zero*. New York: St. Martin's Press, 1987.

Sala, Charles. "La signature à la lettre et au figure." *Poetique* 18 (1987): 119–27.

Salazar, Philippe-Joseph. "Rhetoric and Reconciliation in South Africa: Arguing for Democracy in the New Millennium." Paper presented at Swarthmore College, 1999.

Sarat, Austin. "Between (the Presence of) Violence and (the Possibility of) Justice: Lawyering against Capital Punishment." In *Cause Lawyering: Political Commitments and Professional Responsibilities*, edited by Austin Sarat and Stuart Scheingold. New York: Oxford University Press, 1998.

Scarry, Elaine. *The Body in Pain: The Making and Unmaking of the World*. Oxford: Oxford University Press, 1985.

Schegloff, Emanuel A. "Body Torque." *Social Research* 65, no. 3 (1998): 535–96.

Scheppele, Kim Lane. "Counter-constitutions." Unpublished manuscript, 2002.

————. "When the Law Doesn't Count: The 2000 Election and the Failure of the Rule of Law." *University of Pennsylvania Law Review* 149 (2001): 1361–1437.

Schivelbusch, Wolfgang. *The Culture of Defeat*. Translated by Jefferson Chase. New York: Henry Holt, 2003.

————. "The Loneliest Victors." *New York Times*, April 22, 2003.

Schwartz, Barry. *Abraham Lincoln and the Forge of National Memory*. Chicago: University of Chicago Press, 2000.

————. *George Washington: The Making of an American Symbol*. Ithaca, NY: Cornell University Press, 1987.

————. "The Social Context of Commemoration: A Study in Collective Memory." *Social Forces* 61, no. 2 (1982): 374–402.

Schwartz, Hillel. *The Culture of the Copy: Striking Likenesses, Unreasonable Facsimiles*. New York: Zone Books, 1996.

Schwartz, Stephan A. "A Sacred Space." *Attaché*, September 2003, 51–53.

Schweinfurth, Ludwig. "Velázquez, Goya and Picasso: A Commentary on War." *Atenea*, n.s., 2, no. 2 (1965): 75–87.

Seed, Patricia. *Ceremonies of Possession in Europe's Conquest of the New World, 1492–1640*. Cambridge: Cambridge University Press, 1995.

Silverstein, Michael. "Shifters, Linguistic Categories, and Cultural Description." In *Language, Culture, and Society,* 2nd ed., edited by Benjamin Blount, 187–221. Prospect Heights, IL: Waveland Press, 1995.

Simmel, Georg. *Georg Simmel: Individuality and Social Forms*. Edited and with an introduction by Donald Levine. Chicago: University of Chicago Press, 1971.

Small, Jocelyn Penny. "Time in Space: Narrative in Classical Art." *Art Bulletin* 81, no. 4 (1999): 562–75.

Smith, Christine. "Sources for 'The Surrender of Breda' by Diego Velázquez." *Vassar Journal of Undergraduate Studies* 20 (1966): 5–21.

Steiner, Wendy. *Pictures of Romance: Form against Context in Painting and Literature*. Chicago: University of Chicago Press, 1988.

Stinchcombe, Arthur. *When Formality Works: Authority and Abstraction in Law and Organizations*. Chicago: University of Chicago Press, 2001.

Swidler. Ann. *Talk of Love: How Culture Matters*. Chicago: University of Chicago Press, 2002.

Tabor, James. "Religious Discourse." In *Armageddon in Waco,* edited by Stuart Wright, 263–81. Chicago: University of Chicago Press, 1995.

Teitel, Ruti. *Transitional Justice*. Oxford: Oxford University Press, 2000.

Troyen, Carol. "The Surrender of General Lee to General Grant: Thomas Eakins and History Painting." *Apollo* 495 (2003): 30–31.

Urban, Greg. *Metaculture: How Culture Moves through the World*. Minneapolis: University of Minnesota Press, 2001.

Waelchli, Heinz, and Dhavan Shah. "Crisis Negotiation between Unequals: Lessons from a Classic Dialogue." *Negotiation Journal* 10, no. 2 (April 1994): 129–45.

Wagner-Pacifici, Robin. *Theorizing the Standoff: Contingency in Action*. Cambridge: Cambridge University Press, 2000.

Wainwright, Jonathan M. *General Wainwright's Story: The Account of Four Years of Humiliating Defeat, Surrender, and Captivity*. Edited by Robert Considine. New York: Doubleday, 1946.

Weigley, Russell F. *The Age of Battles: The Quest for Decisive Warfare from Breitenfeld to Waterloo*. Bloomington: Indiana University Press, 1991.

Weinraub, Bernard. "Threats and Responses: Articles of Capitulation." *New York Times,* May 20, 2003.

Whitaker, Shirley B. "The First Performance of Calderón's *El Sitio de Breda.*" *Renaissance Quarterly* 31, no. 4 (1978): 515–31.

White, Hayden. *The Content of the Form: Narrative Discourse and Historical Representation*. Baltimore: Johns Hopkins University Press, 1987.

White, Lorraine. "Spain's Early Modern Soldiers: Origins, Motivation, and Loyalty." *War and Society* 19, no. 2 (2001): 25–43.

Winik, Jay. *April 1865: The Month That Saved America*. New York: HarperCollins, 2001.

Wright, John W. "Sieges and Customs of War at the Opening of the Eighteenth Century." *American Historical Review* 39, no. 4 (1934): 629–44.

Wright, Quincy. "How Hostilities Have Ended: Peace Treaties and Alternatives."
Annals of the American Academy of Political and Social Science 392 (1970): 51–61.

Zelizer, Barbie. *Remembering to Forget: Holocaust Memory through the Camera's Eye.*
Chicago: University of Chicago Press, 1998.

Zerubavel, Eviatar. "Lumping and Splitting: Notes on Social Classification." *Sociological Forum* 11, no. 3 (1996): 421–33.

Zerubavel, Yael. *Recovered Roots: Collective Memory and the Making of Israeli National
Tradition.* Chicago: University of Chicago Press, 1995.

Zurawski, Simone. "New Sources for Jacques Callot's Map of the Siege of Breda."
Art Bulletin 70, no. 4 (1988): 621–34.

Index

Abrams, Ann, 48
Adams, Charles Francis, 157n37
Agamben, Giorgio: on authority and mo-
    nopoly of violence, 102; on etymology
    of "witness," 36–37; on force/law di-
    alectic, 179n28; on lack of witnesses,
    39; on shame, 2–3; on theory of sover-
    eignty, 27, 102, 123
Alberti, Leon Battista, 113, 167n85
Alciati, Andrea, 62, 63, 72
Alexander, E. P., 60
Alexander the Great, 98–99, 116, 126, 137
Alfonso (prince of Aragon), 76, 114–15
Alpers, Svetlana, 27, 33, 34, 162n22
anarchic realms, 130, 183n90
Anderson, Benedict, 103, 164–65n50
Anne of Austria, 55, 105–7
annihilation vs. surrender, 60, 65, 169n16
Appomattox, surrender at: authority to
    surrender and, 66–67; case summary of,
    10; ceremony of, 50–51, 92–93; deictic
    deferral and, 142–44; document of sur-
    render and, 124, 136; first Gulf War
    and, 11; lack of representations of, 149;
    Lee's sword at, 90–91, 125; Nast car-
    toon about, 88, 93, 124–26, 139, 143;
    rejected representations of, 126, 182–
    83n79; site of, 94–95, 124, 149; soldiers
    as witnesses to surrender at, 163n38;
    terms of surrender and, 83. See also
    Civil War (U.S.)

Arcadian Shepherds (Poussin), 164n48
archaism of surrender, 11–13
archetype, surrender as, 3–8
architecture, siege warfare and, 30–31,
    155–56n19
Arditi, Jorge, 8, 95, 155n18
Arendt, Hannah: on distance where politi-
    cal matters reside, 46; on problem of
    founding a republic, 94, 160–61n1;
    on promises in surrender, 25, 55, 108;
    on tenuousness of sovereignty, 107
Arnheim, Rudolf, 60, 92–93, 111, 113,
    157n36
art: changing military conventions and,
    6–8; hybrid aesthetics in, 34. See also
    specific works
articles of capitulation, election of 2000
    and, 11
Art of Painting (Vermeer), 77
asymmetry of surrender. See symmetry and
    asymmetry of surrender
Austin, J. L.: on endings, 2; on performa-
    tive speech acts, 144; on signature acts,
    48–49, 166n67; "speech act" terminol-
    ogy of, 23, 51, 69, 108
authority, symbolic objects of, 90–91
authority to surrender: Civil War (U.S.)
    and, 66–67, 83–84, 110–11; Germany
    in World War II and, 12, 66, 110,
    158n42; Iraq War and, 12, 158n42;
    Japan in World War II and, 84–85;

authority to surrender (*continued*)
military vs. civil, 111; military vs. political, 65, 66–67, 169n18
Axel, Brian, 81, 175n105, 185n19
al-Azraq, 73, 76, 114

Bahia, 123–24, 125, 138
Bailly, Jean-Sylvain, 121
Balfour, Michael, 89
Barry, Gerrat, 31
Bartelson, Jens, 100, 101
Barthes, Roland, 95
Battle of Issus, 98
battle of Montijo, 62
Belgium. *See* Breda, siege of
benefits and risks of surrender, assessment of, 13–14
Benveniste, Émile, 27, 153n4, 177n19, 179n33
Biggs, Michael, 112, 118, 172n56, 172n59
Bird King, Charles, 132
bitterness after surrender, 89, 173n84
Black, Donald, 38, 168n87
Black Hawk, 132
Blau, Peter, 60
Bodin, Jean, 122
Body in Pain, The (Scarry), 130
Boltanski, Luc, 46, 160n61, 165n59, 165n61
Borges, Jorge Luis, 152
Botting, Douglas, 73
Bourdieu, Pierre, 15, 25, 70, 71, 140, 179n28
Branch Davidians, 6
Brazil, recapture of Bahia and, 123–24, 125, 138
Breckinridge, John C., 66, 110
Breda, siege of: case summary of, 9; Dutch loss of Breda and, 44; etymology of surrender and, 21; historical background of, 29–30; keys to city and, 32, 161n11; maps and, 77; reversal of Spanish fortunes after, 32, 63, 146, 161n10; site of surrender and, 95; start of, 30; terms of surrender and, 31, 75, 79–80, 83, 87. See also *Map of the Siege of Breda* (Callot); *Surrender of Breda, The* (Velázquez)
Brown, Jonathan, 30, 41, 92, 163n40, 174n103

brutality in war, disallowing of surrender and, 153n5
Bryson, Norman, 53, 121, 122, 150
Buchenwald, 40
Bureau of Alcohol, Tobacco, and Firearms, 6
Burke, Peter, 6
Burns, Robert, 114, 171n52
Bush, George H. W., 148, 159n47
Bush, George W., 11, 86, 148

Calais, surrender of, 128–29
Calderón de la Barca, Pedro, 32, 33. See also *sitio de Breda, El* (Calderón de la Barca)
Callot, Jacques, vision of Breda of, 119. See also *Map of the Siege of Breda* (Callot)
capitulation, articles of, election of 2000 and, 11
Carroll, Margaret D., 105–6
Carta tercera que vino a un cavallero (anonymous), 32
Carthage, 65
cartography. *See* maps
Casablanca, press conference at, 64, 145
Catlin, George, 132
cease-fires, 23
"Centers, Kings, and Charisma" (Geertz), 111
Ceremonies of Possession in Europe's Conquest of the New World (Seed), 5
ceremonies of surrender: danger of for sovereigns, 138; exchanges of surrender and, 62, 91–94, 174nn102–3, 175n105; setting for surrender and, 96; signatures in, 50–51; weapons and instruments of war in, 91, 174n95
Chamberlain, Joshua Lawrence, 88, 92, 163n38
chaos, as alternative to surrender, 110
Chardin, Jean-Baptiste-Siméon, 43
Chartier, Roger, 26, 75–76, 120, 121, 147, 181n65
Chase, John L., 175n118
Chevedden, Paul, 114, 171n52
"Christian imperialism," 158n45
civilians in war, fate of, 78–82
Civil War (U.S.): Confederate troops' return home and, 24; disallowing of

surrender in, 153n5; documents of surrender and, 83–84, 87, 110, 136–37; Lee urged to surrender in, 157n37; loyalty oaths and, 88, 173n83; reconciliation theme in representations of, 182–83n79; reparations suggested during, 170n31; restoration of southern states and, 78; underrepresentation of, 149. *See also* Appomattox, surrender at

civil wars: lack of representations of, 149; reincorporation of territory after, 77–78. *See also* Civil War (U.S.)

Civil War through the Camera (Elson), 125

Clausewitz, Carl von, 59, 149, 168n1

codification of surrenders, 9, 23–24, 108–9, 155n18

Cohen, Sarah R., 178n21

Collins, Randall, 13, 61, 80, 175n116

colonialism, conquest and possession in, 5

Columbus, Christopher, 158n45

commonweal vs. singular ruler, 101–5

communication, possession claims and, 185–86n20

concentration camps: photojournalism and, 10; visual representation of, 40, 163–64n41

concession speech (election of 2000), 11–12, 148

Conclusion of the Peace, The (Rubens), 105

Concordia (emblem), 62, 63, 72, 93

conditions of surrender, 13–14, 16–17, 135

confession, witnesses and, 40

conflict resolution, impermanence of surrender and, 158–59n46

contestation and recognition of surrender. *See* recognition and contestation of surrender

continuity of kings, 160n67

copies of surrender, 25–28, 147–48, 149, 160n64

Cornwallis, Charles, 95, 138

Corregidor, 131

Coser, Lewis, 61, 74, 171n48, 179n28

Cover, Robert, 179n28

Craig, William, 95–96, 116, 140–41, 184n93, 186n30

Crary, Jonathan, 27, 42, 121, 164n44, 181n65

cross-witnessing: deictics and, 41–44, 139–40, 163n40; gestures of surrender and,

92; network of, 67–68, 170n33; signatories and, 55

cycle of return: anticopies of surrender and, 147; decisiveness of victory and, 145, 158–59n46; exchanges of surrender and, 20, 69, 78; itinerant sovereignty and, 113; mass media and, 159n47; representations of surrender and, 146–48

Dalhousie (British general), 81, 127

Damisch, Hubert, 113, 155n16

dangers of surrender, 61–64, 79, 169n8, 172n65

Darius (of Persia), 98, 99, 116, 127, 146. See also *Queens of Persia at the Feet of Alexander, The* (Le Brun)

David, Jacques-Louis, 121

Davis, Jefferson, 129

Dayton Peace Accords, 12

decisiveness of victory, 12, 156n26, 158–59n46

Declaration of Independence, 166n68

deconstitutive moment of surrender, 60–61

deep structure of surrender, 133–52; antagonists as mirror images and, 136–37; appearance of sovereign and, 137–38; conclusions about, 149–52; deictics and, 139–44; inversions and, 147–48; performatives and, 144–45; representations and, 145–49

deictics, 24, 28, 41–44, 139–44, 157n30

Della pittura (Alberti), 167n85

Derrida, Jacques: etymology of surrender and, 19; on gift as form of exchange, 70; on nature of testimony, 162–63n27; on problem of founding a republic, 94, 160–61n1; on signature events, 49, 166nn68–69; on temporal proximity, 165n56

desirability of surrender, evaluation of, 12–13

Diderot, 43

disarmament. *See* weapons and instruments of war

discourse genres, 3–4, 6, 120, 146, 153–54n6

documents of surrender, 82–86. *See also specific documents; specific surrenders*

Donagan, Barbara, 154n7

Don Fadrique de Toledo, 123
Dönitz, Karl, 79, 110
Dumm, Thomas, 95, 149–51, 171n41, 183n86
Dürer, Albrecht, 127
Dutch Republic. *See* Breda, siege of
Dutch West India Company, 123
dynamic center, itinerant sovereign and, 111–12, 113

Eakins, Thomas, 182n79
effigies, peace medals and, 132
Eisenhower, Dwight D., 66, 73, 128, 138
election of 2000 (U.S.), 11–12, 86, 148
Elias, Norbert, 95, 115, 175n109
Elizabeth I (England), 79, 111–12
Elizabeth of France, 105–7, 167–68n86
Elliott, J. H., 30, 41, 92, 163n40, 174n103
Ellis, Norbert, 8
Elshtain, Jean Bethke, 176n10
Elson, Henry, 125
endings, surrenders as, 2–3, 150–51
England. *See* Great Britain
Essay concerning Human Understanding (Locke), 165n51
etymology of surrender, 17–22, 69, 72, 78, 113, 158nn39–41
Exchange of Princesses at Hendaye, The (Rubens), 105–7, 146, 177–78nn20–21
exchanges of surrender, 59–97; authority and solidarity and, 66, 75, 90–91; capital as symbol of nation and, 171n48; ceremonies and, 62, 91–94, 174nn102–3, 175n105; channels of action and, 75–76; civil wars and, 77–78; coercive violence and, 70, 71, 72; convergence and divergence and, 15–17, 59–60, 96–97; cycle of return and, 20, 69, 78; danger and, 61–64; deconstitutive moment of surrender and, 60–61; documents and, 82–83; emblems in art and, 62–63; erotic, 105–7; etymology of surrender and, 17–18, 19–20; fates of warriors and civilians and, 78–82; gifts and, 20, 69–72, 170n32, 170n35; instruments of war and, 88–90, 94, 173n87; interregnum of surrender and, 24–25; maps and, 76–77; models of exchange relationships and, 69–74; objects of exchange and, 74–76, 79, 80–86, 90–91;

responsibility to end bloodshed and, 73–74; sacred relics and, 75, 171n49; selfhood and, 136; semiotic phases and, 67, 135; sites of, 94–96; symmetry of, 88, 136; temporary terminations of hostilities and, 23–24; territory and, 75–77; transactional objects and, 82–86; two-sided vs. unilateral surrenders and, 59–60, 168n1; types of exchanges, 86–88; unconditional surrender and, 64–69; untranslated surrender agreements and, 73
extermination vs. surrender, 8
Ezawa, Kennosuke, 21

Federal Bureau of Investigation (FBI), 6
feigned surrender, in first Gulf War, 156n24
Felibien, André, 98–99, 122, 137
Ferdinand (Spain), 113
Ferguson, Niall, 14, 21, 156n28
Fifth Amendment (U.S. Constitution), 39
Final Reconciliation, The (Rubens), 105
flags, as tokens of exchange, 80, 81
Florida recount (2000), 11–12
Foch, Ferdinand, 147
force/law dialectic, 108–9, 179n28
Forrest, Nathan Bedford, 153n5
Fortna, Virginia Page, 156n26
Fort Pillow, 153n5
Foucault, Michel, 27, 100, 102, 121, 186n25
France: Calais surrender and, 128–29; Franche-Comté and, 76, 113, 147; French Revolution and, 9; and Germany in World War II, 147, 171n48; military engineering by, 30; political marriages and, 167–68n86; pursuit of land claims by, 5, 7, 76, 160n66; Spain and, 105–7, 113, 178n21, 178n23
Fried, Michael, 43

Gallagher, Gary W., 173n84
Galle, Cornelis, 32
Galle, Theodore, 32, 77, 79
Gallup Poll on unconditional surrender, 64–65, 169n15
Geertz, Clifford, 111–12
"General Orders Number 9" (Lee), 85–86

General Wainwright's Story (Wainwright), 131

Germany: rebellious peasants in, 127; reparations and, 69; World War I surrender of, 147. *See also* World War II

gestures of surrender, 92–94

Gift, The (Mauss), 19

gifts, exchanges of surrender and, 20, 69–72, 170n32, 170n35

Godelier, Maurice, 20, 70, 75

Goemans, H. E., 37–38, 183n90

Goffman, Erving, 39

Gonseth, Ferdinand, 177n19

Gordon, Scott, 122, 178n27

Gore, Albert, 11–12, 86, 148

Grant, Ulysses S.: authority to surrender and, 66–67, 110–11; ceremonies of surrender and, 92; compared to Jesus Christ, 124–25; deictic deferral and, 143–44; documents of surrender and, 83, 136; on Lee's attire at Appomattox, 117; Lee's misrecognition of, 127; as magnanimous victor, 67, 90–91, 96, 152, 159n54; Nast cartoon and, 124–26; as "Old Unconditional Surrender," 65; refusal to allow reproductions of surrender and, 126, 149; on responsibility to end bloodshed, 73–74; scorched-earth policy and, 156n21; Sherman's memorandum and, 110–11; terms of surrender and, 10; unkempt vestments of, 117. *See also* Appomattox, surrender at; Civil War (U.S.)

Great Britain: Calais surrender and, 128–29; emergence of "England" and, 177n13; India and, 127; itinerant sovereignty and, 111–12; Lostwithiel surrender and, 79, 154n7; pursuit of land claims by, 5; Sikh diaspora and, 131–32, 185n19; Treaty of Waitangi and, 76, 120. *See also* World War II

Greece, 169n16

Greenblatt, Stephen, 127, 158n45

Greimas, A. J., 15, 93, 106, 157n36

Greuze, Jean-Baptiste, 43

Guidoriccio da Fogliano, painting of, 80–81, 173n71

Gulf War (first), 11, 12, 148, 156n24, 159n47

Gulf War (second). *See* Iraq War

Habsburg empire, artistic respresentations of, 32

Habsburgs. *See* Breda, siege of

Hall, Bert, 155–56n19

Hall of Realms, artworks in, 116, 124

Hanks, William: on boundary works, 115, 120, 180n47; on discourse genres, 153–54n6; on gestures of surrender, 92; on Mayan referential practices, 165n54; on "spatial field" of surrender, 96–97

Hansen, Reiner, 158n42, 169n18, 181n59

Harney, Michael, 155n15

Harper's Weekly. See Nast, Thomas, Appomattox cartoon

Hayam Wuruk, 111–12

Helgerson, Richard, 162n17, 177n13, 181n58

Henry V (Shakespeare), 117

Henry of Bergues, 96

Hephaestion, 98–99, 119, 137

Hirohito (Japanese emperor): absence of from surrender, 129, 185n8; authority to surrender and, 84–85; declaration of surrender by, 113–14; as a god, 109; with MacArthur after surrender, 107; photograph of surrender and, 129; terms of surrender and, 10, 51–52, 68–69, 116, 167n77

Hiroshima, 10, 148, 186n30

historiography of surrender, bias and, 4

Hitler, Adolf, 104, 109–10, 129, 147

Hobbes, Thomas, 102, 122, 178n27

Homma, Masaharu, 131

Honig, Bonnie, 94, 150, 160–61n1, 166n68

Hourticq, Louis, 177–78n20

Hugo, Hermannus, 45, 79–80, 117, 174n91, 184n93. *See also Obsidio Bredana* (Hugo)

Hull, Cordell, 175n118

Hungary, 171n49

Hussein, Saddam, 12, 158n42

identity of surrenderer: collectivities and individuals and, 47–48, 104–5, 156n28, 158n42; sovereign authority and, 18, 103–5, 158n42

Igarashi, Yoshikuni, 107

Iliad, The (Homer), 63, 152

images of surrender, 25–28, 147–48, 149, 160n64. *See also specific works of art*
India, 127
In dona hostium (emblem), 63, 93
Inoue, Kyoko, 21, 116, 159n48
international law, on surrender as purely military agreement, 169n18
interpretation issues, 6, 73, 114–16, 120, 140–41
interregnum of surrender, 24–25
interstitial action of surrender, 23–25
Iraq. *See* Gulf War (first); Iraq War
Iraq War, 12, 158n42, 179n28
Isabella (Spain): as itinerant sovereign, 113; *Map of the Siege of Breda* (Callot) and, 77, 119; on reverence at Breda surrender, 109; Rubens engraving of, 131, 177–78nn20–21, 184n93
Islam, roots of Spanish "Requirement" in, 5, 137, 154n8, 180n48
Israel, Jonathan, 30
Israeli-Palestinian conflict, 12
Italy, 67

Jamar, Jeff, 6
James (king of Aragon), 73, 76
Japan, self-disarmament and, 89–90. *See also* Potsdam Declaration; Tokyo Bay, surrender at; World War II
Játiva, 75, 171n52
Java, 111–12
Jay, Martin, 34, 53, 167n80
Jerusalem, 124
Jesus Christ, 124, 125, 182n75
Jews, 5
Jodl, Alfred, 73, 110, 128
Johnson, Andrew, 66–67, 84, 111
Johnston, Joseph E., 66, 82–84, 110, 120, 136–37
journalism, spatial and temporal distance and, 165–66n50. *See also* photojournalism
Justin of Nassau: as grateful vanquished, 35; key to city and, 32, 35, 36, 41, 43–44, 56, 62, 146; in *Map of the Siege of Breda* (Callot), 119; negotiations at Breda by, 31; in *El sitio de Breda,* 32. *See also* Breda, siege of; *Surrender of Breda, The* (Velázquez)

Kalisch, Bertram, 156n23, 175n112
Kantorowicz, Ernst: on collectivity as sovereign realm, 103; on kingly immortality, 113; on king's two bodies, 176n2; on *Macbeth,* 176n3; on theory of Phoenix, 176–77n11; on theory of sovereignty, 27, 102, 160n67
Kase, Toshikazu, 129, 151
Kawabe, Masakazu, 94
Kecskemeti, Paul, 8, 88–89, 104
Kemp, William, 121
king's two bodies, doctrine of, 129–30, 137, 176n2
Koh-i-nor, 81–82
Koresh, David, 6
Kuwait, 11. *See also* Gulf War (first)

law, codification of surrenders and, 108–9
Le Brun, Charles, 98
Lee, Robert E.: alternatives to surrender and, 60; attire of at Appomattox, 117; ceremony of surrender and, 51; on Confederate Army, 78; deictic deferral and, 142–44; documents of surrender and, 83, 136; "General Orders Number 9," 85–86; misrecognition of Grant by, 127; in Nast cartoon, 87–88, 124–26; responsibility to end bloodshed and, 73–74; resurgent popularity of, 126; as stateless, 182n74; terms of surrender and, 10. *See also* Appomattox, surrender at; Civil War (U.S.)
legenda nera, rejection of, 35
Leonardo, Jusepe, 35
Letters and Notes on the Manners, Customs, and Conditions of North American Indians (Catlin), 132
Liber emblemata (Alciati), 62, 63, 72
Lincoln, Abraham: as absent from Lee's surrender, 125; on authority to surrender, 66; compared to Jesus Christ, 182n75; loyalty oaths and, 88; as magnanimous victor, 83; reparations suggested by, 170n31; representations of, 125, 131; restoration of southern states and, 78; River Queen Doctrine and, 83; terms of surrender and, 10
Lincoln, Benjamin, 95
Locke, John, 165n51

Lostwithiel, surrender at, 79, 154n7
Louis XIII (France), 55, 105, 167–68n86,
    178n21
Louis XIV (France): appearance of cour-
    tiers of, 118; augmentation of sovereign
    power by, 116; on *The Queens of Persia
    at the Feet of Alexander* (Le Brun), 99; as
    Sun King, 109; territorial control and,
    7, 76, 113, 147

MacArthur, Douglas: authority to surren-
    der and, 84–85; ceremony of surrender
    and, 51, 96; with Hirohito after sur-
    render, 107; Instrument of Surrender
    and, 10, 84–85; painting of Corregidor
    surrender and, 131; photograph of sur-
    render and, 129; Potsdam Declaration
    and, 52
Macbeth (Shakespeare), 176n3
magnanimous victors: Alexander the Great
    as, 98–99; Allies as, 67; Grant as, 67,
    90–91, 96, 152, 159n54; Lincoln as, 83;
    salvaging missions and, 151–52; sites of
    surrender and, 96; Spinola as, 31–32,
    35, 36, 44, 63, 96, 161n9; symmetry of
    surrender and, 136
Maino, Juan Bautista, 123
Mallory, Michael, 173n71
Mansfield, Ernst Graf von, 174n91
Maori. *See* Treaty of Waitangi
Map of the Siege of Breda (Callot), 32–34,
    77, 118–19, 143, 185n15
maps: accuracy of, 172n59; documentary
    value of, 33–34, 162n22; as emblems of
    power, 77; exchanges of surrender and,
    76–77; seventeenth-century role of, 33,
    34, 162n17; of sovereign relations, 118–
    19; territorial claims and, 142; treaty
    documents and, 172n56. See also *Map
    of the Siege of Breda* (Callot)
Marin, Louis, 27–28, 53, 97, 164n48,
    186n25
Marriage of the Virgin (Raphael), 53–54
Martini, Simone, 80
martyrdom, collective suicide as, 5
Masada, 5
Mashbir, Craig, 93–94
mass media, cycle of return and, 159n47
Maurice of Nassau, 30

Mauss, Marcel, 19, 60, 70, 74–75
Maximus, Petronius, 38
Mayan letters, 115, 120, 180n47
Mayer, Arno, 149
McClellan, George, 156n21
McKim-Smith, Gridley, 33, 160n64
McLean, Wilmer, home of, 94, 124, 149
Médicis, Marie de, 105, 106, 167–68n86,
    177–78n20
Meisel, Martin, 42, 44–45
Melo, Francisco Manuel de, 31
melodrama, freezing of time in, 42
Memoirs (Grant), 83, 90, 91, 136, 143–44
Meninas, Las (Velázquez), 57, 58, 121,
    181n63
Merleau-Ponty, Maurice, 177n19
methodology, 3–8, 151
microthemes, 92–93
military conventions: changes in, 6–7;
    codification of, 79; siege warfare and,
    63–64
military engineering, at Breda, 30
military vs. political authority to surren-
    der, 65, 66–67, 169n18
Millen, Ronald Forsyth, 177–78n20
Miller, William Ian, 16, 62, 169n8
Minerva (goddess of war), 123
"Misbehavior before the Enemy" (U.S.
    Military Code), 62
mistranslation, 6, 73, 114–16, 120, 140–41
Mitchell, W. J. T., 45, 148, 159n47,
    165n55
modalities of knowing, witnesses and, 45,
    165n54
Moffitt, John, 63
Molière, 147
Monroe, James, 132
Moran, Gordon, 173n71
Morocco, 112
Mukerji, Chandra, 7, 77, 116, 118,
    160n66, 170n35
Mulay Hasan, 112
mutuality of surrender, qualifying factors
    of, 4, 154n7

Nagasaki, 10, 148, 186n30
Nast, Thomas, Appomattox cartoon, 87–
    88, 93, 124–26, 139, 143
Native Americans, 24, 131–32, 139

Netherlands, The, pursuit of land claims
  by, 5. *See also* Breda, siege of
Nimitz, Chester W., 96
noble vs. ignoble foes, 126–28
notaries, 133–34

oaths, as exchanges of surrender, 86–88
Obsidio Bredana (Hugo), 32, 77, 79, 87,
  174n102
O'Connor, Raymond, 67
Olivares (Spanish count), 31, 123, 161n9
On War (Clausewitz), 149, 168n1
Order of Santiago, 57
Owens, Craig, 181n63, 186n25

Paine, Robert, 183n92
Palestine. *See* Israeli-Palestinian conflict
Palm Sunday (Nast), 139
paradigms of surrender, 4, 5, 6, 114–15
paradoxes of surrender, 3, 4, 153n5
pardons, as exchanges of surrender, 86–88
Paris, fall of, 147, 171n48
Parker, E. S., 124, 139
Parker, Geoffrey, 161n10
Parliamentary Foot, surrender of, 154n7
peace, durability of, 156n26
peace accords, decisiveness of victory and,
  12, 13
peace medals, 132
Perry, Matthew, 81, 148
Persian princesses, representations of, 98,
  121–22, 126–27, 137, 176n1
Peters, John Durham, 45, 165n51
Petersburg, Virginia, 10
Philip III (Spain), 105
Philip IV (Spain): as absent sovereign, 127;
  Breda siege and, 9; at Calais, 129; Hall
  of Realms and, 116; in *Map of the Siege
  of Breda* (Callot), 119; political marriages and, 105; in *The Recapture of
  Bahia* (Maino), 123–24, 131, 138;
  victories during reign of, 32
Philippines, 131
Phoenix, theory of, 176–77n11
photojournalism, 10–11, 40, 129,
  175n112
Picture Theory (Mitchell), 45
pleasure of surrender, 26
pledges, as exchanges of surrender, 86–88

point of view, of the vanquished, 59
political semiotic of surrender, 13–14, 135,
  138–39
political vs. military authority to surrender, 65, 66–67, 169n18
Politica militar (Melo), 31
Porter, Horace, 50–51, 78, 90–91, 127
Portugal, 5, 62, 123–24
Potsdam Declaration: acceptance of, 131,
  140–41, 184n93; Instrument of Surrender and, 84; unconditional surrender
  and, 51–52, 68–69, 109
Poussin, Nicolas, 164n48
premature surrender, penalties for, 162n21
pretenders, 119–20
process of surrender, multiple steps in,
  89–90
promises: as exchanges of surrender, 86–88;
  interregnum of surrender and, 25

Queens of Persia at the Feet of Alexander, The
  (Le Brun), 98, 121–22, 137, 176n1

Rape of the Daughters of Leucippu, The
  (Rubens), 105
Raphael, 53–54
Rather, Dan, 148, 159n47
Recapture of Bahia, The (Maino), 123, 125,
  127, 131, 138
recognition and contestation of surrender:
  Branch Davidians and, 6; Civil War
  (U.S.) and, 126–27; deictics and, 141–
  42; exchanges of surrender and, 59–60,
  168n2; military and political authority
  and, 66; pursuit of land claims and, 5;
  since World War II, 12
refusal to surrender, annihilation and, 65,
  169n16
Reminiscences (MacArthur), 107
Remnants of Auschwitz (Agamben), 2, 39
Renaissance art and theater, 52–55, 97,
  155n16, 167n85. *See also specific works*
reparations, 69, 170n31
repetitions of social actions, functions of,
  148, 151
"Report of the Commission on Truth and
  Reconciliation in South Africa," 39
"Requirement" (Spanish), 5, 137, 154n8,
  180n48

Resignation of General Washington, The
(Trumbull), 48
resignations: forced, 183n86; procedural
quandaries about, 150–51
revenge, legitimation of, 154n7
Revolutionary War (U.S.), 95, 138
Richard II (Shakespeare), 3, 51, 90, 128,
153n4
Richmond, Virginia, 10
risks and benefits of surrender, assessment
of, 13–14
River Queen Doctrine, 83
Roberto, Fra, 167n83
Roman empire, 5, 31, 65, 176n10
Roosevelt, Franklin Delano, 64, 65, 67,
89, 145
Rose, Carol, 185n20
Ross, Marc, 62, 158–59n46
Rotman, Brian, 53
rotunda of U.S. Capitol, paintings in, 150,
186–87n35
Rubens, Peter Paul, 32, 105–6, 131, 177–
78nn20–21, 184n93

Sage, Byron, 6
Sala, Charles, 168n88
Salazar, Philippe-Joseph, 39, 40
Saxton, Christopher, 181n58
Scarry, Elaine, 130
Scheppele, Kim Lane, 171n49
Schivelbusch, Wolfgang, 156n21, 158n42
Schmitt, Carl, 102
Schwartz, Barry, 166n66
Schwartz, Hillel, 38, 134
scorched-earth policy, origin of, 156n21
Seed, Patricia: on municipal charters, 34;
on performative acts, 144; on pursuit of
land claims, 5, 142; on Spanish "Re-
quirement," 137, 154n8, 180n48
self: disappearance of, 51, 128; language
of, 110, 177n19, 178n33; physical body
and, 177n19; from sovereign to sub-
jected, 3, 104, 153n4; undoing of, 90,
134, 136
semiotic phases of surrender, 67–69
Shah, Dhavan, 169n16
Shakespeare, William. See *Henry V*
(Shakespeare); *Macbeth* (Shakespeare);
Richard II (Shakespeare)

shame, 2–3, 28
Sheridan, Philip Henry, 156n21
Sherman, William T., 66–67, 83–84, 110–
11, 120, 136–37, 156n21
Shigemitsu, Mamoru, 52
siege warfare: architecture and, 30–31,
155–56n19; codified forms of surrender
and, 9, 15; as conducive to surrender,
30–31, 63–64; literature and, 8, 155n15.
See also Breda, siege of
Siena, emblems of surrender at, 80–81
signature acts, 48–52, 133–34, 168n88
Sikh diaspora, 131–32, 185n19
Silverstein, Michael, 47, 142, 157n30, 165–
66n62
Simmel, Georg, 61, 70, 71, 99
Singh, Dalip, 81, 132
Singh, Ranjit, 132
singular ruler vs. commonweal, 101–5, 108
sites of surrender, exchanges of surrender
and, 94–96, 175n109. *See also specific
sites*
sitio de Breda, El (Calderón de la Barca),
32, 33, 34, 44
Smith, Adam, 46, 160n61
Smith, Christine, 161n9
Snayers, Peter, 30
soldiers, fate of after defeat, 78–82,
172n65
solidarity, symbolic objects of, 90–91
sovereignty, 98–132; absence of sovereign
from scenes of surrender, 126–28, 138,
185n8; actions of sovereign and, 107–9;
agency without, 119–20; collective vs.
individual, 47–48, 101–5, 109, 156n28,
158n42; definition of, 100–101; deifica-
tion and, 109; dispersion of political
power and, 122–26; identity of surrenderer and, 18, 158n42; indivisibility of,
123; itinerant, 111–14; mapping relations of, 118–19, 180n56, 181n58; origin of, 176n10; plurality of, 98–100,
102, 176n2; recognition of, 114–18,
119–20; representation of, 120–22,
181n62, 181–82n65; responsibility and,
109–11; self and, 3, 104, 153n4; singularity of, 122–24, 129–30; theory of,
27, 160n67; types of, 101–5, 121; unrepresentability and, 128–32; vicarious

sovereignty (*continued*)
surrender and, 105–7. *See also* authority to surrender
space of surrender. *See* spatial considerations
Spain: battle of Montijo and, 62; Brazil and, 123–24; France and, 105–7, 113, 178n21, 178n23; Franche-Comté and, 76, 113; Granada surrender and, 174n103; Mayan letters and, 115, 120, 180n47; military engineering by, 30; political marriages and, 167–68n86; pursuit of land claims by, 5; "Requirement" of, 5, 137, 154n8, 180n48; treatment of enemies by, 31, 161n9. *See also* Breda, siege of; "Requirement" (Spanish)
spatial considerations: deictics and, 157n30; displacement and, 15–16; etymology of surrender and, 17; images of surrender and, 27; journalism and, 165–66n50; location of witnesses, 44–46; neutral space for surrender, 106; orientation and, 15–16, 157n36; perception of battlefield and, 175n116; sites of surrender and, 94–96; social, 15; "spatial field" of surrender, 96–97; support and, 15; typology of spatial relation to event, 46; witnesses to surrender and, 37–38. *See also* temporal considerations
Spinola, Ambrogio: death of, 161n9; keys to city and, 32, 35, 36, 43–44, 56, 62, 93, 161n11, 174n102; as magnanimous victor, 31–32, 35, 36, 44, 63, 96, 161n9; *Map of the Siege of Breda* (Callot) and, 77, 119; negotiations at Breda by, 31; reversal of fortunes of, 32; in *El sitio de Breda,* 32, 33; terms of surrender and, 83, 87; unkempt vestments of, 117. *See also* Breda, siege of; *Surrender of Breda, The* (Velázquez)
Steiner, Wendy, 27, 43, 146
Strategic Surrender (Kecskemeti), 88–89
suicide, 5, 129
Surrender of Breda, The (Velázquez): blank piece of paper in, 56–57, 127; ceremony of surrender and, 62; creation of, 32; dating of, 63, 169n10; deictic

deferral in, 143; distraction and absorption of witnesses in, 43–44; doubling up in, 185n15; focal point of, 56, 168n87; Hall of Realms and, 116; handshake in, 93; *Map of the Siege of Breda* and, 34; military engineering operations in, 30; "nobody" of enunciative modality and, 164n48; portrait of Velázquez in, 58; *El sitio de Breda* and, 34; sources for emblems in, 62–63, 72, 93; victor and vanquished on same plane in, 35. *See also* Justin of Nassau; Spinola, Ambrogio
Swidler, Ann, 184n2
symbolic violence, contingencies of surrender and, 25
symmetry and asymmetry of surrender, 35–36, 88, 115, 116–17, 136
Sysigambis, 98–99

Teitel, Ruti, 69, 72, 88, 108
temporal considerations: cycle of return, 20; deictics and, 157n30; etymology of surrender and, 17, 19; first-order witness and, 45; freezing of time in visual representations, 42–43; images of surrender and, 27; interstitial action of surrender and, 23; interval and delay, 24, 28; journalism and, 165–66n50; phase appropriateness and, 16–17; typology of temporal relation to event, 46; witnesses to surrender and, 37–38. *See also* spatial considerations
Tennis Court Oath, 121
terms of surrender: at Breda, 31; collaboration in producing, 72–73, 171n41; documents and, 82–83; election of 2000 (U.S.) and, 11–12; maps and, 172n56; wording of, 11–12, 21–22, 116. *See also* specific conflicts; specific surrenders
testimony, credibility of, 37, 162–63n27
Theory of Moral Sentiments (Smith), 46
Third Punic War, 65
Thirty Years' War, 9, 30
Tiepolo, Giovanni Battista, 176n1
time of surrender. *See* temporal considerations
Tokyo Bay, surrender at: absence of Hirohito from, 129, 185n8; case summary

of, 10–11; ceremony of surrender and, 51; disbelief about, 109; document of surrender and, 184n3; emblems of exchange at, 81; handshake and, 93–94; as last unmitigated surrender, 10; return of Perry's flag and, 148; terms of, 21–22, 75, 159n48; unconditional surrender and, 51–52. *See also* USS *Missouri*

Treaty of Waitangi, 75–76, 120

Troyen, Carol, 182n79

Truman, Harry S., 131, 184n93

Trumbull, John, 48, 138, 150

Truth and Reconciliation Commission (TRC), 39, 40

turbans, in exchange of surrender, 175n105

twinning, 130, 183–84n92

Ubaldus, Baldus de, 103, 176–77n11

Umezu, Yoshijirō, 89–90

unconditional surrender: absence of sovereign authority and, 66, 120, 181n59; annihilation and, 65; exchanges of surrender and, 64–69; Gallup Poll on, 64–65; Instrument of Surrender (at Tokyo Bay) and, 84; justification for policy, 65–66; lack of modern precedent for, 65, 169n18; postwar implications of, 175n118. *See also* Potsdam Declaration

U.S. Capitol, paintings in rotunda of, 150, 186–87n35

USS *Missouri*, 11, 48, 95–96, 156n23, 175n112. *See also* Tokyo Bay, surrender at

Van Buren, Martin, 132

vanishing point, 52–55, 96–97

Velázquez, Diego: abdication of "author's" role by, 181n63; artistic tradition and, 162n22; attention to attention and, 43; as court painter to Philip IV, 57; creation of *The Surrender of Breda* by, 34, 63, 146; Order of Santiago and, 57; signature of, 56–58; unconventional representation of surrender by, 35. See also *Meninas, Las* (Velázquez); *Surrender of Breda, The* (Velázquez)

Vermeer, Jan, 77

Veronese, 176nn1–2

Victoria (queen of England), 81, 127, 132

victory, decisiveness of, 12, 156n26, 158–59n46

Vietnam War, 12, 148, 159n47

Villani, Giovanni, 128

Waelchli, Heinz, 169n16

Wainwright, Jonathan: ambivalence of about surrender, 52; ceremony of surrender and, 51, 184n3; on Corregidor surrender, 131, 173n87, 184n94; portrait of, 146–47

war on terror, decisiveness of victory and, 12

Washington, George: Farewell Address of, 78; resignations of, 48, 103, 150, 166n66, 187n38; at Yorktown surrender, 138. See also *Resignation of General Washington, The* (Trumbull)

weak legs, surrender on assault and, 16

weapons and instruments of war, 88–91, 94, 173n87, 174n95

Weber, Max, 102, 179n28

Welles, Marcia, 33, 160n64

Whitaker, Shirley, 33

White, Hayden, 146

White, Lorraine, 79, 113, 180n56

Wilson, Woodrow, 88

Winik, Jay, 136–37, 142–43, 153n5, 173n83, 182n74

Winterhalter, Franz, 132

Wise, Henry, 157n37

witnesses, 29–58; activities of, 47–48; anonymous, 32; artistic conventions and, 32–33, 34; at Breda, overview of, 29–36; children as, 43, 164n47; collectivities and individuals as, 47–48; as cosigners and countersigners, 29, 55, 160–61n11; definition of, 36–41; disappearance of self and, 50–52; distraction and absorption of, 43–44; epistemological dilemmas and, 45–46; etymology of "witness," 36–37; first- and later-order, 41–44, 45, 46, 50, 165n61; ideal spectator and, 27, 160n61; journalism and, 40; lack of, 39; paper and responsibility and, 56–58; phase shifting and, 47; protagonists as, 39–41, 163n38; proximity of, 44–46, 165n51; as signatories, 48–52, 166n71; as survivors,

witnesses (*continued*)
38–39; as third parties, 37–38, 41, 45,
163–64n41; vanishing point and, 52–
55. *See also* cross-witnessing
Wizard of Oz, The (film), 182n72
Wolf, Robert Erich, 177–78n20
World War I, reparations and, 69
World War II: Allied broadcasts to Germany in, 21; Allies as magnanimous
victors in, 67; Allies' definition of war,
65–66; atomic bombings and, 10, 148,
186n30; authority to surrender and, 12,
66, 84–85, 158n42; continued fighting
on eastern front in, 79; France's surrender in, 147; Germany's surrender in,

66, 73, 95, 104, 109–10, 120, 128,
181n59; Hungary's surrender in,
171n49; Italy's surrender in, 67; reparations and, 69. *See also* Tokyo Bay, surrender at; unconditional surrender
Wright, John W., 172n65, 174n95
Wright, Quincy, 104

Yorktown, surrender at, 95, 138
Yugoslavia, former, 12

Zelizer, Barbie, 10, 40, 163–64n41, 164n47
Zelizer, Viviana, 70
Zerubavel, Yael, 5